To Ned –
with fondness an...
appreciation for 20
years of conversations
that made this book
possible ;

Charlie

Courting Peril

Courting Peril
The Political Transformation
of the American Judiciary

Charles Gardner Geyh

OXFORD
UNIVERSITY PRESS

OXFORD

UNIVERSITY PRESS

Oxford University Press is a department of the University of Oxford. It furthers
the University's objective of excellence in research, scholarship, and education
by publishing worldwide. Oxford is a registered trade mark of Oxford University
Press in the UK and certain other countries.

Published in the United States of America by Oxford University Press
198 Madison Avenue, New York, NY 10016, United States of America.

Library of Congress Cataloging-in-Publication Data
Geyh, Charles Gardner, author.
Courting peril : the political transformation of the American judiciary /
Charles Gardner Geyh.
p.   cm.
Includes bibliographical references and index.
ISBN 978-0-19-023349-5 (hardcover) — ISBN 978-0-19-023350-1 (ebook)
1. Political questions and judicial power—United States. 2. Judicial process—Political
aspects—United States. I. Title.
KF5130.G488 2016
347.73'14—dc23
2015031644

1   3   5   7   9   8   6   4   2

Printed by Sheridan Books, Michigan, USA

For Emily

... and the University of Wisconsin coffee machine that

introduced us with a steaming cup of its abysmal sludge

CONTENTS

ACKNOWLEDGMENTS

For the ideas developed in a book such as this, publication is their coming out party: Years of schooling and maturation have culminated in this moment, and they want their corsage, gentleman caller, and debutante ball. The author's temptation to indulge his ideas with a lavish, celebratory parade of acknowledgments is considerable. They are, after all, his children—needy, demanding narcissists though they may be, who acquire a sort of demented sentience when they reach puberty. The perennial challenge is to keep these vainglorious impulses at bay, by giving credit to the people who made the book possible without transforming the acknowledgments into an interminable, self-congratulatory, Oscar-style acceptance speech. Wish me luck.

The catalyst for this project was a conference I hosted at Indiana University in 2009, which brought judges, law professors, and political scientists together to discuss recent research on judicial decision-making and its policy implications. I'd like to thank the participants at that conference, from whom I learned much, as well as Stanford University Press, for publishing an edited volume that emerged out of that conference: *What's Law Got to Do With It? What Judges Do, Why They Do It, and What's at Stake.* I contributed no substantive chapters to that book, but editing it served as a kind of home-schooling that informed my perspective in two later articles published by the Cornell and Florida Law Reviews, pieces of which appear in revised form here.[1]

A bevy of scholars has gone to the time and trouble of reading and commenting on chapters of the manuscript at various stages of development. This book has been markedly improved by the insights of Keith Bybee, Steve Burbank, Paul Carrington, Malcolm Feeley, Barry Friedman, Jim Gibson, Steve Gillers, Mark Graber, Steve Lubet, Dave Pozen, Dana Remus, Judith Resnik, Ron Rotunda, James Sample, the late, great Roy Schotland, Greg Sisk, Brian Tamanaha, and Steve Wasby. Publicly, I take responsibility for any errors that remain, although I am not above pointing fingers in private settings. Thanks likewise to the American Bar Association, the Association of Professional Responsibility Lawyers, the

American Association of Appellate Lawyers, the Federal Judicial Center, the First Circuit Judicial Conference, George Washington University, Harvard University, the Indianapolis Law Club, Marquette University, the Pound Institute for Civil Justice, Vanderbilt University, the University of Akron, the University of Georgia, the University of Nevada Las Vegas, and the University of Wisconsin, for hosting forums where I had an opportunity to vet some of the ideas developed here.

I have been blessed with wonderful administrative and research support. My research assistants have been called upon to find, organize, and analyze an eclectic array of materials, to perfect the manuscript for style and form, and to endure countless hours of my geezing in exchange for an hourly wage that is just enough to go bowling on weekends. I appreciate you: Ben Cole, Cristina Costa, Katie Cullum, Anita Foss, Jack Garvin, Chris Hanewald, Brian Lynch, Dan Matheny, Phillip Olsson, Mark Plantan, Andy Williams, and Annie Xie. Among my gifted group of RAs, Katie Thrapp deserves special mention: her exceptional research abilities, chapter edits, and substantive insights at a critical juncture in the project made this a better book. In a related vein, when it comes to research support, our law school's library staff is second to none and was particularly helpful in hunting down materials for chapter 4. Finally, thanks to my administrative assistant, Rita Eads, whose secretarial, organizational, and editorial skills have kept my projects (and me) from running off the rails for nearly a decade, and counting.

I am fortunate to work at one of the most supportive institutions on the planet. Thanks to Indiana University for a sabbatical leave that made this book possible and to the Maurer School of Law for its generous, annual research grants. Thanks likewise to Lauren Robel, Hannah Buxbaum, and Austen Parrish: three terrific deans who have lent unflagging support to this project over a span of years. Special thanks to my colleagues Jeannine Bell and Victor Quintanilla for their advice, and Jeannine Bell (again), Dan Conkle, Leandra Lederman, Ajay Mehrotra, and Gene Shreve for their helpful suggestions and comments on draft chapters. Finally, I'm indebted to the Indiana University Center for the Global Legal Profession, and its director Jay Krishnan, for including me in the Center's ambit and creating a new platform for my work.

I had more fun with this project than any other in recent memory, owing largely to its deeply interdisciplinary character, which furnished me with an excuse to reach out to colleagues in other fields, in search of ideas and source materials. In that regard, many thanks to political scientists Chris Bonneau, Eileen Braman, and Jeff Yates; sociologists Howie Erlanger and Ethan Michaelson; anthropologists Pierre Lienard and David Samson; and English scholar Eric Rasmussen.

Finally, I close with a word of thanks to my family. First, and foremost, I'm grateful to my partner, spouse, and best person ever, Emily Van Tassel, for her critical insights on Kuhnian paradigms, and for enduring me, lo, these many decades. I'd also like to give a shout-out to our daughters, Hallie Geyh and Sarah Van Tassel, who lack Emily's tenacity, and opted to grow up and move out while there was still time, leaving me with a quiet (sometimes too quiet) place to complete my manuscript. Ongoing thanks to my mother, Patricia Geyh, without whom I, and hence this book, would have been inconceivable. Last, and certainly least, to our cat, Bruce: Your best efforts to thwart this project through adverse possession of my computer keyboard have failed—better luck next time.

C.G.G.

CHAPTER 1

Introduction

In public discourse on the American judiciary, crisis rhetoric abounds. Many have targeted judicial selection and its accouterment. Former Justice Sandra Day O'Connor, for example, has written that privately funded judicial elections have given rise to a "crisis of confidence," by creating the perception that "justice is for sale."[1] An eminent legal scholar has argued that Supreme Court decisions invalidating state regulation of speech in judicial campaigns have caused a "national crisis."[2] The Minnesota Chief Justice has expressed the fear that public confidence in the courts will be "dramatically undermined" by "nasty" election campaigns.[3] Federal judicial appointments have likewise come under fire, as scholars have alleged a "vacancy crisis"[4] and argued that the confirmation process is "deeply flawed, if not broken," creating a "desperate need" for reform.[5]

Another cadre of commentators has issued alarmist proclamations on matters of judicial administration and oversight: There are chronic claims of "caseload crisis."[6] A 2011 law review symposium addressed a "state court funding crisis" that, participants argued, had jeopardized the judiciary's institutional and decisional independence.[7] Chief Justice John Roberts has opined that inadequate judicial salaries have provoked a "constitutional crisis."[8] And the Massachusetts Chief Justice (among others) has argued that "state courts are in crisis"[9] because of partisan attacks on judges by pundits and public officials[10]—attacks that include threats to remove judges, disestablish courts, curtail jurisdiction, and cut budgets.

Still others have blamed judicial decision-making for impending crises: The results of a 2005 survey found that 56% of respondents agreed with a Republican congressman, who said that "judicial activism seems to have reached a crisis,"[11] and numerous conservative commentators have argued that judges imperil themselves through lack of judicial restraint. A progressive scholar has made a related point from the other end of the ideological continuum, arguing that the absence of a "persuasive case that the

Court's decisions are rational extrapolations of constitutional meaning as opposed to impositions of the political and moral preferences of the individual justices" has created a "legitimacy crisis" that is "increasingly acute for progressives."[12] Still others have asserted that "pleading standards are in crisis"[13] because recent Supreme Court decisions have "destabilized the entire system of civil litigation"[14] by directing judges to dismiss claims they deem implausible, in light of their "personal feel,"[15] which opens the door to more ideologically driven decision-making.[16]

One possible conclusion to draw from all of this is that the judiciary is on the brink, and that the four horsemen are saddling up. Dire predictions of impending catastrophe notwithstanding, the sky has yet to fall, and public support for the state and federal courts remains relatively stable, which fuels the suspicion that such predictions are overstated. And scholars aplenty have lined up to show just that.[17]

An alternate conclusion, then, is that to get attention, the alarmists are making mountains of molehills and should be sent home with a basket of bran muffins. But that prescription overlooks and thereby trivializes common concerns that animate these seemingly disparate crisis claims.

Between the extremes of a judiciary in crisis and business as usual lies a third possibility that this book explores. For generations, if not centuries, the way in which the bench, bar, media, scholars, public, and their elected representatives conceptualize and evaluate the American judiciary has been structured by what I call a "rule of law paradigm." That paradigm posits that if judges are afforded independence from external sources of interference with their decision-making, they will set extralegal influences aside and impartially apply pertinent law to operative facts. Events giving rise to recurring crisis rhetoric evidence an American judiciary in the midst of a transformation that has caused stress fractures in the rule of law paradigm. Developments of the past fifty or more years have subjected state and federal courts to greater scrutiny and thrust them into the political limelight in new and different ways. One consequence has been to highlight, in an often negative light, the discretion and judgment that judges exercise—discretion and judgment that are informed by life experiences that frame judges' policy perspectives on the world. The public has long internalized what scholars have confirmed: When judges decide difficult cases, they are subject to the influence of ideology, strategic considerations, race, gender, religion, emotion, their life experience, and other extralegal factors despite their assertions to the contrary. In recent decades, judges have been called out for this perceived hypocrisy across a proliferating array of venues.

These developments challenge core tenets of the rule of law paradigm. Why should judges be free (code that: "independent") to impose their policy and other extralegal preferences on the people they serve without fear of consequence, when other public officials are not?

Old paradigms die hard. The realization that the premises underlying the rule of law paradigm are overstated, if not counterfactual, is ancient in origin, and more recent impatience with the paradigm has catalyzed no crisis of confidence in judges or the rule of law. Erosion of the paradigm, however, is another matter, evidence of which can be found in many of the developments that court defenders have exaggerated as crises. With exceptions, the legal community's penchant for Chicken Littling such developments punctuates its increasing dismay with the ways the judiciary is being "politicized" over the legal community's objections, and over its own inability to "depoliticize" the courts by thwarting incursions on the judiciary's autonomy through recourse to the rule of law paradigm.

Over the long term, continued erosion will eventually culminate in a collapse of the paradigm, and with it, the independence and impartiality that the paradigm has promoted. The resulting vacuum will be filled with more aggressive political controls that diminish the distinctiveness of the judge's role relative to that of public officials in the legislative and executive branches. Heightened political control will presumably be for the best, unless a new or revised paradigm emerges to justify, in more defensible terms, a measure of judicial independence from popular and political oversight. This book explores what that new paradigm might look like.

The story begins with the venerable rule of law paradigm. By "paradigm," I mean a model of interaction between law, society, and culture, to which affected communities adhere. Affected communities include: (1) the bench and bar, who implement and explicate the rule of law paradigm; (2) the general public and their elected representatives, who legitimate the paradigm and oversee its implementation by the bench and bar; and (3) the media and scholars who study the paradigm and report on its operation to all affected communities. At its core, the rule of law paradigm posits that the judiciary is rendered distinct from the so-called "political" branches of government by virtue of its independence and impartiality, which enable judges to decide cases on the basis of facts and law, unaffected by "political" and other extralegal influences that color the decision-making of public officials in the executive and legislative branches.

As marketed to other affected communities by the bench and bar, the rule of law paradigm is clear, concise, and unyielding: Independent and impartial judges apply pertinent law to relevant facts—period. Traditional law review scholarship has complemented the rule of law paradigm, with doctrinal work grounded on the premise that understanding why judges do what they do is a matter of parsing legal doctrine—that the decisions judges make should be understood and critiqued with exclusive reference to applicable law. When judges deviate from applicable law, it is (except for rare instances of corruption or other misconduct) simply a matter of getting it wrong—mistakes appellate review and doctrinal scholarship aim to spot and correct.

Meanwhile, in the aftermath of the legal realism movement of the 1920s and 1930s, political scientists began to explore the role of politics in judicial decision-making. Over the latter half of the twentieth century, a dominant cohort within the political science community became increasingly convinced that judges make decisions by following their ideological predilections, and that applicable law has little, if anything to do with the choices judges make.[18] More recently, a cadre of interdisciplinary scholars began to bridge the law-politics divide with a flurry of empirical projects demonstrating that judicial decision-making is subject to a complex array of influences, including law, ideology, and others.[19] Such findings have led these scholars to conclude that the dichotomy itself is false: Law and policy are so inextricably intertwined that to say judges are influenced by one but not the other is to misunderstand both.[20] In that way, the "law versus policy" debate that has dominated scholarship on judicial decision-making for decades has outlived its usefulness.

For experienced lawyers and judges, these conclusions are intuitive. When the law and facts are clear, so too is the outcome, and judges often allude to cases in which they have ruled contrary to their policy preferences because the law required them to do so. But the adversarial process proceeds on the assumption that there are two or more ways to look at the applicable facts and law, and when the "correct" answer is unclear, judges must look beyond "law," narrowly defined, to decide which answer among plausible alternatives is right or best. That calls upon judges to make a kind of policy choice that can be informed by the judge's upbringing, education, religious convictions, philosophical perspectives, emotions, and experience (including experience arising out of the judge's socioeconomic status, race, and gender). Far from a bad thing, exercising judgment and discretion within the boundaries of applicable law to the end of achieving results the judge deems best may be the very definition of justice.

All of this then begs the question of why the bench and bar hew to the rhetoric of an unyielding rule of law paradigm. The answer is multifaceted. In part, this is the way of paradigms: They structure the world for adherents, who will struggle to explain anomalies in ways consistent with the entrenched schema to the extent they can. Psychological factors are also at work. Judges may sincerely believe that the choices they make are based on applicable law, and yet be influenced subconsciously by ideological and other extralegal factors to favor one legal argument over another.

Moreover, judges (like everyone else) regard their own judgments as objective and unbiased, relative to the judgments of others: Hence, judges tend to credit self-assessments that they are following the law and dismiss their critics' claims to the contrary as subjective and ill-informed. In addition to psychological factors that may lead judges to underestimate the impact of extralegal influences on their decision-making, there is a perceived strategic need to disavow such influences when judges defend their role in the public square. If the bench and bar openly acknowledge that independent judges are subject to legal and extralegal influences, it complicates life for the legal community in the public policy debate, as alluded to earlier. Why should the policy choices that judges make be insulated from political controls to any greater extent than the policy choices of Congress, state legislatures, city councils, presidents, governors, or mayors?

The view that judges are subject to extralegal influences is a ubiquitous suspicion dating back millennia. The pivotal role that judicial independence came to play in the rule of law paradigm, thus evolved against the backdrop of an ancient and pervasive understanding, reflected in folktales, plays, biblical passages, novels, poems, polemics, and historical accounts. This understanding posits that the decisions judges make are subject to myriad influences, from financial conflicts of interest and personal relationships, to political pressures, ideological predispositions, and a range of biases. One scholar has explained this curious state of affairs in terms of an "acceptable hypocrisy":[21] The public understands that judges are not perfectly impartial—that they are subject to political and other extralegal influences. But the public embraces the rule of law paradigm and reconciles the cognitive dissonance created by judges whose conduct is at odds with the premises of the paradigm by embracing judges who pledge their allegiance to unqualified, rule of law rhetoric. In this way, institutionalized hypocrisy operates as a coping strategy that responds to a flaw in the paradigm by looking the other way.

Thus, the point is not that "we are all legal realists now"[22] who have suddenly decided that what judges do and what they say they do are two different things, because we have been legal realists of that sort for centuries. The point is that discomfort with the hypocrisy is on the rise. Maintaining the pretense of an independent judiciary that is impervious to extralegal influence in the teeth of contemporary scholarship and long-standing realist suspicions to the contrary is gradually becoming an unacceptable hypocrisy in the wake of persistent and proliferating challenges. Making the case that the political landscape of the American courts is changing in this way is a challenge because history is littered with politicized attacks upon the courts that seemingly belie claims that we are witnessing something new or different. Hence, it is critical to distinguish between those political pressure points best described as chronic or cyclical, and those that are more recent, sustained, and arguably transformative.

Many of the most aggressive challenges to the judiciary's independence have arisen during periods of political realignment, when the political leaders of a new regime come into conflict with holdover judges selected by the outgoing regime. During these cyclical storms, the judiciary has been sheltered by a culture of judicial independence attributable to the rule of law paradigm that the legal community has cultivated for a very long time. And it has averted the brunt of political ire with decision-making that is less "counter-majoritarian" than either court critics condemn as a vice, or court defenders hail as a virtue.

Apart from these chronic, episodic pressures, however, a series of developments more than half a century in the making has changed the landscape of judicial politics in new and different ways and compounded the political pressures under which courts operate. Jury trial rates have declined, diminishing the jury's check on judicial power and transforming trial judges into case managers, settlement brokers, and problem solvers, with respect to whom the need for independence from political control is less obvious. Recent changes in pleading standards have added to the managerial judge's considerable pretrial discretion in controversial ways. Judicial selection wars have ramped up: Judicial elections have become "noisier, nastier, and costlier,"[23] and Senate confirmation battles over nominee ideology have migrated to the circuit and sometimes district courts—developments fueled, in part, by a new era of interest group mobilization. The advent of intermediate state appellate courts, coupled with the elimination of mandatory jurisdiction for supreme courts (in the federal system and most states) has reduced supreme court dockets to fewer, more controversial and ideologically charged cases. And rendering intermediate appellate courts the courts of last resort in virtually all cases in these jurisdictions has elevated the political profile of their work as well. Media coverage and criticism of the courts has changed, with shrinkage of traditional news outlets and the ascent of ideologically aligned cable news networks and Internet reportage. Judicial conduct commissions, armed with enforceable codes of conduct, have been installed in every state, creating new venues for judicial accountability and criticism of judicial conduct. A centerpiece of those codes of conduct is a rule that judges avoid not just impropriety, but "the appearance of impropriety." In an age of appearances, when the media reports news via impressionistic sound bites and the general public often suspects the worst of public officials, regulating how the judiciary is perceived has become a new centerpiece in oversight of the courts.

I am not suggesting that the rule of law paradigm is on the brink of collapse. As noted at the outset, perennial crisis claims are premature and overstated. What we see instead is a paradigm eroded by escalating challenges to the assumptions on which it rests. Perceived crises in judicial decision-making derive from the growing suspicion among court critics that independent judges disregard facts and law, and act upon their ideological and other personal predilections, to the detriment of their impartiality. Election battles, appointments showdowns, and partisan attacks seek to curb the independence of judges who make politically unacceptable, ideologically freighted decisions, by controlling judicial selection, removal, and oversight. Caseload pressures beget the judiciary's need for bigger budgets, and inflation begets the need for upward adjustments to judicial salaries, which create institutional vulnerabilities that legislatures can exploit to the potential detriment of the judiciary's independence and impartiality.

To date, the legal community has remained unyielding in its half of the public policy debate. The bench, bar, and organizations that share their concern argue that capable, honest, impartial, and independent judges uphold the rule of law, and that judges' capacity to follow the law is compromised by political interference with their decision-making. For the legal community, the solution lies in "depoliticizing" the judiciary and opposing proposals that court critics advocate,[24] with the future of the rule of law paradigm hanging in the balance.

The legal community has thus placed itself in a seemingly untenable position: It can cling tenaciously to the rule of law paradigm, pledge allegiance to the paradigm's counterfactual premise that independent judges impartially follow facts and law alone, and weather the paradigm's continued erosion. Or it can acknowledge the hypocrisy of the paradigm, concede that independence liberates judges to do more and less than follow the law, and invite the paradigm's collapse.

If an independent judiciary can only be explained and justified with recourse to a paradigm that embraces a hypocrisy widely regarded as unacceptable, then the paradigm will (and should) crumble along with the independent judiciary that the failed paradigm cultivated. But can judicial autonomy only be explained and justified with recourse to the besieged rule of law paradigm? In this book, I propose not so much a paradigm shift as a paradigm tweak that retools judicial independence and accountability for a judiciary that is subject to legal and extralegal influences. In so doing, my objective is to develop a "legal culture paradigm" premised on a positive theory of judicial decision-making that scholars, the public, and their elected representatives can accept, and that the bench and bar can embrace and defend.

The legal culture paradigm begins with the modest proposition that the legal community has a distinct culture. The norms of the legal culture that are inculcated in law school, entrenched in practice, and perpetuated on the bench, take the role of law as a constraint on judicial behavior seriously. At the same time, the business of "learning to think like a lawyer"— a long-standing mission of legal education—entails an appreciation of pervasive legal indeterminacy inherent in the nature of an adversarial system in which opposing lawyers offer competing perspectives on applicable facts and law. In light of such uncertainty, the notion that judges resolve close cases with reference to policy and other considerations influenced by legal and extralegal factors is utterly unremarkable.

That brings us to the critical question of whether a measure of independence from popular and political controls can be justified for judges who "make policy" in some sense of the term. The answer is "yes" for three reasons.

First, judicial independence still promotes government by law, but in more qualified ways. In easy cases, where the law and facts are so clear they leave little room for judicial discretion, independence insulates judges from political pressure to contort the rule of law, as it is traditionally understood. If the plaintiff files a tort claim in an auto accident case two years after the applicable statute of limitations has expired, the judge will dismiss the case, regardless of her ideological predisposition regarding tort claims. In difficult cases, where outcomes are subject to ideological or other extralegal influence, law still limits the range of contestable issues, acceptable outcomes, and methods of analysis, while independence helps to ensure that judges are not pressured by interested participants or observers to exceed those limits.

Moreover, one can define "law" more flexibly to accommodate ideological and other influences. Few lawyers would argue that there is but one "correct" answer to hotly disputed legal questions; most would freely acknowledge that in close cases, outcomes could go "either way." Conservatives and liberals may answer such questions differently—they may disagree, for example, over the extent to which the text, history, and purpose of the Second Amendment guarantee an individual (as opposed to a collective) right to bear arms, but the answers nonetheless fall within the ambit of law, broadly construed. In this way, independence from external interference with their decision-making enables judges to offer their best judgment of what the law—flexibly understood—requires.

Second, judicial independence promotes procedural fairness, by buffering judges from political pressure to reach preferred results by any means necessary. Independence thus better enables judges who are acculturated to take procedural as well as substantive law seriously, to respect the dictates of fair process required by rules of procedure, rules of evidence, and the due process clauses of the state and federal constitutions. That, in turn, enhances the judiciary's legitimacy in the eyes of litigants, regardless of whether the conclusions of law that judges reach are subject to ideological or other extralegal influences.[25] Hence, for example, in gender discrimination cases, judges who are acculturated to respect rules governing the admissibility of evidence are likelier to abide by those rules in the absence of pressure to reach a result regardless of means, even if liberal judges ultimately tend to be more favorably disposed toward gender discrimination claims than their conservative counterparts.

Third, judicial independence promotes the pursuit of justice. The adversarial process familiarizes judges with the unique circumstances of each case and regulates the manner in which the facts giving rise to those circumstances are presented. That equips judges with a more complete and balanced presentation of the case than is available to outside observers. Independence encourages a pragmatic form of justice by limiting external interference with a judge's capacity to make fact-sensitive decisions she regards as best in the cases before her, regardless of whether ideology and other extralegal factors may affect the judge's assessment of what "best" means.

The default position of the rule of law paradigm is that competent, honest, impartial, and independent judges will set extralegal influences to one side and uphold the law—a position that has proved counterfactual and increasingly difficult to defend. The default position of the legal culture paradigm, in contrast, is that competent, honest, impartial, and independent judges, though subject to extralegal influences, are immersed in a legal culture that takes law, process, and justice seriously enough to constrain judicial behavior.

Independence thus enables judges acculturated to respect law, process, and justice, to protect and promote those objectives, even though their interpretation of those objectives can be colored by their ideological (and other) predilections. By the same token, unchecked independence can liberate judges to stray from the default position and pursue political or other agendas at the expense of the three objectives that independence in the new paradigm aims to further. Hence, a measure of judicial accountability—to the electorate, the public's elected representatives, or other judges—is needed to ensure that independence furthers, rather than thwarts, the purposes it serves.

The legal community's defense of the rule of law paradigm makes room for accountability to guard against the possibility that judges will abuse their independence. Indeed, "independence versus accountability" debates in judicial oversight rival debates over "law versus politics" in judicial decision-making for their intensity and ubiquity. But it is a limited, if not parsimonious, form of accountability that the rule of law paradigm tolerates—one that relies largely on the judiciary to regulate its own decision-making and sharply limits the role that "political" processes should play in curbing judicial excesses. Hence, the legal community's oft-repeated claim is that judges are "accountable to the law," which is to say their oaths of office, appellate processes, and the strictures of the law itself. More aggressive efforts to hold judges accountable to the other branches of government or the electorate are branded threats to judicial independence and elicit calls to "depoliticize" the courts. If, however, we concede the inevitability that judicial decision-making is subject to certain kinds of "political" influences, then the time has come for the legal community to abandon its crusade to "depoliticize" the judiciary and for the legal culture paradigm to step in and manage judicial politics instead.

Put simply, we want good judges. "Good" judges are capable, honest, impartial, and independent, but we have never thought of them as perfectly so. Perfection is neither attainable nor necessary. Rather, judges need only be capable, honest, impartial, and independent enough to further the three systemic objectives enumerated here: (1) upholding the law; (2) respecting rules of process; and (3) rendering justice. Insofar as judicial politics can threaten systemic objectives but cannot be eliminated, the key to managing judicial politics is to ensure that judges remain capable, honest, impartial, and independent enough to further those objectives. Managing judicial politics is thus a line-drawing exercise: If the goal of oversight is to produce judges who are "good enough," then how good is that? Where should independence end and accountability begin, to produce good judges who are independent enough to uphold law, respect process, and do justice in the teeth of external forces intent on contorting their judgment, but not so independent that they are free to indulge their internal preferences at the expense of those goals?

Here is where it gets tricky. As an initial matter, the desired independence-accountability balance can vary between state and federal systems, between trial and appellate tiers, and between states. Context is key. More fundamentally, even in context, where that line between independence and accountability should be drawn will vary, depending on whom one asks and why they care. That is because oversight of the judiciary and regulation of its independence and accountability occur in three distinct dimensions: (1) adjudicative; (2) political; and (3) ethical. In the adjudicative dimension we seek to assure parties a fair hearing under law—an objective that is undermined if judges lack the independence to be fair or the accountability to constrain their biases. In the political dimension, we seek to assure the public a judiciary deserving of its confidence and support—an objective that is compromised if judges are seen as dependent puppets of interested observers, or unaccountable, renegade politicians in robes. In the ethical dimension, we seek to promote the platonic ideal of a good judge who embraces the virtues of law, fair process, and justice—a goal that is thwarted if judges are subject to reprisals for pursuing those objectives or suffer no consequences for flouting them.

The legal culture paradigm I propose seeks to manage judicial politics by balancing independence and accountability to the end of producing judges who are capable, honest, impartial, and independent enough to follow the law, promote procedural fairness, and dispense justice. But the optimal independence-accountability balance can vary by dimension. The independence-accountability blend needed to ensure parties a fair hearing in the adjudicative dimension may differ from that needed to provide the public with judges it trusts in the political dimension, which may differ from that needed to ensure that judges live up to the expectations of their role in the ethical dimension.

An analogy and an example may help to elucidate this balance between the dimensions. First, the analogy: The great impressionist Claude Monet painted a series of landscapes featuring the same haystacks captured from different perspectives in different lights, by blending his palette of colors in different ways. In a like vein, the same subject—the "good" judge who furthers systemic objectives—is painted differently from adjudicative, political, and ethical perspectives, by blending independence and accountability in different ways.

To illustrate how the optimal independence-accountability blend can be combined differently in different dimensions, consider the merits and demerits of selecting judges by contested election. In the political dimension, the judiciary's legitimacy may be enhanced by electoral accountability, which increases the likelihood that the decisions judges make will be acceptable to the body politic. In the adjudicative dimension, however, the parties' interest in a fair hearing may be compromised if the judge is at risk of losing her tenure should her ruling favor an unpopular party or cause. And in the ethical dimension, the compatibility of electoral accountability with the judicial role may vary depending on the political culture of the jurisdiction: Judges in states that have been selected in partisan elections since the 1840s may analyze the question differently than in states where judges have always been appointed.

As a consequence of being dimension dependent, the independence-accountability debate in its current state—like the "law-politics" debate—has exceeded its expiration date. That debate is ultimately intractable because compelling arguments for independence in one dimension of judicial oversight can be countered by equally compelling arguments for accountability in another dimension, to no end. Returning to the judicial election example, electoral accountability is wonderful, because it promotes the judiciary's legitimacy with the voters (the political dimension argument), and awful, because it jeopardizes fair hearings for parties, by hinging the judge's tenure on reaching popular results regardless of facts or law (the adjudicative dimension argument).

A more fruitful course is to pursue a dimension-dependent analysis. Many of the recent changes to the landscape of American courts, and generalized objections that the judiciary has become too politicized, can be better understood in terms of a long-term trend away from regulation of the courts in the adjudicative and ethical dimensions of judicial oversight, toward the political. Cyclical attacks on judges that come and go with transitions of political power, judicial selection battles, interest group mobilization over judicial decisions, the new politics of judicial campaign finance, the elevated policymaking profile of supreme courts, and strategic manipulations of judicial budgets and salaries, are developments with common roots. They reflect a shared recognition that the choices judges make have policy implications, and that public confidence in the courts is promoted by holding judges accountable to the people and their elected representatives, to ensure that the decisions judges make are politically acceptable. But the vigor with which political dimension oversight has been pursued evinces emerging disaffection with judicial independence as rationalized by the rule of law paradigm—independence that can better be explained and defended by the successor paradigm I advocate.

To the extent that more aggressive political dimension tactics have enhanced public confidence, they have sometimes done so by constraining judicial independence in ways that arguably compromise fair hearings for parties and jeopardize judicial integrity in the adjudicative and ethical dimensions, respectively. In the adjudicative dimension, a fair hearing is put at risk if judges must look past achieving just results consistent with the facts and law as they interpret them, and make choices aimed at mollifying the public or their elected representatives. And in the ethical dimension, making judges responsive to the preferences of politicians, public, or pundits can be in tension with the traditional "three I's" embedded in codes of judicial conduct—independence, impartiality, and integrity—as reflected in an ethical directive for judges to disregard "public clamor" that has been in place since the Canons of Judicial Ethics were promulgated in 1924.[26]

Insofar as the objectives of the legal culture paradigm—adherence to applicable law, procedural fairness, and the pursuit of justice—are optimized if preserved in each dimension, this trend toward political dimension hegemony is problematic. Prescriptively, this suggests a need for the ethical and adjudicative dimensions of judicial oversight to recapture some of the turf ceded to the political, thereby restoring needed balance. Unlike the rule of law paradigm, the legal culture paradigm acknowledges the need for a robust political dimension of judicial oversight to manage the judiciary's excesses, but draws a line where oversight in the political dimension impairs the operation of the adjudicative and ethical dimensions.

The path to reform lies in restoring balance between the dimensions. To date, the public has received two messages. One message, from court critics, is that judges are politicians in robes who will disregard the law and make public policy if left to their own devices, and so must be controlled like other politicians. The other message, from the legal community, is that judges are umpires who do not make rules but instead follow them, and who will uphold the rule of law if afforded independence. For a public that has been steeping in judicial politics for a very long time, the legal establishment's message seems antiquated and counterfactual, and recent developments recounted here suggest that the legal establishment is slowly losing the public policy debate.

The time has come for the legal community to revise its message, to the end of adjusting the paradigm that they proselytize: In difficult cases, judges fill spaces in the law by making choices informed by legal and extra-legal considerations—including considerations of public policy. By virtue of their training, experience, and familiarity with the facts presented in carefully controlled settings, judges are better positioned than pundits, politicians, or other self-interested observers to exercise informed judgment that will mete justice under law—provided that judges enjoy a measure of independence from result-oriented kibitzers.

The argument that judges need breathing room to exercise judgment informed by their common sense (which includes their policy predilections) must allow for the possibility that such independence can be abused in ways that compromise the values independence seeks to promote—hence, the need for accountability. But accountability can be ensured and public confidence in the courts maintained without the adjudicative and ethical dimensions of judicial oversight giving so much ground to the political. Unlike the political dimension of judicial oversight, which is controlled by the public and elected officials, the ethical and adjudicative dimensions are largely within the control of the courts themselves. By ramping up their oversight in the adjudicative and ethical dimensions—and advertising those efforts in the political dimension—judges can restore some of the balance lost. Critical to the success of this venture is education and marketing: The bench and bar must enter the political dimension to the end of repositioning the judiciary's role in a legal culture

paradigm and selling the public on the continuing importance and effec-
tiveness of oversight in the adjudicative and ethical dimensions.

In this book, I develop the argument summarized here, across the
remaining chapters. Chapter 2 introduces the rule of law paradigm. It
begins by defining and developing the meaning of a sociolegal paradigm
as I use the term here. I then turn to a description of the core components
of the traditional rule of law paradigm, which posits that judges, armed
with a measure of independence from external encroachments on their
decision-making prerogatives, will bracket out extralegal influences and
follow applicable law.

The chapter then turns to the changing landscape of judicial politics in
American courts, to the end of showing how recent developments challenge the rule of law paradigm. It distinguishes between political pressure
points best described as chronic or cyclical and those that are more recent
and arguably transformative. It recounts the chronic and dichotomous
debate these developments have fueled between court defenders and critics over whether independent judges are impartial exponents of law in the
prevailing rule of law paradigm or politicians in robes who denigrate the
rule of law they are sworn to uphold. And the chapter highlights the ways
in which recent developments expose paradigm vulnerabilities.

Chapter 3 explores the changing academic understanding of judicial
decision-making in American courts. It shows how academic debates—
once dichotomous, like those in the public sphere—have recently yielded
to an emerging consensus among law professors and social scientists that
judges are subject to an array of legal and extralegal influences. The net
effect is to expose the perennial law versus politics debate as simplistic
and outmoded.

Chapter 4 transcends the contemporary law versus politics impasse,
with recourse to cultural understandings of the judicial role dating back
millennia, as reflected in folk tales, poems, polemics, novels, and scrip-
ture. It isolates judicial independence, impartiality, integrity, and competence as widely and deeply regarded values that promote the rule of law,
due process, and justice, which evolved against the backdrop of an ancient
understanding that judges are human beings subject to a host of influences. How and when those influences should be controlled to promote
law, due process, and justice, have varied, the chapter concludes, depending on whether the problem at hand was viewed from the perspective of a
litigant's interest in a fair hearing, the public's interest in the legitimacy of
its courts, or a natural law interest in good and ethical judges.

Chapter 5 then revisits the ailing rule of law paradigm and proposes,
in its stead, a new "legal culture" paradigm, which rests on a different set of assumptions that comport more closely with the traditional

understandings of the judicial role summarized in Chapter 4. This new paradigm posits that judges are immersed in a legal culture that values law, process, and justice—values that independence promotes by insulating judges from external pressures that could undermine their commitment to the norms of the legal culture. Yet, because judges are also subject to internal influences in tension with the values of the legal culture, independence must be tempered by a measure of accountability, the appropriate limits of which vary by dimension: (1) an adjudicative dimension that seeks fair hearings for litigants; (2) a political dimension that seeks public confidence in the courts; and (3) an ethical dimension that seeks good judges who respect their roles.

Chapter 6 reevaluates the transformation of the American judiciary discussed in Chapter 2, in light of the legal culture paradigm and its three dimensions of judicial oversight. This chapter reconceptualizes existing systems of oversight in terms of the three-dimensional structure I have proposed, to the end of documenting a long-term trend away from regulating the courts in the adjudicative and ethical dimensions of judicial oversight, toward the political.

Chapter 7 adds explanatory and prescriptive notes. First, it seeks to show how the legal culture paradigm, and the three-dimensional analysis it subsumes, can help to explain some of the more perplexing questions afflicting the courts and their oversight. Second, it details the normative underpinnings for each of the three dimensions of judicial oversight, to the end of underscoring the importance of each and the value of preserving balance between the dimensions. Trends documented in chapter 6 show that the adjudicative and ethical dimensions of oversight are being eclipsed by the political—an imbalance in need of correction. The chapter concludes by outlining ways in which the ethical and adjudicative dimensions of judicial oversight can recapture some of the turf ceded to the political, through education, reclamation, and moderation, thereby restoring needed balance.

Chapter 8 then brings the book to conclusion.

CHAPTER 2

The Rule of Law Paradigm
in a Changing Landscape

The traditional conception of the judicial role in American government is an essential component of a larger rule of law paradigm. It is a role that features competent, honest, impartial, and independent judges who interpret and apply the rules that we the people have created to govern ourselves, by bracketing out extralegal influences from within and without, and following the law on a case-by-case basis. In the first part of this chapter, I elaborate on the traditional rule of law paradigm and the role it envisions for judges. In the second part, I review the changing landscape of American courts, to the end of showing that the fabric of the traditional rule of law paradigm, as it concerns judges and the judiciary, is under stress and beginning to fray.

THE RULE OF LAW PARADIGM

In his influential book, *The Structure of Scientific Revolutions*, Thomas Kuhn explained how paradigms emerge, develop, crumble, and shift.[1] In Kuhn's schema, scientists in given fields organize their thinking around dominant models or paradigms that synthesize and describe how their piece of the world works to the satisfaction of those who study it. The prevailing paradigm structures how a field of study is conceptualized until practitioners within that field identify anomalies that the paradigm cannot explain. These practitioners struggle to rationalize such anomalies within the framework of the existing paradigm until a critical mass concurs that the paradigm is unsustainable. As the old paradigm crumbles, the hunt begins for a new, more satisfactory paradigm that can explain what its predecessor could not. When found, the relevant scientific community shifts its focus to developing the new paradigm, until that paradigm crumbles as well and gives way to a successor. Hence, Copernicus yielded to Newton, who yielded to Einstein.[2]

Kuhn's analysis was confined to the hard sciences, where changes in scientific thought could be explained in terms of shifting descriptive models around which the community of researchers galvanized itself over time. Kuhn did not think that the structure he described could be exported to the social sciences, where researchers resisted unifying paradigms to understand social phenomena at a metalevel.[3] But a bevy of scholars has tweaked, borrowed, and sometimes contorted Kuhn to conceptualize myriad subsets of social science study in useful and not so useful ways. In this book, I likewise borrow selectively from Kuhn, by exporting his approach to sociolegal paradigms.

I define sociolegal paradigms in a squishy kind of way—as templates of interaction between law, society, and culture with descriptive, normative, and aspirational elements that affected communities follow. Broadly conceived, the rule of law has operated as a dominant sociolegal paradigm in western thought for millennia. Books have been written on the rule of law and its origins, and I do not presume to do justice to that body of work in a paragraph or two. For purposes here, it is enough to render a thumbnail sketch of the history, before bearing down on the details of its current incarnation.

The western edition of the rule of law origin story is disjointed and nonlinear. It typically begins with the ancient Greeks. Whereas Plato advocated government by philosopher kings, the narrative begins, Aristotle was less trusting. "We do not allow a man to rule, but the law," Aristotle declared, because:

> He who bids law to rule seems to bid God and intelligence alone to rule, but he who bids that man rule puts forward a beast as well; for that is the sort of things desire is, and spiritedness twists rulers even when they are the best of men. Accordingly law is intelligence without appetite.[4]

Rome followed suit with its own rule of law tradition. As Cicero put it, "we are all servants of the law for the very purpose that we may be free men."[5]

Following the collapse of Rome, antiquity's experience with the rule of law was lost for half a millennium. As Brian Tamanaha explained, the rule of law's eventual return, "congealed into existence in a slow, unplanned manner that commenced in the Middle Ages, with no single source or starting point."[6] Greco-Roman political philosophy later rejoined the conversation, and was integral to the democratic theory of John Locke in the late Renaissance, and subsequently Montesquieu, who in turn, were highly influential upon early American writers, such as Thomas Paine and John Adams.[7]

James Madison, architect of the American Constitution, sided with Aristotle over Plato in his distrust of leaders with political power and saw the challenge as being to design a government that implemented the rule of law in practice:

> If men were angels, no government would be necessary. In framing a government which is to be administered by men over men, the great difficulty lies in this: you must first enable the government to control the governed; and in the next place oblige it to control itself.[8]

The key for Madison and his cohort was to divide the powers of government into three separate and independent branches. Those branches would simultaneously exercise executive, legislative, and judicial powers to control the governed and wield checks over the coordinate branches to control the government itself.

With respect to the judicial branch, the judicial power concerned the impartial application of law to facts on a case-by-case basis. Subsumed within the judicial power was the courts' primary check on the other branches of government: the power to declare acts of the executive and legislature unconstitutional. Several early state courts exercised judicial review prior to the 1787 constitutional convention,[9] and Alexander Hamilton, as coauthor of the *Federalist Papers*, asserted that the power would be available to the federal courts as well—a power the Supreme Court first exercised in the 1803 case of *Marbury v. Madison*.[10]

Insofar as "law is intelligence without appetite," to borrow Aristotle's phrase, when exercising judicial power it has long been a defining feature of the judge's role to eschew extralegal influences and uphold the law. Hence, Blackstone warned that a judge is "sworn to determine, not according to his own private judgment, but according to the known customs and laws of the land."[11] To ensure that judges hewed the rule of law, the framers of the United States Constitution afforded judges a measure of independence by guarding against encroachments upon judicial tenure and salaries, which Alexander Hamilton regarded as "peculiarly essential in a limited Constitution":

> In a monarchy it is an excellent barrier to the despotism of the prince; in a republic it is a no less excellent barrier to the encroachments and oppressions of the representative body. And it is the best expedient which can be devised in any government, to secure a steady, upright, and impartial administration of the laws.[12]

In response to the concern that independence could have the opposite effect of unfettering judges to disregard the law and aggregate power to themselves, Hamilton argued that the prospect of impeachment would serve as an accountability-promoting deterrent:

> There never can be danger that the Judges, by a series of deliberate usurpations on the authority of the Legislature, would hazard the united resentment of the body intrusted with it, while this body was possessed of the means of punishing their presumption, by degrading them from their stations.[13]

Reduced to its essence, then, the rule of law paradigm envisions a government of laws established (directly and indirectly) by the governed, that an independent judiciary, unsullied by extralegal influences, interprets and applies, subject to limited accountability. In the modern era, the bench, bar, and their helpmates (who together comprise the legal community) have taken the lead in developing and defending rule of law architecture.

The general proposition that we are a nation operating under the rule of law enjoys pervasive structural and rhetorical support. It is a point too obvious to belabor that the organization of the federal and state governments is oriented to satisfy the basic structural requirements for the rule of law that scholars of jurisprudence have identified. First, delegating the task of lawmaking to the people and their elected representatives guards against arbitrary, idiosyncratic exercise of power by despotic rulers, which ensures that government is limited by law.[14] Second, the legislative process and the constitutional strictures legislation must satisfy, seek to ensure that laws are clear, public, and prospective, so that the people know what is expected of them.[15] Third, assigning the task of applying the law to a separate and independent judicial branch aims to ensure that laws are fairly enforced by open and accessible tribunals.[16]

Ubiquitous and often florid rhetoric by political and legal community leaders reinforces the rule of law as a guiding paradigm. President John F. Kennedy declared that "only respect for the law makes it possible for free men to dwell together in peace and progress";[17] President Ronald Reagan effused that "we've promised the world a season of truth—the truth of our great civilized ideas: individual liberty, representative government, the rule of law under God."[18] The day after his inauguration, President Obama promised that "transparency and the rule of law will be the touchstones of my presidency."[19] In 2002, American Bar Association President A. P. Carlton opined that "our society remains intact, based on the rule of law."[20] And in his acceptance speech as American Bar Association president, Michael Greco enthused that the "greatest democracy the world has ever known has survived only because of the rule of law."[21]

Bearing down on the role of the judiciary in the rule of law paradigm, structural and rhetorical elements converge to emphasize that judges must disregard extralegal influences and follow the law on a case-by-case basis. Structurally, the U.S. Constitution delegates the judicial power to Supreme and inferior courts; limits its jurisdiction to cases and controversies; and requires that all federal and state officials (including judges) take an oath to support the constitution.[22] By statute, federal judges swear to discharge duties under the "laws of the United States" "faithfully and impartially," and state systems require comparable oaths.[23] A virtually universal right to appellate review positions appellate courts to correct accidental and intentional failures to follow the law by lower courts under their supervision. And codes of conduct declare that judges "shall uphold and apply the law."[24]

The legal community's rhetoric reinforces the judge's inflexible duty to follow the law and disregard internal and external sources of interference with that unyielding mandate. A federal circuit judge explained that a "judge's responsibility is to interpret and apply the Constitution, legislative enactments and the decisions of higher courts. . . . This function must be performed by relying on legal training, and cannot, in any conscious way, be dependent upon personal or public opinion."[25] Similarly, Iowa's Chief Justice opined that "[i]n our system of government, we expect judges to rule according to the law, regardless of their personal views."[26] Similarly, the Constitution Project has declared that "[j]udges are supposed to be responsive only to the rule of law and the Constitution, not to majority will or public, political or media pressure."[27] And American Bar Association President William Paul echoed that the "public expects its judges to put aside their own partisan political views and to make impartial decisions based on the rule of law rather than on the transitory popular will of the political branches or the people."[28]

To buffer judges from external sources of interference with their duty to follow the law (and nothing but), the rule of law paradigm calls for an independent judiciary. Federal judges are afforded decisional independence by life tenure and a salary that is not subject to being cut, which insulates them from threats to their livelihood; and the judiciary's constitutional monopoly over "the judicial power" affords the judicial branch some institutional independence from external encroachments on judicial functions.[29] In state systems, many constitutions explicitly provide for a separate and unified judicial branch.[30] And while few states provide judges with tenure during good behavior, and most subject them to some form of periodic election instead, the movement away from appointive to elective systems that began in the 1830s was motivated by a desire to render judges independent from the governors or legislatures who appointed them.[31] Finally, codes of conduct call upon judges to act with independence, by directing that a judge "shall not be swayed by public clamor, or fear of criticism";[32] "shall not permit family, social, political, financial, or other interests or relationships to influence the judge's judicial conduct or judgment";[33] and "shall act at all times in a manner that promotes public confidence in the independence . . . of the judiciary."[34]

As a matter of structure and rhetoric, the paradigm tethers judicial independence tightly to the rule of law. Independence is thus positioned as an instrumental value that makes impartial decision-making under the rule of law possible. The U.S. Constitution provides that neither the state nor federal governments may deprive a citizen of life, liberty, or property without due process of law.[35] And the U.S. Supreme Court has held that an independent adjudicator is core to a citizen's right to due process under law.[36] In other words, an independent judge is an essential attribute of the rule of law. The preamble to the Model Code of Judicial Conduct (some variation of which has been adopted by all fifty state judiciaries and the lower federal courts) emphasizes this linkage:

> The United States legal system is based upon the principle that an independent, impartial, and competent judiciary . . . will interpret and apply the law that governs our society. Thus, the judiciary plays a central role in preserving the principles of justice and the rule of law.[37]

The bench and bar aggressively market the linkage between independence and the rule of law. Justice Stephen Breyer has opined that "judicial independence revolves around the theme of how to ensure that judges decide according to law, rather than according to their own whims or the will of the political branches of government."[38] A federal district judge has echoed that "judicial independence . . . ensures that judges are free to follow their oaths, free to follow the Rule of Law."[39] The Wisconsin Chief Justice adds that independence enables judges to decide cases "fairly, impartially, and according to the facts and law, not according to whim, prejudice, or fear, the dictates of the legislature or executive, or the latest opinion poll."[40] In a like vein, an American Bar Association president explained that judicial independence "mean[s] that judges can decide cases before them without fear or favor, based on the law and the facts of that particular case."[41] And a report of the Defense Research Institute adds that, "for our system to work, a judge must be free to make decisions based on the facts and law without undue influence or interference."[42]

Accordingly, the bench and bar are often critical of court critics, whom they characterize as seeking to intimidate or threaten judges in ways that undermine judicial independence and the rule of law.[43] Modern apostles of the rule of law paradigm acknowledge that judicial independence is not absolute and should be tempered by accountability to control its excesses. But it is a constrained form of accountability that exponents of the rule of law paradigm advocate. In an oft-repeated mantra, we are told that judges should be "accountable to the law," and not to the "popular will," "whims of the day," or the desires of "political supporters or special interests."[44] New York's Chief Judge pushed back against a "distorted concept of accountability" that has led interest groups on a campaign "to convince Americans that the judiciary is no different than the political branches of government."[45] In other words, judges should not be accountable in the same ways and to the same extent as officials in the legislative and executive branches. When it comes to judicial rulings, the legal community is at peace with the conclusion that judges should be accountable to their oaths of office and legal processes (such as appeal, mandamus, constitutional amendments, and statutory overrides), but it typically goes no further. Proposals to chasten judges for their rulings by (1) removing them from office via impeachment, disciplinary, or election processes; (2) disestablishing their courts; (3) cutting their budgets; or (4) curtailing their jurisdiction are opposed as unwarranted threats to judicial independence and the rule of law.[46]

The foregoing discussion underscores an important difference between the paradigms that Kuhn described in the hard sciences and sociolegal paradigms. Unlike Kuhnian paradigms, the communities that operate within the sociolegal rule of law paradigm are not confined to the social scientists who study it. Rather, they include all communities guided by the paradigm: (1) those who design and implement it; (2) those who abide by it; and (3) those who study and report on it. That includes rule of law practitioners: the bench, bar, and other public officials (including the political parties with which those officials are affiliated), who are delegated by the people to design, build, and repair rule of law structures. It includes rule of law beneficiaries: the public generally and litigants specifically. And it includes rule of law analysts: not just scholars but interest groups and the media as well.

In the hard sciences, the paradigms Kuhn isolates fail as they lose descriptive force among the scholars who work within them. If that were true of sociolegal paradigms, the rule of law paradigm, as constructed and defended by the legal community, would be a goner: As chapter 3 elaborates, scholars are in general agreement that judicial decision-making is subject to extralegal influences, and that categorical claims to the contrary are exaggerated or wrong—even if minimizing such influences is a worthy goal.

The rule of law paradigm, however, is more complicated, because it includes normative and aspirational elements. Paradigm adherents include but are not limited to researchers interested in the model's descriptive accuracy. For communities that embrace the rule of law as a guiding model—not because they study it, but because they live by it—descriptive accuracy may be neither necessary nor sufficient. The rule of law paradigm could retain influence after losing descriptive force, if an affected community thinks that the rule of law is a helpful myth or desirable aspiration. Thus, for example, to preserve social order or promote a rule of law ideal, the public may acquiesce to the rulings of judges on the pretext that they implement the rule of law and nothing else, even if they regard that pretext as exaggerated. In this context, descriptive failures can simply elicit calls for judges to redouble their efforts to abide by the rule of law ideal. Conversely, the rule of law paradigm could fail without losing descriptive force if the affected community rejects the paradigm's underlying normative premise that judges should follow the law. For instance, even if the affected community thinks that independent judges do follow the law, the paradigm would fail if the community rejects the premise that judges should follow the law, in favor of the premise that they should follow the ad hoc policy preferences of the electorate or legislature instead. Thus, voters could oust a judge at the ballot box for ruling that a given state action is unconstitutional because they favor the state action regardless of what the constitution says.

That, in a nutshell, is the rule of law paradigm. It serves as a template or mission statement for the varied communities operating within it, and so, by its nature, lacks the subtlety and detail of a fully developed jurisprudential construct or model. Indeed, as I argue later, its failure to account for the complexity and elasticity of law is among the rule of law's primary failings. The balance of this chapter explores how the landscape of the American judiciary has changed in recent generations, and the ways in which those changes have strained the rule of law paradigm.

THE CHANGING LANDSCAPE OF THE AMERICAN COURTS

In 1906, amid Progressive Era attacks on state and federal courts, Roscoe Pound addressed the American Bar Association at its annual meeting, where he spoke on "the causes of popular dissatisfaction with the administration of justice."[47] Among the causes he identified was "putting courts into politics and compelling judges to become politicians," which "in many jurisdictions has almost destroyed the traditional respect for the Bench."[48] Ultimately, however, he attributed politicization of the courts to "an age in transition," concluded that the problems it caused "will take care of themselves," and focused his attention on other issues—specifically, court administration and procedure—which he regarded as more pressing.[49]

Cyclical Ages of Transition

In one respect, Pound's assessment was right: Political interest in the courts waxes and wanes with the era. When a new political regime wrests power from the old, holdover judges appointed or elected under the old regime become political targets of the new, until more politically compatible judges are selected, less politically compatible judges retire or recede, or the attacks run their course and lose momentum. Thus, "putting courts into politics" has tended to spike after major transitions of political power.

The first round of American anti-court sentiment coincided with the initial transition of political power in the fledgling nation's history, after Jeffersonian Republicans bested the Federalists in the 1801 elections. Jeffersonian loyalists led successful campaigns to disestablish sixteen judgeships that the ousted Federalist Congress had created, to impeach and remove Federalist District Judge John Pickering, and to impeach Federalist Supreme Court Justice Samuel Chase, with the Senate vote on the final Article of impeachment against Chase falling two votes short of that necessary for removal.[50]

In 1828, the Jacksonian Democrats ushered in a new, populist era with their defeat of the Whigs and sparked a second spate of anti-court agitation. President Jackson challenged the holdover Marshall Court's supremacy as expositor of the Constitution, declaring that "[t]he opinion of the judges, has no more authority over Congress than the opinion of Congress has over the judges and on that point the president is independent of both."[51] And while the war Jackson waged was largely one of words, Georgia took those words to heart by openly defying Supreme Court orders in a series of cases involving the Cherokee Indian tribe. In response to one such case, Jackson is reported to have said, "John Marshall has made his decision, now let him enforce it."[52] Although the statement is likely apocryphal, it captures the tense tenor of the times.

A generation later, in the aftermath of the Civil War, the "Radical Republican" Congress took control of the newly reunited nation. The Republicans had neither forgiven nor forgotten the Supreme Court's 1856 decision in *Dred Scott v. Sanford*, which deprived Congress of the power to prohibit slavery in the territories. As Congress undertook to reconstruct the South, their leaders threatened to "annihilate" the Court if it interfered.[53] In this third cycle of court-directed animus spanning a dozen years, Congress stripped the Court of jurisdiction to review the constitutionality of a pending piece of Reconstruction legislation, and (although Congress's motives were unclear) decreased the Supreme Court's size from ten justices to seven, which deprived Democratic President Andrew Johnson of the opportunity to fill pending and impending vacancies, only to increase its size to nine after his Republican successor, Ulysses S. Grant, took office.[54]

At the turn of the twentieth century, a fourth barrage against the courts began with the Progressives' ascension to power. The Progressives launched a crusade against conservative, laissez-faire courts that obstructed the Progressive agenda—most notably, courts that invalidated legislation regulating the workplace on the grounds that such restrictions deprived employers of their property without due process of law.[55] Pound thus delivered his seminal address to the American Bar Association amid a blizzard of Progressive Era proposals to end life tenure for federal judges, subject them to popular election, shrink their jurisdiction, abolish judicial review, disestablish the unpopular Commerce Court, and subject state judges to recall elections.[56]

A fifth wave of court-directed hostility descended in the 1930s, with the arrival of Franklin Delano Roosevelt's New Deal. Vexed by a Court that invalidated pieces of his legislative agenda on the same substantive due process grounds that angered Progressives in the 1890s, Roosevelt proposed to "pack" the Supreme Court by increasing its size to ensure a majority sympathetic to New Deal initiatives.[57]

In the 1950s and 1960s, congressional Republicans, joined by southern Democrats, criticized the Warren Court for the perceived liberal excesses of its decisions on civil rights and civil liberties issues. Such criticism culminated in calls to impeach Chief Justice Earl Warren and Justice William O. Douglas, attempts by southern states to defy Supreme Court rulings, and bills to strip the federal courts of jurisdiction to hear school prayer cases.[58] This sixth cycle came to a crescendo with the election of President Richard Nixon, who pledged to appoint "strict constructionists" to the bench and realigned the Supreme Court with four new appointments in his first term.[59]

Round seven arrived a generation later, in 1994, when the Republican Party gained control of both houses of Congress for the first time in over a generation and embarked on a campaign against liberal "judicial activism."[60] House Republican leaders threatened "activist" district and circuit judges with impeachment, proposed to disestablish or cut the budgets of uncooperative courts, introduced legislation to curtail federal court jurisdiction over controversial issues, and enacted legislation curbing judicial review in immigration cases, prison litigation, and habeas corpus petitions.[61] And Senate Republicans and Democrats alike sought to delay or reject nominees of presidents from the opposing political party whose ideologies they challenged as too extreme.

The New Age of Perpetual Transition

As right as Pound was in observing that courts are under greatest pressure during times of transition that come and go, in another respect, he was quite wrong. For state and federal courts, the "age of transition" to which Pound referred in 1906, came but never went. Rather, the courts have been in a state of perpetual transition that accelerated in earnest beginning in the latter half of the twentieth century, which has heightened the political salience of their work, put them under ever more scrutiny, and challenged traditional conceptions of judges as disinterested neutrals or "umpires."

The Changing Role of the "Trial Judge"

The American judiciary serves a population that has grown from 85 million in 1906, when Pound gave his speech, to 205 million in 1970, to 309 million in 2010.[62] This growth in population has coincided with an increase in caseloads. In 1977, the National Center for State Courts reported 70.1 million cases filed in state courts.[63] In 2010, that number had increased to 103.5 million.[64] In 1977, the Administrative Office of the United States Courts reported that 172,208 cases had been filed in federal courts the previous year.[65] By 2010, that number had grown to 361,323.[66]

Expense and delay were among the sources of dissatisfaction with the administration of justice that Pound identified over a century ago, which he sought to ameliorate with improved administration and procedure.[67] With populations and caseloads perennially on the rise, complaints of docket congestion and delay have become fixtures of the litigation landscape.[68] And with the arrival of modern discovery and complaints concerning its attendant expense, cost and delay have been cast as the omnipresent evil twins of civil litigation.

Driven in part by a desire to reduce cost and delay, legislatures, courts, and litigants have developed an array of coping strategies. First, the obvious remedy for caseload problems is to add new judgeships, and indeed, the number of judges has increased over time: In recent years, the number of judicial officers across state systems has increased at a rate of 110 judges per year.[69] Typically, though, that number has increased at only half the rate of the caseload.[70] And in the federal system, the infusion of judges aimed at easing caseload pressures has included a significant number of nontraditional judicial officers: administrative law judges, magistrates, special masters, and so on. These judicial officers lack the tenure and salary protections of traditional Article III judges, and operate as adjuncts to Article III judges, or as "Article I" judges who serve on adjudicative bodies specially created by Congress. Because this new wave of judicial officers lacks the independence of Article III judges, it raises a question revisited later in this chapter: Is an independent judiciary losing its relevance?[71]

Second, judges have been authorized, encouraged, and sometimes directed to play a more aggressive role in managing litigation and settling disputes. Rule 16 of the Federal Rules of Civil Procedure, for example, promulgated in 1938, was amended six times between 1983 and 2015.[72] As amended, it requires district judges to issue scheduling orders that "limit the time" for joinder, amendments, discovery, and motions, and authorizes district judges to schedule pretrial conferences for the purposes of "expediting disposition of the action," establishing "early and continuing control" of the action so that it "will not be protracted because of lack of management," "discouraging wasteful pretrial activities," and "facilitating settlement."[73] The Civil Justice Reform Act, enacted by Congress in 1990 (pieces of which were discontinued in 1997), directed district courts to devise case "expense and delay reduction plans" and report decision-making delays.[74] Procedural rules have been amended in an effort to reduce excesses in the discovery process, by limiting the discovery that can be taken without court permission, requiring unsolicited disclosure of basic information about the parties' claims and defenses, and articulating the court's role in managing electronic discovery.[75]

Third, beginning in the 1980s, scholars, legislators, judges, and lawyers joined a movement to promote mediation, arbitration, and other alternative dispute resolution (ADR) mechanisms, "as a solution to crowded dockets and an inexpensive panacea for the ills of an overly litigious society."[76] In the 1980s, the number of ADR providers increased tenfold;[77] in 1998, Congress enacted legislation requiring every federal judicial district to establish ADR mechanisms;[78] and in 2013, a study of Fortune 1000 companies reported that American businesses had expanded their use of ADR mechanisms.[79]

Fourth, courts have resorted to rules at their disposal to end litigation before trial with increasing frequency. Case termination rates via summary judgment rose from 1.8% in 1960, to 4% in 1975, to 8% in 2000. When partial summary judgments are included, rates doubled from 6% to 12% between 1975 and 2000. In cases decided in 2007 and 2009, the Supreme Court relaxed dismissal standards at the pleading stage, for the explicit purpose of sparing defendants the expense of unnecessary discovery when plaintiffs fail to articulate a "plausible" claim.[80] On a related

front, federal courts revised litigation sanctions rules multiple times, subjecting lawyers and parties to penalties for pleadings and motions filed for
"any improper purpose, such as to . . . cause unnecessary delay, or need-
lessly increase the cost of litigation."[81]

Fifth, courts and the legislatures that oversee them, confronted with
the advent of modern complex litigation and the influx of multiparty, multiforum cases that complex litigation has spawned, have explored ways
to manage the resulting costs and delays through manipulation of aggregation mechanisms. In 1966, the Judicial Conference rewrote the class-
action rule, accompanied by commentary that sought to exclude mass
tort actions from its purview.[82] In 1968, Congress enacted legislation
establishing a judicial panel on multidistrict litigation (MDL) enabling
the transfer of related cases filed in different districts to a single forum,
where they could be consolidated for pretrial proceedings only.[83] Over the
succeeding decades, the "pretrial" limitation on MDL was circumvented,
and mass tort proceedings were certified as class actions with increasing
frequency.[84] Efforts to manage the proliferation of class actions led to hybridized forms of class actions or class-action surrogates: In 2002, Congress increased the availability of consolidation devices in mass-accident
litigation;[85] in 2003, the class-action rule was revised to accommodate its
use in facilitating settlements;[86] in 2005, the Class Action Fairness Act
expanded the availability of federal forums in class-action litigation (less
a manifestation of enthusiasm for class actions than of antipathy toward
state class actions in some jurisdictions);[87] even more recently, MDL proceedings have been exploited to create settlement classes, and contract-
based settlements of aggregate claims that may not meet class-action
requirements.[88] Aggregation critics argue that hinging the outcome of
multiple cases on a single proceeding raises the stakes to such an extent
that plaintiffs effectively "blackmail" defendants into a favorable settlement. Empirical support for such "blackmail" claims is contested,[89] but
the unassailable point remains that aggregation—like civil litigation
generally—has become a process aimed more at facilitating settlement
than readying for trial.[90]

In light of these developments, it is unsurprising that the incidence of
trials has been in a long, slow state of decline. As of 1936, 19.8% of federal
cases filed ended in trial.[91] By 1962, that percentage had declined to 11.5%,
and to 1.8% by 2002.[92] In state systems, trials have become scarcer still,
with only 0.6% of 2002 cases filed culminating in trial.[93] The "trial judge"
has thus become an oxymoron, who looks less like an archetypal umpire,
than a case manager.[94] But more is at work here than continuing efforts
to combat excessive cost and delay. This movement away from the trial as
the traditional form of dispute resolution is driven to an uncertain extent

by an emerging view that justice is ill-served by judges cast as coldly detached umpires who declare winners and losers in protracted disputes between two combatants in a zero-sum game. From this perspective, judges who encourage settlement and ADR promote a kinder, gentler, and fairer resolution of disputes. Judges who facilitate aggregation improve access to justice for those who cannot afford to litigate individually. And judges who resort to dispositive motions fulfill the potential of modern discovery to facilitate the just, speedy, and inexpensive determination of civil actions, by sparing blameless defendants and wronged plaintiffs unwarranted angst, uncertainty, expense, and delay.

Emblematic of emerging norms that celebrate nontraditional forms of judging is the so-called "problem-solving courts" movement, which began in the late 1980s with drug courts, and later expanded to mental health courts, domestic violence courts, veterans courts, and courts of more general jurisdiction. It proceeds from the premise that the administration of justice will be more effective if judges seek to address the substance abuse, mental health, domestic violence, and other problems at the root of many cases that judges adjudicate.[95] Thus, the problem-solving judge is less a detached referee than an engaged troubleshooter. She interacts with the parties, their lawyers, health care professionals, service providers, and others, to the end of addressing the problems that brought the parties to court in the first place. And she does so in cases where the prospect of trial is usually beside the point because the underling legal issue, such as the defendant's guilt, is a foregone conclusion.

The transformation of the trial judge into a settler, manager, and problem-solver has created a rift within the legal community. That rift is born of a tension between the twin missions of the courts as forums for public vindication of legal rights, for which trial remains a symbolic centerpiece, and forums for the effective and expeditious resolution of private disputes, for which trial is increasingly viewed as anathema. For those who regard the courts as public guardians of their legal rights, the proliferation of aggregation mechanisms, alternative dispute resolution, heavy-handed settlement pressures, aggressive recourse to dispositive pretrial orders, and the profusion of problem-solving courts, endanger the parties' time-honored right to their "day in court" by eclipsing the opportunity to have their individual claims and defenses fully adjudicated.[96]

As judges mutate into case managers, settlement negotiators, and problem solvers, the need for judicial independence from political oversight becomes less obvious. It is one thing to say that we should buffer the rule of law from political encroachment by enabling umpire judges to make their calls without interference. It is quite another to say that judges should enjoy comparable freedom from oversight when managing and settling claims, or remediating drug and alcohol dependencies, where judicial independence cannot be defended on traditional rule of law grounds.[97] Hence, the new, nontraditional judge who manages, settles, and fixes is not above the fray, but part of it—a role that the rule of law paradigm is ill-equipped to accommodate.

Controversy has not been confined to judges in their emerging, nontraditional roles. The transformation of trial judges into problem solvers, case managers, and settlement negotiators diminishes the role of the trial judge "umpire," but has not heralded the demise of the umpire judge altogether. The consummate case manager who never presides at trial must nonetheless officiate at innumerable pretrial hearings on contested motions to dismiss, suppress evidence, certify class actions, compel discovery, grant summary judgment, and so on, where she must apply facts to law and issue rulings. Such a role is no less umpire-like than ruling on objections at trial. Moreover, the appellate judge's umpiral role as arbiter of contested legal questions—at issue in the next section—remains largely unchanged.

All of this begs the larger question of what it means to be an umpire when the metaphor seems apt. Even if we indulge Chief Justice Roberts and accept that when judges interpret the constitution, they "call balls and strikes," we must come to terms with the observation of a major league umpire, that calling balls and strikes is "like [interpreting] the Constitution. The strike zone is a living, breathing document."[98] Judges, like umpires, subject the rules they apply to different interpretations. When the results of a judge's interpretations are sharply at odds with public policy preferences, political fallouts can follow. But unlike umpires, more is at stake in those fallouts than the outcome of a sporting event.

At the epicenter of these controversies surrounding judges in their varied roles is a struggle to manage the choices judges make. How far and in what ways should the need for accountable, cost-effective access to justice intrude on a judge's prerogatives to dismiss complaints, sanction litigation misconduct, manage discovery, grant summary judgment, certify class actions, settle disputes, ameliorate a defendant's drug problem, or rule on questions of law? Managing judicial prerogatives, in turn, implicates the larger question of the extent to which the choices judges make should be independent of popular or political control. That is particularly so when those choices are fraught with partisan-aligned policy implications that affect the relative rights and responsibilities of corporations versus consumers, management versus unions, law enforcement versus accused, rich versus poor, men versus women, blacks versus whites, and so on. Why should the judge's preferences in such cases trump those of the public she ostensibly serves?

As discussed in chapter 3, empirical study of the extent to which the decisions judges make are influenced by their policy predilections and other extralegal factors was catalyzed by the legal realist movement of the 1920s and continues apace to this day. But claims that judges are subject to such influences are of far more ancient origin, as chapter 4 elaborates. Being as old as the hills, such claims are not part of the "changing landscape" that I describe here. What has changed is that there are new, different, and proliferating outlets for airing claims of judicial choices run amok. That, in turn, has added urgency to questions concerning the continuing value of judicial independence, even when judges are serving as "umpires" in some sense of the term.

Proliferating Forums for Challenging the Choices Judges Make

Emerging forums for airing grievances against judges and courts include some new ones and some old ones that have been repurposed or reenergized. They include: (1) changes wrought by the establishment of intermediate appellate courts; (2) the shifting focus of the federal judicial appointments process; (3) the new politics of state judicial elections; (4) the emerging use of procedural reform to influence substantive case outcomes; (5) the transformation of media outlets and courts reportage; (6) the advent of codes of judicial conduct and systems of judicial discipline; and (7) intensifying battles over state judicial budgets.

Changes in Appellate Structure

Changes spanning decades, and sometimes generations, have created new forums for challenging the decisions that federal and state judges make. Some of those forums target trial courts or, more aptly (given the dearth of trials), courts of original jurisdiction. Indeed, all cases with hotly contested policy-laden questions of law must, of necessity, begin in courts of original jurisdiction. Such cases, however, are dwarfed by the deluge of garden-variety disputes those judges decide, making political maelstroms a relative rarity for trial judges. Moreover, when the occasional, ideologically freighted issue arises, political attention and ire usually shift from the trial to the appellate court, where the buck stops after an appeal is taken. Hence, when thinking about the proliferating forums for challenging the choices judges make, appellate courts are often a focal point.

There may be nothing new to the critique that judges allow extralegal factors to influence if not supersede their duty to uphold the law, but changes in appellate structure and practice have rendered courts of last resort more vulnerable to such claims. In 1891, Congress interposed intermediate appellate courts between the federal district courts and the U.S. Supreme Court, in an effort to alleviate the backlog on the Supreme Court's docket.[99] In 1988, Congress went further still and made nearly all appeals to the Supreme Court discretionary.[100] In 1880, there were over 1,200 pending appeals before the Supreme Court—all of them mandatory.[101] In 2010, that number had dwindled to 86 cases that the Court, in its discretion, had scheduled for oral argument and decided from over 9,000 petitions received.[102]

State systems have followed a similar path. In an effort to relieve docket congestion on their high courts, a handful of states introduced intermediate appellate courts as early as the 1890s; many followed suit beginning in the 1950s, and today they are in place in forty states.[103] Most jurisdictions with intermediate appellate courts have likewise opted to make appeals to their highest courts discretionary.[104]

Establishing intermediate appellate court systems has had a threefold impact. First, it has enabled supreme courts to limit their dockets to significantly fewer cases than before, which has elevated the political attention those cases have received through sheer paucity of numbers. Second, and more important, the one-two punch of establishing intermediate appellate courts and eliminating mandatory appeals to the supreme courts has transformed high courts from courts of error correction to courts of law clarification, if not lawmaking. Gone is the steady, bland diet of non-controversial cases in which a typically unanimous high court methodically corrects trial court mistakes—which helped to keep the occasional controversy in perspective. In its stead is a spicier fare of supreme court cases featuring more hotly contested and often policy-laden questions of law with respect to which the intermediate appellate courts are often divided.[105] Third, the net effect of making circuit courts the courts of last resort in virtually all cases heightens the political salience of their work. It is probably impossible to quantify the impact of these structural reforms on judicial politics, but they add context that may help to explain when and why the forums for challenging the choices judges make have proliferated.

Federal Judicial Appointments

President Richard Nixon's dismantling of the Warren Court with four appointments in three years mobilized liberals and conservatives alike. The newly constituted Burger Court disappointed Christian conservatives with decisions that recognized abortion rights, perpetuated restrictions on school prayer, and invalidated other religious observances on public property. Beginning in the late 1970s, organizations such as Baptist Minister Jerry Falwell's "Moral Majority" mobilized Christian conservatives, who agitated to overturn judicial decisions they deemed antithetical to their values,[106] while liberal organizations, such as "People for the American Way," mobilized in response.[107] The confirmation process became the battlefield of choice for newly mobilized interest groups on both sides of the emerging culture war over judicial decision-making.

Partisan wrangling had always been a part of the Supreme Court confirmation process. Disputes over nominee ideology, however, did not emerge until the 1880s, when the agricultural lobby, the Grange, interceded to oppose the Supreme Court nomination of Stanley Matthews, whom the populist group regarded as a corporate lackey.[108] Nominee ideology was a factor in several confirmation proceedings in the early twentieth century, but became increasingly salient as interest group mobilization intensified, reaching its apogee 1987, with the nomination of Robert Bork, when ideology became the sole basis for Senate rejection of a Supreme Court nomination.[109] Political ideology has remained a primary—and sometimes the exclusive—focus of every Supreme Court confirmation in the years since.

Partisan battles over nominee ideology subsequently spilled over into circuit court confirmation proceedings. Appointments to the lower courts have always been partisan affairs: Presidents have traditionally chosen nominees from within the ranks of the president's political party, and since the early nineteenth century, the practice of "Senatorial courtesy" has afforded senators considerable power to designate nominees for district court judgeships in their states.[110] In the 1980s, President Ronald Reagan committed himself to appointing ideologically conservative judges; with respect to the lower courts, he made good on that promise by requesting that Senators supply him with lists of proposed nominees for the White House to vet.[111] The Democrats responded by rejecting the Bork nomination, the reverberations from which began to shake the circuit court confirmation process soon thereafter. Every administration since has witnessed acrimonious circuit court confirmation battles over nominee ideology, featuring an impressive array of dilatory tactics by senators from both political parties.[112]

State Judicial Elections

During the Warren Court era, federal courts were the forums of choice for public interest or cause lawyers intent on pursuing civil rights and civil liberties agendas. By the late 1970s, progressives, most notably Justice William Brennan, frustrated by the conservative turn of the Burger Court, began urging liberal cause lawyers to take their campaigns to state courts.[113]

Meanwhile, elections in southern and New England states—long Democratic strongholds—became more competitive affairs in the aftermath of the Lyndon Johnson administration, and reached their denouement with the 1980 election of President Ronald Reagan.[114] The reemergence of two-party politics portended new conflict and competition in judicial elections,[115] starting with Texas in the early 1980s, when trial lawyers and the defense bar grappled to control how their supreme court was constituted. President Reagan's popular campaign to "get tough" on crime and drugs furnished additional grist for the judicial campaign mill, and in 1986, California Chief Justice Rose Byrd and two of her colleagues lost their retention elections for their perceived refusal to uphold the death penalty.[116] In 1996, Tennessee Justice Penny White and Nebraska Justice David Lanphier lost retention elections because of their votes in criminal cases and the "soft on crime" mantra became a durable campaign issue for conservatives in the years that followed.[117] In the 1990s, judicial campaigns over candidate ideology proliferated to include issues ranging from abortion and same-sex marriage, to school funding and water rights.[118]

This upsurge of political interest in state courts was not lost on the Chamber of Commerce. During the latter half of the twentieth century, state courts had enabled a plaintiff-friendly revolution in the personal injury arena that transformed the substantive law of products liability and punitive damages.[119] At the end of the twentieth century, the Chamber of Commerce began pouring unprecedented sums into supreme court races, in the hope of electing more business-friendly judges.[120] In an effort to bootstrap their campaigns to more salable political issues, the Chamber and other tort reform advocates often targeted disfavored incumbents with soft-on-crime campaigns.[121] The plaintiff's trial bar responded in kind, throwing its financial support behind pro-consumer plaintiff candidates.

So began the "new politics of judicial elections,"[122] in which supreme court campaign spending doubled between the 1990s and the first decade of the new millennium. Prominent organizations and individuals, most notably retired Justice Sandra Day O'Connor, launched initiatives decrying the perception that campaign dollars were buying influence among judges.[123]

Procedure Reform

Litigation procedure has likewise become a venue for skirmishes with ideological overtones, affecting trial judges and the appellate courts that supervise them. Beginning in the 1970s, procedural rulemaking became a new forum for litigants and interest groups angling to improve their position in litigation, as disputes erupted over procedural rules regulating such issues as evidence, litigation sanctions, class actions, and discovery.[124] A trilogy of Supreme Court cases decided in 1986, which appeared to relax the showing needed for defendants to seek summary judgment, elicited widespread criticism from lawyers and interest groups sympathetic to causes championed by plaintiffs.[125] In 2005, Congress enacted the Class Action Fairness Act to address perceived pro-plaintiff bias in state class actions, by making it easier for defendants to remove state class actions to federal court.[126] In two cases decided in 2007 and 2009, the Supreme Court reinterpreted pleading standards in ways that provoked political interest. Previously, district judges were authorized to dismiss a plaintiff's suit for failure to state a claim at a preliminary stage in the proceedings, only if there was "no set of facts" that could sustain the claim. In *Atlantic Bell v. Twombly* and *Ashcroft v. Iqbal*, however, the Court instructed district judges to dismiss any claim that their "common sense" and "experience" tell them is "implausible."[127] Insofar as a judge's "common sense" is influenced by her ideological (or other) inclinations, "Twiqbal" opened the door to a new politics of pleading.[128]

The politicization of procedure intersects with two issues previously raised in this chapter. First, it continues the story that began with the emergence of cost and delay as perennial sources of disaffection with the administration of justice, which has contributed to the changing nature of the judicial role. Whether civil justice is too expensive or time-consuming can depend on whose ox is being gored. Consumer plaintiffs and their counsel, who oppose a "plausible" pleading standard that facilitates early dismissals, who resist rigorous litigation sanctions rules that discourage putatively marginal claims, and who decry restrictions on liberal discovery, typically regard the cost and delay such measures aim to reduce as a price worth paying for access to justice. Corporate defendants and their counsel, of course, often feel otherwise. Thus, corporate defendants aligned with conservative partisans, have challenged consumer plaintiffs aligned with liberal partisans in policy debates so vituperative as to obscure answers to such basic questions as what the relevant costs and delays of civil litigation actually are.[129] Second, these ideological alignments that have besieged federal procedural law are functionally the same as those that have driven debates over substantive state tort law in judicial election campaigns.

Media Outlets

Television, almost by definition, reorients viewer focus toward issues of image or appearance. As early as the 1960s, Daniel Boorstein observed that covering news stories with an eye toward their appearance and entertainment value had led to the reporting of manufactured or "pseudo events," as news.[130] In the years since, the time that traditional news outlets have devoted to hard news has diminished. Between 1977 and 1997, entertainment and "human interest" stories in television news programs and major newspapers increased from 15% to 43% of the total.[131] News about politics and government became correspondingly compressed. In 1968, the average "sound bite" from presidential candidates in televised election stories was 42.3 seconds long; by 1988, it had diminished to less than ten seconds, and by 2000 it had dwindled to seven.[132] Insofar as the news is communicated in short, image-oriented segments, the public's understanding of judges and the judiciary will, of necessity, be impressionistic; and to the extent that public opinion influences how policymakers regulate the judiciary, the public's impressions of judges become very important.

Cable news networks and the Internet, which emerged in the last two decades of the twentieth century, had the potential to counter the long-term trend toward compressed, image-oriented sound bites, by virtue of cable's twenty-four-hour format, and the Internet's capacity to supply unlimited information on demand. But the primary cable news networks orient their programming toward filtering news through commentators with openly partisan or ideological alignments.[133] Similarly, Internet sites featuring court reportage are typically hosted by organizations with preordained perspectives supportive or critical of the courts.[134] The net effect is not to add factual details that contribute to a more nuanced understanding of the courts, but to add an ideological spin aimed at changing how viewers (or readers) perceive and interpret the few snapshots of information they are handed.

This changing media landscape has created new outlets for dissemination of information about the decisions judges make that render those decisions easier to attack and harder to defend. Image-oriented squibs or sound bites in traditional media accommodate pithy condemnations of unpopular judicial decisions. Defenses of judicial decisions, in contrast, which often require an explanation of the court's counter-majoritarian role in protecting constitutional rights from violation by fleeting majorities of the electorate, take more time than blurbs or bites allow. Cable news stations and the Internet now disseminate information on judicial decisions to a worldwide audience—information that previously went unreported for want of an outlet. Much of that information is critical of the judges involved: One need not be a hardened cynic to appreciate that sound and unexceptional decisions are less newsworthy than controversial ones, regardless of whether such controversies are real or pseudo. While the forums for criticizing courts and judges have thus proliferated, the opportunities for judges to respond to such criticism remains limited and largely unchanged: Ubiquitous ethical rules prohibit judges (upon pain of discipline) from commenting on pending or impending cases.[135]

Traditional media outlets have likewise contributed to the judiciary's changing political landscape. When journalists report on decisions of the U.S. Supreme Court, they routinely explain outcomes with reference to the ideological alignments of the justices in the majority and dissent.[136] The implication: To understand why justices vote as they do, it is not enough to understand the legal reasoning reflected in the opinions they write; one needs to know their ideological orientations.

It is not new for the press to explain Supreme Court decisions with reference to extralegal influences, but increased incidence of concurring and dissenting opinions, beginning in the 1940s,[137] has served as fodder for such explanations. Justices who proselytize the rule of law paradigm on their days off fuel skepticism of the paradigm in dissenting opinions when they openly accuse the majority of disregarding the law and substituting their policy preferences. Justice Antonin Scalia's colorful dissents have charged the Court with grounding this opinion or that in "philosophical predilection" that has "no foundation in American law and barely pretends to," that "vandalizes . . . our people's traditions," or implements a "homosexual agenda."[138] In *Obergefell v. Hodges*, one of the most important cases of the century, the Supreme Court invalidated state laws that denied same-sex couples the right to marry.[139] Chief Justice Roberts, who became a poster child for the rule of law paradigm during his confirmation proceedings when he declared that judges are "like umpires" who "do not make rules; they apply them,"[140] dissented in *Obergefell*. He did not confine his dissent to disagreement with the majority's constitutional analysis of underlying text and precedent. Rather, he proceeded to accuse the majority of confusing its "own preferences with the requirements of the law," to the end of "seiz[ing] for itself a question the constitution reserves to the people," and concluded that the Constitution had "nothing to do" with the Court's ruling.[141] Such inflammatory rhetoric (in the *Federalist Papers*, Alexander Hamilton characterized "deliberate judicial usurpations on the authority of the legislature" as an impeachable offense[142]) sends a powerful message about the nature of judicial decision-making that the press reports to the public—a message sharply at odds with the rule of law paradigm.

Judicial Conduct and Discipline

Codes of conduct and disciplinary processes create forums for evaluating a different kind of judicial decision: one concerning a judge's personal or professional conduct and its implications for the judge's independence, impartiality, integrity, and competence. The American Bar Association first promulgated Canons of Judicial Ethics in 1924, but they were unenforceable exhortations that judges violated at the peril of a disapproving glower and were paid little more than lip service for decades.[143]

Between 1969 and 1970, Justice Abe Fortas resigned, the Senate rejected President Nixon's nomination of Judge Clement Haynsworth to the Supreme Court, and the House initiated an impeachment inquiry into the conduct of Justice William O. Douglas, for reasons relating in part to alleged ethical transgressions of the judges involved.[144] The American Bar Association responded by promulgating a Model Code of Judicial Conduct in 1972.[145] States began to adopt versions of the Model Code and to establish judicial conduct commissions to enforce standards of conduct that their codes created. When the 1960s began, no state had an enforceable code of conduct or a formal disciplinary process. By 1981, all fifty states had disciplinary processes in place, and by 2008, all fifty states had adopted codes of judicial conduct.[146] The federal judiciary followed suit: In 1973, the Judicial Conference of the United States adopted a "Code of Judicial Conduct for United States Judges," based on the 1972 American Bar Association Model, which governed federal judges below the Supreme Court; and in 1980, Congress created a disciplinary process for federal judges, albeit one that did not link discipline to violation of the Code.[147]

Because they are administered by and for judges, state and federal codes of conduct and disciplinary processes have not become sites for politicized battles over the ideology of judicial decision-making (with disqualification being a notable exception). But they have created another venue for the scrutiny of judicial conduct of interest to policymakers and the media. Congress, which oversees the federal disciplinary process, periodically seeks to invigorate that process, by showcasing episodes of under-regulation in oversight hearings, and by proposing reforms, such as to establish an inspector general within the judicial branch.[148] Interest groups have agitated for the Supreme Court to bind itself to a code of conduct, and the Chief Justice has resisted those proposals as unnecessary.[149]

One exception is judicial disqualification, where judicial ethics has become a field for ideological combat. The need for judges to disqualify themselves when their impartiality is compromised is both an ethical obligation and a procedural requirement. At the turn of the twenty-first century, commentators, interest groups, and litigants turned to disqualification in attempts to remove judges and justices from a series of hotly contested and ideologically divisive cases. In 2004, Justice Scalia declined to disqualify himself from a Freedom of Information Act case in which Vice President Dick Cheney was a named defendant, after Scalia spent a weekend hunting with Cheney at the Vice President's invitation while the case was pending.[150] In 2008, West Virginia Justice Brent Benjamin declined to disqualify himself from a case in which the defendant's CEO had spent three million dollars in support of Benjamin's election while the appeal was pending. (The U.S. Supreme Court subsequently ruled that Benjamin's failure to disqualify himself violated the plaintiff's due process rights.)[151] In 2010 and 2011, opposing parties unsuccessfully sought to disqualify the district judge and a member of the circuit court panel from a case challenging the constitutionality of a California initiative banning same sex marriage, because the district judge was a gay man in a long-term relationship and the circuit judge's spouse headed an ACLU chapter that supported same-sex marriage.[152] In 2011, commentators and interest groups called for the disqualification of Justices Clarence Thomas and Elena Kagan from a case challenging the constitutionality of the Affordable Care Act ("Obamacare"), on the grounds that Thomas's wife worked for the Heritage Foundation, which opposed the Act, and Kagan served as President Obama's Solicitor General while the legislation was pending.[153] Meanwhile, Chief Justice John Roberts, in his 2011 year-end report on the federal judiciary, pointedly observed that the constitutionality of legislation subjecting Supreme Court justices to standards of disqualification (in place since 1948) had never been tested.[154]

Race

American courts played the role of enabler in the Jim Crow era, by interpreting the equal protection clause of the Fourteenth Amendment to the U.S. Constitution to permit state-sanctioned segregation, as long as separate treatment of the races was nominally equal. The U.S. Supreme Court reversed course in the 1954 decision of *Brown v. Board of Education*, and the federal judges who assisted in desegregation by implementing *Brown* in the teeth of southern resistance were portrayed as the "unlikely heroes" of the civil rights era.[155]

Continuing suspicion that African Americans were subject to disparate treatment in the courts (particularly state courts) led to the creation of racial bias task forces in a number of states, beginning in the 1980s. Those task forces found numerous manifestations of racial bias and recommended a variety of reforms, including education and training, diversification of the bench, and revisions to codes of judicial conduct. In 1990, the Model Code of Judicial Conduct was amended to include a canon directing judges to perform their duties without bias on the basis of race; accompanying commentary warned against bias "in any form"—including demeanor and body language.[156] In 2003, the American Bar Association adopted a series of recommendations to improve minority representation on the bench.[157] Meanwhile, empirical research confirmed significant racial disparities across the administration of justice from arrest rates[158] to incarceration rates[159] and the imposition of death sentences in capital cases.[160] Unsurprisingly, survey data from the turn of the twenty-first century revealed that African Americans reported significantly lower rates of confidence in the courts and the impartiality of judges than the general population.[161]

The tension between these developments and the premise underlying the rule of law paradigm—that impartial, independent judges are impervious to so pernicious an extralegal influence as racial bias—is obvious. To date, the implications of systemic racial bias in the courts have been explored within the legal community but have not led to public agitation on an order of magnitude sufficient to constitute a transformative challenge to the rule of law paradigm. That, however, may be changing. A police officer shot an unarmed African American man in Ferguson, Missouri, in 2014, which culminated in massive protests that proliferated to other states and accelerated following reports of similar episodes in other jurisdictions. Anger at law enforcement spilled over to prosecutors and grand juries in Ferguson and elsewhere, when officers involved in the shootings were not indicted. Although judges have for the most part remained out of the spotlight, that was not the case in Ferguson, where a municipal court judge resigned following a scathing Justice Department report, and the Missouri Supreme Court reassigned all Ferguson municipal court cases to the circuit court in an effort to restore public confidence.[162]

In 2001, then Circuit Judge Sonia Sotomayor gave a speech in which she said that race and gender "may and will make a difference in our judging," adding that "I would hope that a wise Latina woman with the richness of her experiences would more often than not reach a better conclusion than a white male who hasn't lived that life."[163] The notion that race is a component of life experience that informs judicial decision-making for the better is as antithetical to the rule of law paradigm as the notion that it informs judicial decision-making for the worse, and in her Supreme Court confirmation testimony, Sotomayor struggled to distance herself from her earlier remarks. Reducing the tension to its essence, the rule of law paradigm posits that race is irrelevant to a nation where it is not.

Budgets and Salaries

In this age of perpetual transition, intensified scrutiny of judicial ideology, selection, conduct, and administration is the new normal. This new normal, when combined with post-Watergate skepticism of government motives, post-Reagan revolution skepticism of government spending, and post-2008 recession-era budgetary shortfalls, has resulted in a perfect storm of factors, the eye of which has settled over judicial budgets and salaries. Judges have no natural constituency to lobby for their budgetary needs, except the bar, whose track record in defending the judiciary is mixed, and whose influence may be diminished by a declining percentage of lawyers in legislatures. When judges lobby for themselves, they appear self-interested; when they do not, they are ignored; when they exploit their inherent powers to order adequate funding, they provoke constitutional crises.[164] Because legislatures understand that budgets and salaries are the judiciary's Achilles heel, it is not unusual for legislators to exploit the budgetary process as a means to retaliate against unpopular judicial decisions.[165]

The Polarized Public Policy Debate on Judges

There is continuity to the critiques of judges that cuts across the proliferating forums just described. The recurring complaint is that too often judges disregard applicable law or misuse their discretion to the end of implementing their policy preferences or personal feelings. Former Judge Robert Bork, for example, complained that the nation is "increasingly governed not by law or elected representatives, but by unelected, unrepresentative, unaccountable committees of lawyers applying no laws other than their own will."[166] Pennsylvania Senator and presidential candidate Rick Santorum characterized the problem as one in which "judges have decided to go off on their own tangent and disobey the statutes of the United States of America."[167] And the Center for a Just Society opined that "[t]here is nothing wrong with our existing federal and state constitutions. What is wrong is that judges are wrongly misrepresenting the requirements of these documents. Indeed, they are rewriting the documents by misconstruing them in order to satisfy their own social and political agendas."[168]

Proceeding on the assumption that too often judges disregard the law and implement their personal preferences, court critics have argued that only by curbing the freedom of "activist" judges can the rule of law be preserved. "If we're going to preserve our Constitution," declared Congressman Steve King, "we must get them in line."[169] Similarly, in proposing legislation calling on federal judges to report their deviations from federal sentencing guidelines to Congress, Representative Tom Feeney opined that his amendment followed from the "simple precept" that "judges should follow, not make the laws," and that "if insisting on that precept 'intimidates' federal judges, then perhaps that is a good thing."[170]

And so, court critics, rallying behind the nom de guerre of judicial accountability, have targeted such judges across the gamut of proliferating forums: (1) federal confirmation proceedings; (2) state judicial election campaigns; (3) procedural reforms aimed at curtailing judicial discretion; (4) websites and cable news programs; (5) disqualification proceedings; and (6) legislative appropriations.

The bench and bar have countered this recurring critique with recourse to the rule of law narrative, which posits that independent judges set their ideologies aside and apply the law. Hence, for court defenders, the "problem" lies not with the judges, but with their detractors. To protect judicial independence and the rule of law from incursion, the bench and bar advocate some variation on the theme that courts and judicial systems must be depoliticized. The American Bar Association's Commission on the 21st Century Judiciary declared categorically that its mission was to "defuse the escalating partisan battle over American courts."[171] In the realm of state judicial selection, some reformers propose to "take the politics out of the system by setting up nonpartisan elections";[172] others advocate public funding of judicial elections to "take politics out of judicial races";[173] and still others would replace judicial elections with an appointive system to "depoliticize the judicial process."[174] With respect to federal judicial selection, the American Bar Association has advocated the use of nominating commissions for federal judges to "alleviate excesses" of "polarized combat that fosters the view that judges are in office simply to carry out ideological agendas of those involved in putting them there."[175] Similarly, we hear calls to "take politics out of the debate over judicial salaries,"[176] and to depoliticize the rhetoric of judicial criticism generally, because "if this current, often politically motivated drumbeat against judges continues unchallenged, more and more people . . . will lose faith not just in the courts but in the rule of law itself."[177]

CONCLUSION

For centuries, the legislative and executive branches of government have been denominated the "political" ones, which implies that the judicial branch is something else. But the judiciary has never been an apolitical place, as evidenced by the periodic partisan attacks it has weathered throughout its history. Against this backdrop, the claim that the American judiciary is now experiencing a "political transformation," rather than another incarnation of a perennial phenomenon, warrants a measure of skepticism. In laying the groundwork for such a claim, this chapter has described developments generations in the making, the confluence of which suggests the possibility that something new, different, and more sustained is taking place.

Chapter 4 elaborates on the perennial critique that judges are subject to inappropriate extralegal influences, by exploring the manifestations of that critique dating back millennia. That invites the question of why these ancient complaints have acquired new urgency in recent decades. Professor Steven Teles and Sarah Staszak have done a marvelous job of describing the changing legal landscape in the broader context of a changing sociopolitical culture.[178] To replicate those efforts here would double the size of this work and to improve upon them would be impossible. That said, two possibilities come to mind. First, distrust of American government catalyzed by the Vietnam War and Watergate, which took a more immediate toll on public confidence in Congress and the executive branch, may gradually be spilling over into the judiciary.[179] Second, the advent of orchestrated political campaigns that use civil litigation as a tool for law reform, beginning in the mid-twentieth century with civil rights, and later school prayer, abortion rights, affirmative action, same-sex marriage, and tort reform, may have subtly shifted the real and perceived role of courts in the political process.[180] Either way, the developments discussed in this chapter have spawned a dichotomous, polarized, and shrill public policy debate on judicial decision-making. This debate stands in contrast to a very different trend in the academic scholarship on law and courts, elaborated on in the next chapter, away from binary arguments and toward greater nuance and consensus.

CHAPTER 3

The Changing Academic Understanding of American Courts

C hapter 2 described the changing political landscape of American courts in the twentieth and twenty-first centuries, a landscape where the venues for challenging judges and the choices they make have been proliferating. In that same time, those who study the courts have changed their views on what influences the choices judges make. Recent developments have reconciled, to an extent greater than in decades past, the competing views of scholars across academic disciplines of what influences judicial decision-making. Thus, as the public policy debate is becoming more fractious, the scholarly debate is moving in the opposite direction.

The consequences are twofold. First, social science confirms what court critics suspect: Judges are subject to an array of extralegal influences, which shows that the premises underlying the rule of law paradigm are exaggerated, if not counterfactual. Second, by charting a middle course between the legal establishment, which claims that law means everything to judges, and court critics who claim that law means nothing to judges, the emerging scholarly consensus offers a more defensible foundation for a new legal culture paradigm developed in later chapters.

To appreciate the significance of recent developments in the scholarship of judicial decision-making, it is necessary to embed those developments in historical context. A logical starting point is with the advent of formalism in the nineteenth century, which gradually gave way to conflicting and, more recently, unifying approaches to understanding judicial decision-making.

THE ASCENDANCE OF FORMALISM

In the United States, the first half of the nineteenth century was a time of geographical and economic expansion. To accommodate that expansion, merchants and entrepreneurs were keen to modernize the common law by "forg[ing] an alliance with the legal profession to advance their own interests through a transformation of the legal system."[1] To facilitate this transformation to a more business-friendly common law, courts often resolved close cases with reference to public policy and conceptions of economic justice.[2]

By the mid-nineteenth century, however, this transformation was close to complete.[3] To shore up the gains of the previous half-century, the simple solution was to lock those gains in place with a new, more formalistic way of looking at the law, which "gave common law rules the appearance of being self-contained, apolitical and inexorable, and which, by making 'legal reasoning seem like mathematics,' conveyed 'an air ... of ... inevitability about legal decisions.'"[4]

When economic elites and the legal order they had cultivated were challenged by populists and progressives in the latter third of the nineteenth century, mainstream judges of the era found refuge in the new formalism. "For judges of this stamp," Lawrence Friedman writes, "formalism was a protective device. They were middle-of-the-road conservatives, holding off the vulgar rich on the one hand, and the revolutionary masses on the other. The legal tradition represented balance, sound values, and a commitment to orderly process."[5]

Meanwhile, Harvard Dean Christopher Columbus Langdell revolutionized legal education in the last quarter of the nineteenth century, by reorienting the focus of the law school classroom away from lectures on legal principles, toward questions and answers that divined legal principles from cases.[6] Implicit in the case method was the notion that legal principles could be deduced from scientific analysis of cases, and that legal scholarship should be devoted to isolating and classifying those principles in exhaustive articles and treatises.[7] The net effect was to inculcate new generations of lawyers with the values of formalism, or more neutrally, "classical legal thought."

THE EMERGENCE AND DECLINE OF LEGAL REALISM

During the Progressive Era, the dictates of classical legal thought were challenged from various quarters. Justice Oliver Wendell Holmes opined that:

The language of judicial decision is mainly the language of logic. And the logical method and form flatter that longing for certainty and for repose which is in every human mind. But certainty generally is illusion, and repose is not the destiny of man. Behind the logical form lies a judgment as to the relative worth and importance of competing legislative grounds. . . . We do not realize how large a part of our law is open to reconsideration upon a slight change in the habit of the public mind.[8]

Dean Roscoe Pound, in turn, complained about the prevailing "mechanical jurisprudence," in which "premises are no longer to be examined," and "[e]verything is reduced to simple deduction from them," to the point where "social progress" is "barred by barricades of dead precedents."[9]

In the 1920s, academic lawyers at Columbia and Yale, persuaded by the critiques of Holmes, Pound, and others, renounced formalism, proposed a more "functional" curriculum that deemphasized technical legal doctrine, and argued that law was better studied empirically, as a social science—an agenda of projects that Columbia law professor Karl Llewellyn collectively denominated "realism."[10] The Realist critique of formalism could be scathing, as illustrated by the following excerpt from Jerome Frank's *Law and the Modern Mind*:

Myth-making and fatherly lies must be abandoned—the Santa Claus story of complete legal certainty; the fairy tale of a pot of golden law which is already in existence and which the good lawyer can find, if only he is sufficiently diligent; the phantasy of an aesthetically satisfactory system and harmony, consistent and uniform, which will spring up when we find the magic wand of rationalizing principle.[11]

For this new realist, then, law was not transcendental; rather, law was what law did. To understand how judges decided cases, the realist deemphasized parsing the abstract legal principles upon which judges purported to rely and devoted more time to studying what judges really did—which was to balance the competing policies at stake in the cases that came before them.[12]

Legal Realism's campaign to reorient the study of law away from a body of rules and toward empirical, social science analysis of judicial behavior never gained traction in American law schools and, by the end of the 1930s, had run its course. John Henry Schlegal explains why Realism was menacing to the legal academy, in terms that apply equally to judges:

Science was too threatening. It suggested that the words of law might not be too important, that the special preserve of the law professor might not be too special and that, since law was not just rules, the rule of law might not be just a matter of following rules either. That threat was simply too much for the professional identity of the law professor; it could only be attacked mercilessly or distanced with derisive laughter.[13]

This chapter has told the traditional story of formalism and its confrontation with realism in stark terms, to highlight the origins of differences in approach to judicial decision-making that persist to this day. The traditional story, however, arguably exaggerates the extent of the "formalist-realist divide."[14] In a careful study of the period, Brian Tamanaha found that "many of the most prominent lawyers, judges and academics of the day[] described judging in consummately realist terms,"[15] while many legal realists "believed in the law,"[16] sought to "increase the certainty and predictability of law,"[17] and "did not assert that judges routinely manipulate the law to produce desired outcomes."[18]

These competing narratives can be reconciled if participants in the formalist-realist debate are placed on a continuum, rather than in boxes. The difference between formalists at their staunchest and realists at their most strident was as stark as the traditional narrative describes, but the range of views within the legal community was far more nuanced. While Realists at the fringe challenged the rule of law paradigm (and were marginalized for their heresy), mainstream Realists were still operating within it. Hence, the seeds of the law-policy schism were sewn by the realists, but the harvest came later, with the rise of the attitudinal model.

THE REBIRTH OF REALISM AND THE RISE OF THE "ATTITUDINAL MODEL"

The demise of the legal realism movement signaled an end to widespread agitation within the legal academy for teaching, writing, and thinking about law as a social science rather than a system of rules. Legal realism did, however, influence some academic lawyers to explore the ways in which related disciplines illuminated the analysis of law—disciplines that gradually worked their way into law schools as "law and" subfields. Thus, legal realism is credited with catalyzing the law and economics movement, partly because legal realism paved the way by challenging formalism's monopoly on legal analysis, and partly because realism was vulnerable to the critique that it lacked a well-defined methodology, which economic analysis sought to supply.[19] Law and psychology is more clearly rooted in the realist tradition and came into its own in the early 1950s, when the University of Chicago Law School initiated a Law and Behavioral Science Program that undertook path-breaking research into the psychology of jury behavior.[20] And devotees of law and sociology—a subfield that made its first real splash in the 1960s with law school projects at the University of California at Berkeley and the University of Wisconsin—likewise trace their empirical tradition and interest in the interrelationship between law and society back to the realists.[21]

In law schools, consigning a discipline to "law and" status can operate as a means of marginalization that keeps it at a distance from the study of "real" law, which has remained focused on the rules that judges interpret and apply.[22] Such was not the fate of law and politics, however, where interest among political scientists was sufficient to ensconce the study of judicial behavior as a political science subfield (courts and constitutional law, or public law), wholly independent of legal education.[23] While many academic lawyers were uncomfortable with the implications of legal realism, political scientists of the realist era were not. So-called "old institutionalist" political scientists of the day, such as Edward Corwin, Robert Cushman, and Charles Grove Haines, were realists of a moderate stripe who "believed that politics entered the judicial process in subtle and complex ways."[24] In other words, they did not think that "policy preferences or individual 'interests' determined how judges decided cases," even though "they recognized such preferences could affect judicial decisions."[25] In the 1940s, however, C. Herman Pritchett introduced a more aggressive behavioral strain of legal realism to the study of courts.[26] Pritchett and his successors set out to demonstrate, through empirical research, that judges were "motivated by their own preferences."[27] Exhibit A in Pritchett's analysis was the tendency of majority and dissenting Supreme Court opinions to reach divergent conclusions from the same facts and law—a divergence that he explained with reference to differing policy preferences of the individual justices.[28]

Two phenomena facilitated the epiphany of Pritchett and his cohort. First, Pritchett's work coincided with the onset of a gradual collapse of consensus norms (measured in terms of an increased frequency of separate opinions) on the U.S. Supreme Court, which law professor Cass Sunstein traces to 1941.[29] Thus, Pritchett was positioned to observe these more visible ideological divisions on the Court as they emerged. Second, aspiring political scientists opt into a disciplinary microculture that seeks to understand and explain governmental action with reference to political influences. This acculturated predisposition has been described as a form of "path dependence," that leads political scientists to devalue the relevance of law in judicial decision-making.[30] American political scientists, to no less an extent than anyone else, are immersed in a sociopolitical milieu that reveres the rule of law paradigm, but they have self selected into a group that is inclined to be more skeptical.

Unencumbered by the norms of a legal community that proceeded from the premise that law operates as a constraint on judicial behavior, political scientists who followed in Pritchett's footsteps devoted themselves to describing what judges do in terms that marginalized law as a variable in the judicial decision-making equation.[31] In the 1960s,

Glendon Schubert coined the term "attitudinal" to describe a model that explained how Supreme Court justices voted with reference to their attitudes or ideological preferences.[32] And in the 1990s, Harold Spaeth and Jeffrey Segal summarized the current state of political science research on Supreme Court decision-making in an influential book that pitted the "attitudinal model" against the "legal model," and in no uncertain terms declared the former victorious, characterizing the legal model as "meaningless."[33] Against this backdrop of what many political scientists regarded as overwhelming evidence in support of the attitudinal model, the traditional view perpetuated by lawyers, judges, and law schools that the Supreme Court decides cases in light of applicable law was relegated to the status of myth.[34]

In light of data generated by proponents of the attitudinal model, by the 1990s few political scientists would dispute that votes on the U.S. Supreme Court were influenced by the policy preferences of the individual justices. But in the minds of some, "studying the Supreme Court . . . as little more than a collection of individuals who were pursuing their personal policy preferences" failed to take adequate account of other influences on judicial behavior.[35] In two important books, Howard Gillman and Cornell Clayton collected and promoted the recent work of "neo-institutional" scholars (which linked these scholars in spirit to "old institutionalists" of the realist age), who argued that judicial decision-making is more fully understood against the backdrop of the political, legal, social, and cultural institutions of which judges are a part.[36]

Thus, for example, neo-institutionalists such as Lee Epstein and Jack Knight, who advanced a quasi-economic "strategic choice" theory of judicial decision-making, argued that while judges are indeed "seekers of legal policy," as devotees of the attitudinal model posit, their "ability to achieve their goals [primarily policy goals] depends on a consideration of the preferences of other actors."[37] In other words, from a strategic choice perspective, judges do not vote reflexively in accord with their personal policy preferences, but think strategically about how Congress, the President, and others may react to given case outcomes and adjust their decision-making accordingly to better effectuate preferred policy outcomes.

In contrast, Rogers Smith, another neo-institutional scholar who advocated a "historical interpretive" approach to understanding judicial decision-making, argued that historical accounts of institutional development are critical to understanding the values of decision-makers within those institutions.[38] Smith, joined by Thomas Burke, Lief Carter, and Mark Graber (whose work is discussed at greater length in chapter 5), showed how the judiciary's institutional setting helps to create and frame the values that judges seek to implement when they make decisions—values that can include, among others, a commitment to the rule of law. For their part, ardent proponents of the attitudinal model initially responded less by trying to accommodate the neo-institutional critique, than by conducting new studies that set out to prove the neo-institutionalists wrong.[39]

Meanwhile, back at the law schools, the lessons of legal realism enjoyed a brief renaissance in the 1970s with the critical legal studies movement, which posited that elite judges perpetuate the domination of their class by exploiting the fiction of the law's rationality and even-handedness— thereby entrenching preexisting inequalities.[40] But the movement was derided by traditionalists, and leading "crits" sought neither to verify their intuitions empirically nor to propose a meaningful alternative to the status quo they berated. By the mid-1980s, critical legal studies had lost momentum.[41]

As the attitudinal model came into its own, one might suppose that the deluge of studies purportedly demonstrating the irrelevance of law to judicial decision-making would have been of acute interest and concern to law professors, judges, and lawyers. But as the twentieth century drew to a close, the sweeping conclusions of attitudinal studies that were creating a cacophonous din in political science circles were being greeted in the legal profession by the sound of crickets.

Professor Frank Cross, writing in 1997, was among the first to decry this "unfortunate interdisciplinary ignorance" in a law review article.[42] "The political science research and the attitudinal model are significant in that they could potentially obliterate the foundations of much current and past legal scholarship," Cross noted, but "[t]o date, legal scholarship has been remarkably oblivious to this large and mounting body of political science scholarship on courts."[43] Professor Michael Gerhardt attributed the obliviousness to a fundamental difference in worldview: "Law professors believe the Constitution and other laws constrain the Court, while most political scientists do not. These different perspectives on justices' fidelity to the law ensure that legal scholars and political scientists have little to say about the Court that is of interest to each other."[44]

Judge Patricia Wald went further, suggesting that the legal community was not oblivious, but dismissive: "I register something of a ho-hum reaction to the notion that judges' personal philosophies enter into their decisionmaking when statute or precedent does not point their discretion in one direction or constrain it in another."[45] In other words, to the extent that the attitudinal model stood for the softer proposition that judges are influenced by their policy preferences, it told the legal profession nothing it did not know already.[46] To the extent that it stood for the harder proposition that law does not operate as a constraint on judges, the attitudinal model reflected a difference in perspective so fundamental as to foreclose a productive exchange of ideas.

THE NEW EMPIRICISTS

For generations, law professors and political scientists had developed contradictory, dichotomous conceptions of judicial decision-making that they happily cultivated in relative isolation. Persistent calls for more serious cross-disciplinary engagement, however, gradually intruded upon their solitude.[47] Some law professors and judges argued that political scientists were not taking law seriously enough.[48] Others critiqued attitudinal studies, arguing that such studies delineated the scope of "law" so narrowly and rigidly as to render its irrelevance to judicial decision-making a preordained conclusion.[49] Still other legal scholars embarked on empirical research agendas of their own, eliciting criticism, if not potshots from some political scientists as to their methodology, but simultaneously giving rise to a renaissance of interest among academic lawyers in the empirical study of judicial behavior.[50] This "Quantitative Moment" in the legal academy[51] has, in a very short time, all but obliterated the study of judicial decision-making as an either-or enterprise, in which scholars must choose sides and explain judicial behavior with reference to law or policy preferences as if they were mutually exclusive alternatives.

Studies in Law and Politics: The Supreme Court

By the time the quantitative moment arrived, political scientists had already established an all but irrefutable empirical case for the proposition that a justice's policy preferences influence his or her votes on the U.S. Supreme Court. Segal and Spaeth reported that they could predict 74% of individual justices' decisions on the basis of their attitudinal predispositions,[52] and another study by Segal and Albert Cover found that in civil liberties cases, the correlation between the ideological predilections of individual justices and their voting behavior was 80% or higher.[53]

Subsequent interdisciplinary work has, however, yielded important nuances. In 2003, two law professors and two political scientists published the results of a "Supreme Court Forecasting Project" in which man squared off against machine in a twenty-first-century remake of the Ballad of John Henry.[54] Overall, the "machine"—a statistical model—outperformed the predictions of legal experts, by correctly forecasting case outcomes 75% of the time, as compared to 59.1% for the experts.[55]

While this project would seem to have pitted political scientists against lawyers in a kind of celebrity death match, in reality, it went a long way toward demonstrating that the long-standing law versus attitude debate presented a false dichotomy. In order for the machine to work, the computer model could not base its predictions on naive "attitudinal assumptions," which the authors found "insufficient to generate specific forecasts prospectively."[56] Rather, to maximize its predictive capabilities, the model employed classification trees that forecast a justice's future decisions in light of how that justice had previously decided cases similar in six semi-specific respects (which implicated ideological predilections in subtler ways).[57] At the same time, to maximize their predictive capabilities, the experts were not confined to naive doctrinal analysis of pending cases, but were free to take attitudinal factors into account when making their predictions.[58]

Insofar as "legal experts" appreciate that a justice's policy preferences influence how he or she analyzes the law in close cases, they cannot be surprised to learn that sophisticated statistical models aimed at isolating the justices' policy predilections often predict Supreme Court decisions correctly—particularly since the experts likely tried to identify those same predilections when making their own predictions. Consistent with this latter supposition, the researchers found that the experts performed comparably to the model (indeed, slightly better) in predicting the votes of individual justices overall, but that the model did much better at predicting "swing votes," where the researchers fairly suspect that the complex and idiosyncratic preferences of Court moderates were too difficult for the experts to divine without the benefit of a computer model.[59] Rather than thinking about this study as another data point in a dichotomous debate over the primacy of law or attitude in Supreme Court decision-making, the authors suggested that the complex interplay between law and attitude, revealed by the study, may warrant a reconceptualization of law itself: "[U]nder any theoretical conception that regards law as consisting at least in part of what judges do, proxies that reliably predict what they will do in the future are worth considering as . . . guideposts of 'law,' whether or not we can imagine them as 'law' themselves."[60]

Recent studies of related issues have further underscored the need for an increasingly hybridized and eclectic understanding of Supreme Court decision-making. Academic lawyers have explored the correlation between a judge's policy preferences and legal preferences.[61] Thus, for example, conservative justices typically favor methods of interpretation—such as originalism—that yield conservative policy outcomes, while progressives are more partial to "living constitutionalism," which facilitates liberal policy outcomes.[62] The net effect of this insight is twofold: (1) it shortens the analytical distance between law and attitude; and (2) it suggests the possibility that on those infrequent occasions when legal and policy preferences diverge, institutional rule of law norms could lead justices to opt for the former—which may explain at least some case outcomes that statistical models do not predict.[63]

In a related vein, studies of precedent conducted by attitudinal scholars in the 1990s confirmed what lawyers had long suspected—that there is typically precedent on both sides of close cases, and that a justice will usually rely on precedent that supports a result consistent with her ideological preferences.[64] More recent work, however, has added important qualifications by exploring the role that respect for precedent plays in preserving the Court's institutional legitimacy and by distinguishing run-of-the-mill precedent that is often manipulated in the service of implementing policy objectives from more enduring, "super" precedent that constrains Court decision-making in identifiable ways.[65] Finally, two studies with overlapping authorship found that the ideological preferences of most justices "drift" over time.[66] Apart from complicating the task of correlating a justice's future votes to her political predilections at the point of confirmation, this finding raises the questions of why drift occurs, whether changing policy preferences correlate to changing legal preferences, and if so, which is the chicken and which the egg? Such questions take on added importance in light of other research finding that the Court is likeliest to render "consequential" decisions, meaning decisions with a greater impact on the law, when the preferences of the majority are homogeneous, which liberates the opinion writer to speak more stridently without fear of losing his or her majority.[67]

Law and Politics: Lower Courts and State Courts

Early attitudinal studies focused on the U.S. Supreme Court, which made sense. To show that a judge's view of what the law (or public policy) should be influences her view of what the law is, the Supreme Court—which decides close cases where the law is unclear and has declared itself "supreme in the exposition of the law of the Constitution"[68]—is an obvious place to start. But thoughtful analysts understood that the findings of Supreme Court studies did not necessarily extend to district and circuit courts, where judges are subject both to appellate review and possibly to a different set of norms that respect the constraints of controlling precedent.

In the 1990s, attitudinal scholars posited that lower court judges acted as agents for the Supreme Court by implementing the latter's policy preferences, on pain of reversal.[69] To explain how the Supreme Court controlled the lower courts despite increasingly trivial rates of review, some political scientists theorized that the Supreme Court establishes "doctrinal intervals" within which circuit courts may deviate from the Supreme Court's preferred policy outcomes without reversal, and that circuit judges act on their own policy preferences strategically by implementing them to the extent they can within the confines of those intervals.[70] In other words, a circuit court's decision will attract the Supreme Court's attention only if the decision's departure from the Supreme Court's policy predilections is sufficiently flagrant. Consistent with core tenets of the attitudinal and strategic choice models, this approach acknowledges neither law nor legal norms as meaningful constraints on decision-making below the Supreme Court.

More recent work, however, has added law to the factors influencing lower court decision-making. In a study of circuit court decisions on standards of deference in appellate review,[71] "procedural thresholds" (e.g., justiciability requirements),[72] and adherence to precedent,[73] Frank Cross found that "[j]udicial decision making clearly involves a mix that includes some ideological influence, considerable legal influence, and undoubtedly other factors."[74] Correlations of case outcomes to applicable law were consistently "robust"; as to ideology, he concluded that "it appears to be a factor in judicial decision making," but that "the available evidence can demonstrate only that it is a relatively small factor."[75] More recently, Lee Epstein, William Landes, and Richard Posner have likewise found that the influences on judicial decision-making at the intermediate appellate court level are complex and multifaceted, with law and ideology both in play.[76] Other circuit studies have been corroborative.[77]

Studies of judicial decision-making in state court systems have added important nuances. One study found that high courts with fewer members are significantly less likely to overturn established precedent than courts with more members.[78] That finding corroborates a form of strategic choice, in which judges find safety in numbers and are willing to make bolder choices contrary to established law when accompanied by more, ideologically like-minded colleagues. A meta-analysis of multiple studies found that ideological predilection, measured in terms of a justice's party affiliation, exerted less influence on judicial decision-making among state high courts than on the U.S. Supreme Court.[79] Different explanations are possible, but one is that ideological ardor is dampened by periodic elections—to which over 80% of state judges are subject. Put another way, impending elections create an incentive for state judges to moderate their views and vote strategically. Hence, several studies have shown that criminal sentences spike in the months leading up to an election, presumably owing to incumbent fear of being labeled "soft on crime."[80] And elected supreme courts overturn their own precedent at twice the rate of their appointed counterparts, suggesting that the need to make choices acceptable to the electorate can trump adherence to settled law.[81]

It would miss the point to employ recent studies summarized here in support of an argument that law is "winning" or "losing" its competition with ideological preferences and strategic choices for control of lower court decision-making. Sisk, Heise, and Morriss came closer to the mark when they concluded their analysis of district court decision-making with the observation that "as is often the case with empirical research, our study provides both comfort and challenges to all camps, again reminding us that judicial behavior is too complex for easy conclusions about influences and patterns."[82] I would go further still and suggest that it is time to break camp altogether. We have now reached the point in the study of judicial decision-making, where distinguished law professors openly acknowledge the influence of attitudes and strategic choice;[83] where distinguished political scientists openly acknowledge the influence of law;[84] and where law professors and political scientists alike reject the law-politics dichotomy as false.[85] The law versus politics debate offered an important point of scholarly focus when the cross-disciplinary divide was wide and deep. Now that the chasm has narrowed and bridges are built, the "do judges follow law or make policy?" debate has outlived its usefulness. There is an emerging consensus that law and politics both influence judicial decision-making. They are inextricably interwoven. Rather than defending one and attacking the other, leading scholars rightly reorient their focus toward learning more about how law and policy relate to each other and how they interact with additional influences on judicial decision-making.

Beyond Politics: Studies in Economics and Psychology

When studying what influences the decisions judges make, law is a sensible place to start because the opinions judges write explain the decisions they make with exclusive reference to the rule of law. Because law seeks to implement public policy objectives and because ambiguous legal texts accommodate competing ideological perspectives on what those texts mean and what policy objectives they implement, studying the influence of ideology (and its proxies) on judicial decision-making is a logical second step. But there are other influences too—influences that devotees of both law and economics and law and psychology have explored.

Within law and economics, scholars have struggled to overcome the "embarrassment" of "explain[ing] judicial behavior in economic terms, when almost the whole thrust of the rules governing the compensation and other terms and conditions of judicial employment is to divorce judicial action from incentives . . . that determine human action in an economic model."[86] To overcome this problem, exponents of law and economics have defined self-interest more broadly and posited that judicial decision-making is variously influenced by desires to maximize popularity, prestige, power, public interest, affirmance, reputation, and voting as a source of judicial utility.[87]

The strategic choice model of judicial decision-making, discussed earlier, emerged out of the political science camp. Its principal proponents are political scientists, and the choices of primary interest to strategic choice scholars have been "political" ones, aimed at maximizing a judge's prospects for implementing the policy outcomes she prefers. But at its core, strategic choice is rooted in law and economics. It proceeds from the premise that judges are self-interested actors who adjust the choices they make to maximize what they value. What self-interested judges value can include implementation of their preferred policy outcomes, but need not be so limited. Thus, studies discussed earlier showed that state judges desirous of reelection stiffen the criminal sentences they impose when elections are impending.[88] In a like vein, other studies have shown that judges moderate their decision-making to increase their chances for appointment to higher courts.[89]

To this point, the question of judicial motivation has been left conveniently murky. Positive theories devoted to showing that judges do more and less than follow the law necessarily imply that judges are dissembling or delusional when they say that they follow the law and nothing else. But positive theories seek to explain what influences judicial behavior without much regard for what motivates it. Attitudinal scholars borrow heavily from behavioral psychology by positing, in effect, that a case stimulus elicits an ideological response, but have been largely indifferent to whether the influence of ideology is conscious.[90] The phrase "strategic choice" implies purposive direction or motivation, but even here, the success of the model does not depend on it. Whether judges consciously moderate their interpretations of law to avoid confrontations with or resistance from legislators, governors, presidents, voters, or fellow judges matters less than that their interpretations of law are so moderated. The same may be said generally of efforts to view judicial behavior through the lens of economic analysis: If judicial self-interest can be shown to influence the choices judges make, whether judges sincerely believe that they are setting their own interests aside and following the law is neither here nor there.

But American judges take an oath to uphold the Constitution. Codes of conduct direct judges to "uphold and apply the law,"[91] not to be "swayed by public clamor or fear of criticism"[92] and not to "permit family, social, political, financial, or other interests or relationships to influence the judge's judicial conduct or judgment."[93] For those who care whether judges are doing their best to honor their oaths and follow their codes of conduct, motivation matters.

What psychology brings to the conversation is an informed perspective on judicial motivation and bias, and how various biases can affect conduct, consciously and not. Notwithstanding an emerging scholarly consensus that law, policy preferences, and other factors combine to influence judicial decision-making, one gleans none of that from reading judicial opinions, which convey the impression that law alone drives the opinion writer inexorably to the conclusion reached. Whether judges sincerely believe that they are following the dictates of law is a question of cognitive psychology that a cadre of psychologists, law professors, and political scientists began to explore in earnest as another component of the new quantitative moment at the turn of the twenty-first century.

In their landmark study, political scientists Rowland and Carp advanced a "cognitive approach" to district court decision-making, which questioned the "unpalatable image" inspired by attitudinal and rational choice scholars, "of judges who, if they think they can get away with it, will consciously impose their policy preferences on their evaluations of disputed facts."[94] Multidisciplinary studies of what judges do focus on "hard" cases, "when facts give rise to legal indeterminacy"[95] (i.e., when specific outcomes are not clearly dictated by applicable law). As one psychologist explains, in such cases, a judge's preexisting attitudes "can affect the forming of impressions, the evaluating of evidence, and the making of decisions."[96] Hence, judges subconsciously frame or interpret ambiguous facts and law in light of their policy preferences.[97]

When confronted with a choice between plausible alternative constructions of law or facts, judges are likely to find more plausible those constructions that are compatible with their ideological predilections.[98] In her empirical study of legal reasoning among law students, Eileen Braman found substantial evidence of subconscious, ideologically motivated reasoning across a line of experiments.[99]

Motivated reasoning likewise helps to explain why judges often resolve uncertain legal questions in terms that reveal no trace of uncertainty. When faced with credible arguments for a conclusion contrary to the one that judges often are motivated to make, Dan Simon explains the "cognitive system *imposes coherence* on the arguments so that the subset of arguments that supports one outcome becomes more appealing to the judge and the opposite subset, including arguments that previously seemed appropriate, turns less favorable."[100] As a consequence, the "factual patterns, the authoritative texts, and the resulting propositions are *restructured*," which "*spreads apart* the opposing arguments" and enables one decision to become "dominant over the other."[101] What began as a close and difficult case with no obvious right answer culminates in a majority opinion that betrays none of the original uncertainty, and often declares the correct result to be clear, notwithstanding a dissenting opinion that reaches an opposite conclusion stated with comparable certitude. The result is what one scholar has described as the "rhetoric of constitutional absolutism."[102]

Cognitive psychology therefore suggests that judges may not be motivated by a desire to implement their ideological or other predilections and may sincerely believe that their rulings are grounded in an analysis of law alone, even though their predilections influence their rulings.[103] Psychology, however, does more than rationalize the role of ideology in judicial decision-making. It takes us beyond politics to explore other extralegal influences on judicial decision-making.

Chapter 2 highlighted racial bias as an issue that has challenged the rule of law paradigm. Social psychology research has shown how implicit bias and aversive racism can influence judicial decision-making. Studies show that people tend not to regard themselves as biased and report that they are less biased than others.[104] To measure the presence of subconscious bias, Kenneth Greenwald developed an Implicit Association Test.[105] Subjects are first shown words they classify as pleasant or unpleasant, and photographs of faces they classify as black or white. They are then put through two time trials: In one trial, they push a button when they see a pleasant word or a black face, and a different button when they see an unpleasant word or a white face; in the other time trial, they press one button when they see a pleasant word or a white face, and a different button when they see an unpleasant word or a black face. The results reveal that white subjects take significantly less time to correlate unpleasant words with black faces than white.[106] In another study of mock jurors, white subjects associated black defendants with guilt more quickly than white defendants—a result that bore no correlation to the jurors' self-reported levels of explicit racial bias.[107] In a test run on judges, 87% of white judges implicitly associated pleasant words with white faces more quickly than black faces.[108] In studies of implicit bias in the field, Victor Quintanilla measured the impact of Supreme Court decisions that granted district judges the discretion to dismiss claims they deemed "implausible," in the context of race-based employment discrimination cases.[109] He found that under the new plausibility standard, white judges were more than twice as likely to dismiss race discrimination claims than under the old standard and were more than twice as likely to dismiss such claims than black judges (a result that could not be explained on the basis of ideological differences).[110]

Borrowing from social psychology more broadly, another scholar has argued that judges can be influenced by the audiences whose approval they seek, including fellow judges, the legal community, the media, and the general public.[111] With respect to the influence of other judges, in particular, one study has found that the longer their tenure together, the less likely judges are to overturn their own precedent.[112] A second study found that circuit courts are more likely to adopt as precedent the rulings of prestigious judges.[113] A third study found that mixed appellate panels comprised of judges appointed by Democratic and Republican presidents were more likely to follow applicable legal doctrine over policy preferences than panels comprised entirely of judges appointed by Democratic or Republican presidents.[114] For judges, there is nothing nefarious in these findings. Judge Harry Edwards has written about the moderating influence of collegiality on courts.[115] And Judge Alex Kozinski has argued that judges' desire for the respect of their colleagues operates as a brake on decision-making that strays too far from the rule of law.[116]

Yet another subfield of law and psychology has explored the influence of emotion on judicial decision-making. It is a subfield that gained sudden prominence in 2009, when President Obama identified "empathy" as a relevant qualification for service on the Supreme Court. For the most part, law and emotion scholars have not been interested in quantifying the impact of emotion on judicial decision-making. Rather, they have parsed opinions and transcripts and interviewed judges to explore how emotion influences judicial decision-making, often to the end of challenging the traditional assumption (born of the formalist notion that law is circumscribed by rules and logic alone) that emotion can or should be purged from the decision-making process.[117] In a study of decision-making on the U.S. Supreme Court, however, four political scientists and law professors did employ quantitative methods to verify the intuitive suspicion that emotion influences judicial decision-making.[118] In that study, they found a strong, positive correlation between unpleasant comments by Supreme Court justices during oral arguments, and the subsequent votes of those justices and case outcomes.[119] This study may simply stand for the proposition that when a judge feels strongly enough to say something snarky, her mind is made up, but it nonetheless corroborates an interaction between emotion and decision-making.

Finally, in the separate but related subfield of heuristics, several scholars have studied the ways in which judicial reasoning can be unwittingly influenced and distorted by cognitive biases or illusions that occur when the mind takes shortcuts in the reasoning process.[120] While not directly germane here, heuristics studies emphasize the extent to which judicial reasoning, like human reasoning generally, is subject to influences that are often subconscious and perhaps hard-wired.

CONCLUSION

Much remains to be done in the ongoing, multidisciplinary empirical movement to analyze influences on judicial behavior. Nevertheless, there is an emerging consensus that judges are subject to an array of factors that influence their interpretations of law, including but not limited to applicable legal text. More fundamentally, perhaps, is that this empirical work informs and deepens conceptions of law itself—conceptions transcending antiquated notions of law as mathematical formulas that dictate invariable outcomes, and embracing law as an elastic vessel that constrains available choices while accommodating, if not incorporating, a variety of extralegal influences.

Given the deluge of data showing that judicial decision-making is influenced by the judge's ideological predilections and other extralegal factors, persistent claims by judges that they follow the law and nothing else are greeted with understandable cynicism. Cognitive psychology explains how such influences can hold sway subconsciously—how a judge's ideological and other preferences can affect what she sincerely believes the law is. It is one thing, however, for judges, in the context of deciding cases, to think that they are following the law when they are subconsciously influenced by extralegal considerations. It is another thing for judges, in the context of public policy debates, to claim categorically that judicial decision-making is influenced by law alone, in the face of data to the contrary. In these public forums, judges seek to preserve public support and avoid political backlash by downplaying the data, disavowing the influence of extralegal considerations, declaring themselves umpires, and hewing to rule of law rhetoric. When the changing political landscape of the American courts, animated by public skepticism of the premises underlying the rule of law paradigm (as discussed in chapter 2), is paired with social science data justifying such skepticism, the long-term future of the rule of law paradigm is imperiled.

CHAPTER 4

The Rule of Law Paradigm's Popular Antecedents

Chapter 2 discussed the legal community's perspective on the changing landscape of the American judiciary, and its recurring calls to depoliticize the courts. The bench and bar's perspective is animated by the view that independent judges bracket out extralegal influences and follow the law. Political scientists determined to test (and ultimately discredit) this view have dubbed it the "legal model." But as perceptive scholars have noted, the "legal model" is not a model in the social science sense of the term because it is not a construct designed by researchers seeking to articulate a positive theory that can be verified or falsified.[1] Rather, this piece of the rule of law is a different kind of model—a paradigm with descriptive and normative elements that seeks to explain how the world works in terms that embody the ideals and aspirations of those who embrace it.

There are no meaningful data to show that the core communities operating within the rule of law paradigm (the bench, bar, public, and their elected representatives) have lost their reverence for the rule of law. What the evidence does show is that the paradigm is under stress. The venues in which factual premises underlying the paradigm have been challenged are proliferating. The resulting disconnection between how independent judges should decide cases (according to law alone) and how judges do in fact decide cases (not according to law alone) fuels the suspicion that the rule of law paradigm is eroding. If the descriptive and normative components of the rule of law paradigm are visualized as the rungs of a ladder, then the rails that stabilize the rungs are descriptive force and mythic value. Without disputing the power of myth and the extent to which faith in the rule of law paradigm has helped to sustain it at a time when its descriptive force is under assault, if the paradigm is left to balance on the rail of mythic value alone, its long-term future is rendered more precarious.

Keith Bybee characterizes persistence of the rule of law paradigm as an "acceptable hypocrisy."[2] Likening the rule of law to common courtesy, where we feign kindness despite thinking unkindly, Bybee suggests that we feign allegiance to a rule of law paradigm despite awareness that it is counterfactual. In both instances, Bybee argues, we preserve hypocrisy to ameliorate the cognitive dissonance that arises when we confront evidence of who we are that is in conflict with who we think we are and wish to be.[3]

Bybee's analysis offers valuable insights into our current state of affairs, but proceeds on an implicit assumption I do not share: that the rule of law paradigm is in a stable and steady state. The developments recounted in chapter 2 reveal a dynamic environment, in which the American judiciary is undergoing a multifaceted political transformation. That transformation features a series of developments a century in the making, in which judges have been called to task for their perceived hypocrisy again and again, in ways calculated to challenge the paradigm. Borrowing Bybee's analog, it is as if "Nice to see you, my friend—how are you today?" had begun to elicit the predictable reply, "Just shut up—you don't want to see me, you know I'm not your friend, and you couldn't care less how I'm doing, you duplicitous git." Under such circumstances, one might well begin to worry for the future of common courtesy.

It is tempting to explain recent developments with a caricature drawn from events recounted in chapters 2 and 3, to the effect that a public that once embraced naïve formalism has, over the course of the twentieth century, become jaded by realism, thus bringing the rule of law to the brink of crisis. But it is not that simple. Without disputing that realism is an accelerant fueling the brushfires that have transformed the judiciary's political landscape, realist sentiments did not begin with the realists.[4] As the remainder of this chapter is devoted to showing, widespread recognition of extralegal influences on judicial decision-making runs long and deep, dating back millennia. The rule of law paradigm, as crafted by the legal community, emerged and evolved in the shadow of a long-standing, pervasive public appreciation for the complexity of judicial motivations and conduct. The problem is not that the public has suddenly discovered that the rule of law paradigm is hypocritical. The problem is that, in an age when the public is disenchanted with its government and suspicious of public officials, when interest groups exploit courts and judges as tools for law reform in politically charged litigation campaigns, and when the venues for critiquing and controlling the politics of judicial decision-making are increasing in numbers, the hypocrisy of a paradigm that disavows the existence of judicial politics is becoming less acceptable.

To better understand what the wider world has traditionally thought about judges—in contrast to what the legal community has wanted the wider world to think about judges—one must look beyond legal texts to sources that reflect broader public concerns. In the absence of survey data from the distant past, accounts of judges portrayed in folktales, poems, novels, polemics, and other nonfictional accounts may be the next best proxy, for they illuminate how judges (for better and worse) were portrayed by authors of the time—portrayals aimed to resonate with contemporary readers. Literary depictions are, by their nature, exaggerated, unsystematic, and unrepresentative. But they serve my purpose here, of exploring the different ways in which judges have been portrayed over time, to the end of isolating oft-mentioned attributes of a good judge, identifying the objectives those attributes have been portrayed to further, and categorizing the different perspectives that have been employed to assess whether those objectives are met. Armed with this textured and deeply embedded vision of the judicial role, it will then be possible to revisit and reformulate the ailing rule of law paradigm to the end of constructing a new model that the public can embrace, social scientists can accept, and the legal community can implement.

THE ATTRIBUTES OF A GOOD JUDGE

Good judges have long been portrayed as possessing four essential attributes: (1) they are honest; (2) they are capable; (3) they are impartial; and (4) they are independent. Equally important for purposes here is that good judges are often defined in the obverse—by what bad judges lack— meaning that the qualities of a good judge have long been understood as goals, aspirations, or ideals, rather than as descriptions of empirical reality.

Honest and Dishonest Judges

The archetype of the dishonest judge is the corrupt jurist who solicits or accepts bribes. Shudraka, suspected to be the pen name of an Indian king who lived within a century or two of the Christian era, wrote of the need for judges to be "untouched by avarice."[5] William of Nassington and John Gower each complained of fourteenth-century English judges siding with whichever party gave the judge the larger gift.[6] A folktale of that period, widely told across the Eurasian continent, recounted this phenomenon in humorous terms: A carpenter and a butcher took each other to court over a will. The carpenter bribed the judge with a wagon and the judge sided with the carpenter until the butcher bribed the judge with four oxen to pull the wagon, whereupon the judge entered judgment for the butcher. "Turn the wagon!" called the carpenter to the judge, but the judge replied, "[T]he wagon cannot be turned for the oxen want to go the other way."[7] Three centuries later, concerns persisted: In England, *A Poem of the Times* wryly observed that "[t]he ambidextrous judges, bribed, rebrib'd and lesser gifts to greater still subscribed."[8] In the eighteenth-century Chinese novel, *Celebrated Cases of Judge Dee*, the anonymous author wrote that "the amelioration of the common people depends on the honesty of the magistrate."[9] While the personal interest at stake for the dishonest judge is typically economic, that is not always so: In Shakespeare's *Measure for Measure*, for example, the corrupt quid pro quo featured a judge who sought to trade a decision for sexual favors.[10]

Dishonest judges have also been portrayed as abusing judicial power for personal gain by means other than the traditional quid pro quo. Chaucer's *Physician's Tale* concerned a judge who paid a "churl" to falsely claim that a "noble knight's" daughter was the churl's slave, so that the judge would have a pretext to take custody of the knight's daughter and have his way with her.[11]

Capable and Incapable Judges

The "capable" judge exhibits an array of traits variously described to include competence, diligence, wisdom, and intelligence. Plato recounts that in 399 B.C.E., Socrates included among the attributes of a judge, "to hear courteously, to answer wisely, to consider soberly."[12] Shudraka declared that a judge should be "[l]earned, and skilled in tracing fraud's sly path, [a]nd eloquent, insensible to wrath."[13] Similarly, in *The Commission in Lunacy*, published in 1836, Honoré De Balzac described Judge Popinot's virtues in terms of an array of capabilities: He had "lips which spoke to the heart and proclaimed the man's intelligence and lucidity, a gift of second-sight" and "superior knowledge of the law" that earned him an early appointment to Napoleon's Imperial High Court.[14] In his 1751 novel, *Amelia*, Henry Fielding, like Balzac, singled out competence in law for special mention, observing that "this office of a Justice of Peace requires some knowledge of the law: for this simple reason; because in every case which comes before him, he is to judge and act according to law."[15] Of the judge he was describing, however, Fielding added sarcastically that "I cannot conceive how this knowledge should be acquired without reading; and yet certain it is Mr. Thrasher never read one syllable of the matter."[16]

Being learned in the law pairs naturally with possessing the wisdom and intelligence necessary to extract the truth from relevant facts. And so in the biblical account, King Solomon divined which of two claimants was a baby's mother by proposing to split the baby in two to see who would concede defeat rather than see her child killed.[17] In a similar vein is a Dutch folktale, in which a judge determined a child's capacity for criminal culpability by asking him to choose between an apple and a gold coin: By choosing the apple, the child's naïveté (and innocence) was revealed.[18]

Impartial and Partial Judges

Impartiality is an attribute of a good judge with ancient origins and several variations. In the fourth century B.C.E., Socrates is reported to have listed "to decide impartially" among the four essential attributes of a judge.[19] Writ large, impartiality is associated with a judicial temperament: being open-minded and even-tempered.[20] More specifically, partiality has been depicted in two ways: (1) partiality of the judge in relation to a party; and (2) partiality of the judge in relation to an issue.

Partiality of a judge vis-à-vis a party is typically depicted in terms of the judge's preexisting relationship with a party or preexisting bias toward a group of which the party is a member. The concern that impartiality could be corrupted by a judge's preexisting relationship with parties to a proceeding is long-standing. As early as the second century B.C.E., Shudraka urged judges to show "equal grace" to "friend, foe, kinsman."[21] The peril of judges being influenced by their friendships was a topic of concern in fourteenth-century Europe—John Gower, writing in the 1370s, noted how difficult it was to bring suit against anyone who had ties to the judge and criticized the practice of litigants finding nobles who were friendly with the judge to write letters vouching for litigants in court.[22]

Authors have likewise chronicled the peril of partial judges presiding over trials of their enemies. In the fifteenth century, Thomas Hoccleve recounted the story of a Persian judge who the king ordered to be flayed alive for sentencing a personal enemy to death.[23] And in his quasi-historical work, *Personal Recollections of Joan of Arc*, Mark Twain wrote of Bishop Cauchon, who presided at Joan's trial for heresy notwithstanding his vested interest in her demise, observing that "this proposed judge was the prisoner's outspoken enemy, and therefore he was incompetent to try her."[24]

Then, there are relatives. In Lewis Carroll's *Alice in Wonderland*,[25] the King was doubly encumbered: He was a judge presiding over a trial in which his tyrannical wife was the victim of an alleged tart theft; and he was a nincompoop. The resulting partiality problem manifested itself as a race to judgment: No sooner was the indictment read against the Knave of Hearts, than the King-Judge, with the queen scowling at his side, directed the jury to "consider your verdict," prompting the herald (the white rabbit) to admonish the King: "Not yet, not yet!. . . There's a great deal to come before that!"[26] As the proceedings continued, the King passively abided the queen's mid-trial exhortations to declare the knave guilty and have him beheaded, before calling upon the jury to render a verdict "for about the twentieth time that day."[27] Contrast the conduct of King Arthur, in Marie de France's twelfth century poem, *Lanval*. Given his anger at a knight who stood accused of slandering the queen, Arthur agreed that it would be "wrong to hold the trial with only the king's household to judge the case."[28]

In other stories, a judge's partiality toward a party is attributed to the party's membership in a favored or disfavored race, ethnicity, class, gender, or other identifiable group. The forms of status or group-based judicial bias with the most distinguished pedigree are wealth and class. At its basest level, judicial bias in favor of the wealthy and against the poor has one foot in dishonesty and corruption, discussed earlier: When judges award decisions to the highest bidder, rich parties win and poor parties lose. But the problem, as depicted over time, has transcended corruption. One scholar has described the work of medieval poets who decried "class justice," in which "a poor man can hardly ever win against a rich man or a nobleman, no matter how just his case may be."[29] To counter the perceived problem, English judges took an oath as early as the fourteenth century, to "do equal law and execution of right to all . . . rich and poor"[30] and in the seventeenth century, Sir Matthew Hale's code of judicial conduct addressed this ongoing concern with the rule that "I be not biassed with compassion to the poor, or favor to the rich."[31]

In *Amelia*, Henry Fielding described a day in the court of Justice Thrasher, who: convicted a "poor woman," falsely accused of streetwalking, after rejecting her truthful defense; dismissed charges against a "genteel young man and woman," after "declar[ing] with much warmth that the fact [recounted in the charge against them] was incredible and impossible"; and convicted a "shabbily drest" man, rejecting his truthful claim that the crime had been perpetrated by two others who "appeared to be men of fortune."[32] While Fielding noted that some of these proceedings were tainted by bribery, his final, sarcastic indictment of Thrasher went not to his corruption but to his bias against the poor: "In short, the magistrate had too great an honour for truth to suspect that she ever appeared in sordid apparel; nor did he ever sully his sublime notions of that virtue, by uniting them with the mean ideas of poverty and distress."[33]

In William Godwin's *Things as They Are; or, The Adventures of Caleb Williams*, published in 1794, the protagonist was a secretary whose employer was a wealthy man that committed murder and framed the secretary for robbery.[34] When the secretary defended himself by reporting the truth, the judge summarily rebuffed him:

> A fine time of it indeed it would be, if, when gentlemen of six thousand a year take up their servants for robbing them, those servants could trump up such accusations as these, and could get any magistrate or court of justice to listen to them! . . . There would be a speedy end to all order and good government, if fellows that trample upon ranks and distinctions in this atrocious sort, were upon any consideration suffered to get off.[35]

Ethnic, racial, and gender bias have likewise been featured in depictions of judicial conduct. In *Amelia*, Justice Thrasher found a defendant guilty, explaining: "Sirrah, your tongue betrays your guilt. You are an Irishman, and that is always sufficient evidence with me."[36] In the 1898 nonfictional polemic, "J'Accuse!," Emile Zola attacked the French administration of justice for its court martial of Captain Alfred Dreyfus, which Zola attributed to a "'dirty Jew' obsession, which is the scourge of our time."[37] In perhaps his most infamous tale, Judge Roy Bean purportedly acquitted a defendant of murder, reasoning that "I find the law very explicit on murdering your fellow man, but there's nothing here about killing a Chinaman. Case dismissed."[38] And in the climactic trial scene of Mary Wollstonecraft's eighteenth-century novel, *The Wrongs of Woman*, a misogynist judge trivialized the protagonist's suffering at the hands of an abusive husband in a marriage she could not escape. "What virtuous woman thought of her feelings?" he asked rhetorically, answering that "[i]t was her duty to love and obey the man chosen by her parents and relations, who were qualified by their experience to judge better for her, than she could for herself."[39]

Finally, there are examples of partiality in which the judge's bias is directed less at a party than at an issue, thereby exposing the judge's lack of an open mind. Emblematic of such cases is the storied "hanging judge." Robert Louis Stevenson's description of Lord Hermiston, in *The Weir of Hermiston*, is illustrative: "[H]e did not affect the virtue of impartiality; this was no case for refinement; there was a man to be hanged, he would have said, and he was hanging him. Nor was it possible to see his lordship, and acquit him of gusto in the task."[40] The hanging judge's impartiality is thus undermined by his predisposition to convict and execute, reflected in his indifference to the rule of law. A vivid, if disturbing, illustration comes from the story files of Judge Roy Bean:

> "Carlos Robles, this court finds you charged with a grave offense against the peace and dignity of the sovereign State of Texas, to wit: cattle rustlin'. How do you plead?"

> Unable to understand a word of English the defendant uttered a few sentences in Spanish.

> "Court accepts your plea of guilty. The jury will now deliberate, and if'n it brings in a verdict short of hangin' it'll be declared in contempt. Gentlemen, what's yore verdict?"

> "Guilty as hell, your honor."[41]

Independent and Dependent Judge

Illustrations abound of judges whose judgment has been compromised or corrupted by dependence on public officials, the general public, or others in a position to bend judges to their will. In *The Celebrated Cases of Judge Dee*, the author criticized judges who, "fearing lest they lose their position if they do not dispose quickly of a great number of cases, pronounce hasty verdicts on the basis of confessions obtained by torture, or from some shreds of evidence."[42] An infamous example comes from the crucifixion in the New Testament: Pontius Pilate judged Jesus blameless, but acquiesced to calls for his crucifixion after "the Jews cried out, saying 'if you release this man, you are no friend of Caesar.'"[43] In Tolstoy's *Resurrection*, a panel of judges imposed a harsh sentence on the accused, notwithstanding its recognition that the jury had convicted her inadvertently by bungling the verdict forms, because the judges feared adverse publicity if they were perceived as lenient.[44] And returning to Judge Roy Bean's acquittal of a defendant because the victim was Chinese, this episode, made notorious for its grotesque racial bias, was complicated by an overlay of judicial dependence: At the hearing, Bean was surrounded by an angry group of the perpetrator's friends, who were intent on violence if their comrade was convicted.[45]

Conversely, Charles Dickens took the opportunity to applaud an independent judge in *A Child's History of England*. There, he told a story of a "brave and generous," though "wild and dissipated" Prince who drew a sword on the chief justice "because [the judge] was firm in dealing impartially with one of [the prince's] dissolute companions."[46] The justice had the prince arrested, and the prince acquiesced, which offered King Henry (and Dickens) a teaching moment: "Happy is the monarch who has so just a judge, and a son so willing to obey the law."[47]

Similarly, in Marie de France's poem, justice was done when Lanval was exonerated for slander of King Arthur's wife, after Arthur assured those assembled to try the case that "without fail, the judges' decision would prevail."[48]

Old stories celebrating independence and decrying its absence notwithstanding, in England, formal judicial independence from the crown did not arrive until the 1701 Act of Settlement.[49] In systems where the judicial power was exercised by the king and his designees, judicial independence from the monarch to whom judges reported presented a ticklish situation, as evidenced by Shudraka's admonition to judges, that "an open door to truth, his heart must cling ... yet shun each thing that might awake the anger of the king."[50] Although dependent judges have long been criticized, during the centuries in which the tradition of judges serving as an extension of the crown was in place, independence was often relegated to the status of unfulfilled wish.

THE OBJECTIVES OF GOOD JUDGING

The four attributes of a good judge—being honest, capable, impartial, and independent—can be viewed as positive-seeming qualities that are ends in themselves. But as applied to judges, these attributes have been portrayed not as ends, but as instrumental values that further other ends, namely: upholding the rule of law, implementing a fair process, and doing justice. As with the attributes of a good judge, which are often highlighted by their absence, the objectives that good judges further are often depicted in the context of flawed or bad judges subverting such objectives.

Upholding the Rule of Law

When judges have been portrayed as corrupt, incompetent, biased, or under another's thumb, the rule of law is often cast as the casualty. In these stories, one or more of the judge's failings leads him to misapply relevant facts to applicable law and reach a wrong result. The implications for the "good judge" are obvious: Honest, capable, impartial, and independent judges uphold the law as they construe it to be written, in light of the facts as they find them.

Judge Roy Bean's racism led him to contort the law by excluding a Chinese victim from the definition of "human being" under a murder statute. In Fielding's *Amelia*, the dishonest Justice Thrasher, who "was never indifferent in a cause, but when he could get nothing on either side," after "having received a wink from the clerk," promptly acquitted the codefendants in the teeth of the accuser's sworn testimony.[51] And Pontius Pilate's dependence on the madding crowd led him to wash his hands of the facts and acquiesce to an innocent's crucifixion. Conversely, in *Lanval*, the judges got to the truth because King Arthur recused himself from a case in which his wife was the alleged victim, and promised not to interfere with the independent decision of the judges.[52]

Implementing a Fair Process

In a second group of stories, the focus has been on bad judges who truncate due process, often to the end of producing bad results. The focal point of these stories is not the outcome per se, but the process that effectively deprives parties of a fair hearing. Good judges, by negative inference, take process seriously, treat parties fairly, and afford them their day in court.

In Anton Chekhov's *A Malefactor*, for example, a defendant was on trial for the crime of intentionally derailing a train by unscrewing metal nuts from the rails. The judge, who was too confused (code that: incapable) to understand that the defendant had not meant to derail the train and had removed the nuts to weight his fishing line, ordered the defendant to "[h]old your tongue; don't interrupt" before he could explain, and sentenced him to prison.[53] In Twain's *Joan of Arc*, Joan's conviction was depicted as the fait accompli of a biased judge who "carefully suppress[ed] all evidence that came to hand in her favor," and used "limitless ways and means and powers at his disposal for preparing and strengthening the case for the prosecution."[54] And in *Alice in Wonderland*, the King's repeated exhortations—before, during, and after the time that testimony was taken—for the jury to decide the fate of the knave who had allegedly victimized the King's wife, culminated in the Queen's iconic directive: "Sentence first—verdict afterwards."[55]

Doing Justice

Finally, there is a third cluster of stories, in which bad judges produce results that, while technically compatible with applicable facts and law, are unjust. These stories differ from those previously described in that here the judge neither misapplies the facts to law, nor deprives the parties of an opportunity to be heard. Rather, these judges follow applicable law and procedure slavishly, without regard to justice, because they are unwise, indifferent, or biased. By negative implication, good judges do more than mindlessly follow the rules. They do justice.

In *Antigone*, the well-intentioned but unwise King-Judge Creon was ruined for disregarding the higher justice of the gods' will, by upholding a law that forbade proper burial to traitors, thus vindicating Antigone's warning that "I didn't think a mortal man's decrees possessed sufficient strength to nullify the deities' secure, unwritten laws."[56] Other stories feature judges compromised by indifference. In the *Spoon River Anthology*, Edgar Lee Masters depicted a judge who reports from the grave that "I in life was the Circuit Judge, a maker of notches, [d]eciding cases on the points the lawyers scored, [n]ot on the right of the matter."[57] Similarly, in *Bleak House*, Charles Dickens portrayed the High Court of Chancery as "tripping one another up on slippery precedents, groping knee-deep in technicalities . . . and making a pretence of equity with serious faces," in the context of litigation over a will that ended only when legal fees exhausted the estate.[58] Conversely, in *Merchant of Venice*, Portia is presented as a good judge who deprived the plaintiff Shylock of his contractual right to a pound of the defendant's flesh through a tortured construction of their agreement, thereby circumventing the law to achieve just results.[59]

PERSPECTIVES ON WHEN THE OBJECTIVES OF GOOD JUDGING ARE MET

Whether a given jurist is a good judge who upholds the law, adheres to due process, and does justice is a question that literature has addressed from three different perspectives. The first is from the perspective of parties to adjudication; the second is from the perspective of the public or body politic; and the third is from the perspective of an idealized virtuous or ethical judge.

The Adjudicative Perspective

In many stories, readers step into the shoes of parties to the adjudication and are invited to evaluate a judge's conduct in terms of its implications for participants in court proceedings. In these stories, the reader is made to feel the weight of a bad judge's conduct through the incarceration, execution, or mistreatment of blameless parties or witnesses. Jesus, Joan of Arc, Chekhov's hapless fisherman, and the many victims of Justice Thrasher's court are examples where readers are invited to evaluate the bad judge's conduct from the adjudicative perspective of parties whose day in court has been denied or corrupted.

The Political Perspective

Other stories have appealed to readers from a second perspective, as members of the general public. The public may be moved by stories of injustice to individual litigants at the hands of bad judges, but unlike parties, the public is victimized by bad judgments less directly. Rather, for the public, the issue is ultimately one of institutional legitimacy and the trust and confidence of the body politic in judges and the judiciary. Thus, for example, in *The Celebrated Cases of Judge Dee*, the author explained the importance of honest judges in terms of their impact on public confidence, opining that a corrupt judge "should never be appointed as ruler[] over others," because "how could such men make their subordinates honest, and bring peace to the common people[?]"[60] And in *Bleak House*, which revolved around the smug, indifferent, and inefficient Court of High Chancery, Dickens was not oblivious to the court's adverse impact on parties, but he reserved special condemnation for how the court's conduct had ruined its institutional legitimacy, chiding the judges for "looking . . . as if nobody had ever heard that all over England the name in which they were assembled was a bitter jest: was held in universal horror, contempt, and indignation; was known for something so flagrant and bad, that little short of a miracle could bring any good out of it to anyone."[61] From this public or "political" perspective, then, bad judges flout law, process, and justice to the detriment of the public's faith in the courts.

The Ethical Perspective

Then there is a third perspective that evaluates judicial conduct in terms of the intrinsic qualities of a good judge. This "ethical" perspective is focused less on the judge's conduct in relation to its impact on the parties or public, than in relation to a Platonic ideal or Aristotelian virtue, in which judges are to comport themselves in a manner dictated and delineated by the roles of a good or virtuous jurist. Thus, Plato, quoting Socrates, observed that "[f]our things belong to a judge: to hear courteously, to answer wisely, to consider soberly, and to decide impartially"—not because the rights of parties or public support depends on it, but because these qualities "belong to a judge."[62] Similarly, Balzac rhapsodized about Judge Popinot in terms of his intrinsic virtues—characteristics that reflected the "noblest sentiments": his intelligence, lucidity, "gift of . . . heavenly temper," and "second-sight."[63]

IMPLICATIONS OF JUDGES IN LITERATURE

Storybook hour yields two relevant insights. First, these stories show that audiences around the world have been alert to extralegal influences on judicial decision-making for a very long time. Second, these stories illuminate a structure for analyzing judicial conduct.

The Ubiquity of Extralegal Influence

The rule of law paradigm, which proceeds from the premise that judges disregard extralegal influences and follow the law, emerged against the backdrop of popular culture that took such a premise with several grains of salt. In the stories retold here, the presence of extralegal influences on judicial decision-making is usually evidence of weak or flawed judging. Sometimes, as with Judge Roy Bean, these are simply tales of a defective judge—the isolated bad (if colorful) apple, whose miscreance is meant to say nothing about judges generally. If anything, such stories arguably reaffirm the rule of law paradigm by marginalizing deviants.

Oftentimes, however, the defective judge is portrayed as a representative sample from a bad barrel. Of Justice Thrasher, Fielding remarked that "[t]he higher we proceed among our public officers and magistrates, the less defects of this kind will, perhaps be observable"[64]—which by negative implication meant that Thrasher's defects were widely observable among "lower" magistrates. Godwin's magistrate was the foil for an even more systemic indictment: "And this at last was the justice of mankind!" Caleb Williams railed, despairing that wealth "shall protect a man from accusation," while "the validity of an impeachment shall be superseded, because the author of it is a servant!"[65] Similarly, Wollstonecraft's misogynist judge was written into the climax of *The Wrongs of Woman* as a representative of his gender who sat in biased judgment over women.

These categorical claims challenge the rule of law paradigm: The rule of law is illusory—judges are captured by their own appetites and will further their interests at the expense of those over whom they sit in judgment. The sentiment is expressed succinctly in the African proverb: "Corn can't expect justice from a court composed of chickens."[66] In the *Spoon River Anthology*, published in 1916, Edgar Lee Masters made a similar, if narrower point in an anecdote about a diminutive judge for whom "it was natural" to "ma[k]e it hard" on the "giants" who appeared before him, given the teasing the judge had endured earlier in life.[67]

Lighthearted as Masters's story was, it is but a short walk from there to the darker conclusion that judges are ensnared by the same prejudices that afflict us all—prejudices attributable to the influences of their class, gender, race, ethnicity, ideology, and life experiences. Some nineteenth-century thinkers made this point well before legal realism was so much as a twinkle in Karl Llewellyn's eye: In the 1880s, Robert Green Ingersoll declared that "[w]e must remember . . . that we have to make judges out of men, and that by being made judges their prejudices are not diminished and their intelligence is not increased."[68] That same decade, David Dudley Field echoed: "Judges are but men, and are swayed like other men by vehement prejudices. This is corruption in reality, give it whatever other name you please."[69] In other words, many of the stories recounted here reflect an embedded understanding that honest, capable, impartial, and independent judges should follow the law, but that human frailty ensures that judges will never live up to the rule of law ideal.

Typically, judges who succumb to extralegal influences are portrayed in a negative light, while those who bracket out such influences and follow the law are lionized, but that is not always so. Judges who uphold the law without regard to justice are portrayed as missing the point: Sophocles' Creon is condemned for imposing man's law over what the gods have decreed is right; Dickens's Chancery court is made a laughing stock for mindlessly following legal precedent and procedure without doing justice; and Shakespeare's Portia is applauded for contorting the law to reach a just result.

In sum, to the extent that the rule of law paradigm posits that judges bracket out extralegal influences and follow the law alone, it is both over-inclusive and under-inclusive of storied understandings. As a descriptive matter, the paradigm is over-inclusive because it posits that judges categorically eschew extralegal influences, in the teeth of myriad stories to the contrary, dating back millennia. As a normative matter, the paradigm is under-inclusive because it fails to accommodate circumstances in which judges massage indeterminate law to do justice.

A Framework for Analyzing Judicial Conduct

In addition to highlighting a pervasive understanding that judges are subject to myriad extralegal influences, the study of judges in literature illuminates a structure for analyzing judicial conduct that I develop more fully in the next chapter. As reflected in the stories summarized here, there are four attributes of a good judge that recur in literature over time: They are honest; they are capable; they are impartial; and they are independent. In the context of evaluating judicial conduct, these four attributes are not ends in themselves, but are instrumental values that further three objectives: (1) implementing the rule of law; (2) following due process; and (3) doing substantive justice.

These stories make clear that judges as a group are not perfectly honest, capable, impartial, or independent, but are human beings who have their flaws. Whether judges are honest enough, capable enough, impartial enough, or independent enough to uphold the law, respect due process, and do justice is a question that has been analyzed from three distinct perspectives. From an adjudicative perspective, one evaluates whether these objectives have been furthered through the eyes of the parties, who seek a lawful, fair, and just resolution of their disputes. From a political perspective, one evaluates whether the objectives of good judging have been achieved through the eyes of the body politic, or general public, for whom fidelity to law, process, and justice as they perceive it are critical to the judiciary's institutional legitimacy. From an ethical perspective, one evaluates whether the objectives of good judging have been achieved through the eyes of a platonic ideal of a good judge, for whom respect for law, process, and justice is intrinsic to good judging.

CONCLUSION

A perspective-dependent approach to sorting good judges from bad, in the context of a judiciary that is subject to legal and extralegal influences, sets the stage for reassessing the rule of law paradigm. To this point, the value of a perspective-dependent analysis remains unclear, because in literature, where judges are usually portrayed as obviously good or obviously bad, all three perspectives lead to the same conclusion. But as chapter 5 aims to show, at the margins, differences between these perspectives ultimately help to explain the political transformation of the courts described in chapter 2 and why the public policy debate over judges and their roles has been so unproductive and intractable. Armed with this new framework for analysis, it is now possible to revisit and ultimately replace the ailing paradigm with something better.

CHAPTER 5

The Legal Culture Paradigm

The preceding chapters have been devoted to describing the rule of law paradigm, its counterfactual premises, and the extent to which its long-term vitality is in doubt. This chapter, in turn, introduces a new legal culture paradigm that seeks to address the problems of its predecessor.

Chapter 2 showed how the rule of law paradigm rests on the premise that judges who are afforded independence enough to make choices without fear or favor will decide cases with exclusive reference to applicable law and operative facts. Chapter 3 showed how social science data challenge this premise by showing that judges are subject to an array of legal and extralegal influences. When the "law versus politics" debate was in full flower and was presented as an either-or proposition, it was easy enough for the bench and bar to side with law, deny the relevance of extralegal influences, and marginalize arguments to the contrary. As this binary academic debate has yielded to a more nuanced, interdisciplinary consensus in the past decade, denying the impact of extralegal influences in the teeth of such an emerging consensus has become increasingly problematic.

To complicate matters further for the bench and bar, the public thinks (and has long thought) judges are subject to an eclectic array of legal and extralegal influences, consistent with the emerging scholarly consensus, and the thrust of chapter 4. First, the public thinks judges are fair and impartial arbiters of law. In a survey conducted in 2001, 79% thought that "dedicated to facts and law" described judges well or very well; 76% thought the same of the term "fair," and 63% of "impartial."[1] And 58% agreed with the statement that judges "make decisions based more on facts and law" than "on politics and pressure from special interests."[2]

Second, the public thinks judges are influenced by their ideologies. The same 2001 survey found that 76% of respondents thought that "political" described judges well or very well.[3] In 2005, another national poll found that 85.5% of those surveyed thought that judges' partisan backgrounds influenced their decision-making some or a lot.[4] That 2005 survey found that 57.9% agreed with the statement that "judges always say that their decisions are based on the law and the constitution but in many cases judges are really basing their decisions on their own personal beliefs."[5] And in 2006, yet another survey found that 75% of respondents thought that judges were influenced by their personal political views to a great or moderate extent.[6] In 2010, one author reported on survey data showing that 70% of the public thinks that politics are at work in state judicial processes, and 60% think that federal judges are more apt to make decisions that reflect their "own political leanings" than to "hand down fair decisions."[7]

The public's understanding of "law" is merged with politics in ways consistent with a broader and more flexible construction of law proposed by interdisciplinary scholars. One major study, based on interviews with over 400 people, found that the public simultaneously regards law as disinterested, objective, and operating by "fixed rules," and as "a game, a terrain for tactical encounters."[8]

At the same time, the public has retained confidence in courts peopled with judges whose motives it regards as mixed and has favored insulating judges from external controls. A 2006 survey revealed that 64% of the public trusts the Supreme Court a "great deal" or a "fair amount."[9] In another survey, 76% expressed some or a great deal of confidence in the U.S. Supreme Court, followed by 74% for federal courts and 71% for state courts.[10] Moreover, in one survey, 73% thought that judges should be shielded from outside pressure,[11] while in another survey, 83% thought judges should be shielded from congressional intimidation.[12]

In short, the public has internalized what recent scholarship demonstrates—and centuries of literature illustrates—that judges are subject to legal and extralegal influences—but continues to express considerable confidence in the courts. In that light, the pretense of the legal establishment's argument in the public policy debate, that judges are moved by law and facts alone, seems otherworldly, unnecessary, and a bit silly. The bench and bar, however, are between a rock and a hard place. Citizens may think that judges are influenced by their personal feelings and ideological predilections, but that does not mean they like it. For example, a 2005 poll found that 75% of respondents thought a judge's rulings are influenced by his or her politics to a great or a moderate extent. That same poll found that only 29% thought it was appropriate for a judge's ruling to be influenced by her political views.[13] The public is more closely divided on the question of whether, when deciding "an important constitutional case," the Supreme Court should consider only "the legal issues" or take "what the majority of the public thinks" into account.[14] When it comes to judges acting on their own ideological predilections, however, surveys reveal that the vast preponderance of the American public expects judges to apply the law impartially and does not trust judges who advance their own ideological interests."[15]

Perhaps as a consequence, judges have stuck to the rule of law script. The 2005 confirmation of Chief Justice John Roberts offers a useful illustration. Roberts's conservative political bent was widely reported, and Senate Democrats did their best to portray him as an ideological extremist.[16] The Democrats had succeeded with a similar strategy in defeating the Supreme Court nomination of Robert Bork two decades earlier.[17] One critical difference, however, was the extent to which the two nominees hewed to the rule of law rhetoric. Bork was quite willing to elucidate his judicial philosophy with the Senate Judiciary Committee.[18] From his vantage point, he was merely elaborating on his understanding of the law. In so doing, however, he made plain the influence that his ideology was likely to have on the decisions he would be making as a justice, which enabled Senate Democrats and interest groups to sour the public—and ultimately the Senate—on his candidacy.[19] Roberts, in contrast, like every Supreme Court nominee to testify after Bork, was less forthcoming, declined entreaties to discuss his views on any legal issues and repeatedly sounded the theme that he would follow the law.[20] "Judges are like umpires," he testified. "Umpires don't make the rules. They apply them."[21] Against the backdrop of social science learning, the claim that the Supreme Court "applies" but does not "make" rules of constitutional law when it decides hotly contested questions of first impression that have split the lower courts, is something of a whopper. And given the public's readiness to believe that judges are influenced by their personal views, it seems unlikely that the public was so fatuous as to assume that Roberts's widely publicized conservative ideology would have no bearing on his decision-making. Nevertheless, the ease with which Chief Justice Roberts was confirmed was widely attributed to the appeal of his simple and consistent rule of law message.[22]

In 2009, President Barack Obama indicated his intention to replace retiring Justice David Souter with someone who possessed—among other qualities—"empathy."[23] The comment drew a sharp rebuke from critics who claimed that empathy was "code" for activism and had no place on a Supreme Court that should decide cases with reference to applicable law alone.[24] When President Obama later announced the nomination of Sonia Sotomayor, gone was any reference to empathy, and in its stead was a statement that stressed the nominee's commitment to the rule of law.[25] What controversy surrounded her nomination was limited almost exclusively to prior statements she had made implying that judges are subject to extralegal influences (e.g., that a Latina judge might decide matters differently—and better—than a white male, and that circuit courts make policy).[26]

In short, while the public is cognizant of extralegal influences on judicial decision-making, it is uneasy about them. That helps to explain the continuing appeal of unqualified rule of law rhetoric, and the resonance of policy arguments aimed at discouraging ideological and other influences. For their part, judges are acutely aware of the relationship between public perception and the judiciary's institutional legitimacy, and to the extent the public wants judges whose commitment to the rule of law is unwavering, it behooves judges and the legal establishment to profess such a commitment.[27] And so, the bench and bar have stayed on message, declaring that independence enables impartial judges to follow the law—period. Full stop.

Although aware of allegations that independent judges are influenced by their personal preferences (policy-related and otherwise), the bench and bar seek to marginalize those allegations in a variety of ways. Some judges continue to deny or dismiss the relevance of such influences. As one state supreme court justice put it: "What's law got to do with it? Everything. . . .[T]he criticism of some in the political science academy that judicial decision-making is not based on law, but politics, is disheartening—and I think it is wrong."[28] Other judges concede that they are subject to such influences, but downplay their significance. One state court of appeals judge, for example, likened ideological influence to the gap between noted celebrities' teeth: small but noticeable.[29] Still other judges concede that extralegal influences sometimes get the best of their brethren, but relegate the problem to other, misguided judges.[30] Finally, some accuse the accusers, asserting that inflammatory accusations of "activism" and partisanship undermine the rule of law and are part of the larger problem remedied by depoliticizing the courts.[31]

We thus confront a situation in which judges and their defenders say that judges follow the law and nothing else, while scholars, the media, the general public, and its elected representatives appear to understand that such claims are not, strictly speaking, true. For a very long time, these counterfactual declarations may have been tolerated if not embraced as an "acceptable hypocrisy," in which it was enough for judges to pledge unyielding allegiance to the rule of law, even if their performance inevitably fell short of the ideal.[32] What the political transformation of recent generations has done, has been to call out this hypocrisy across an escalating array of venues to the end of rendering it less acceptable. Hence, judges are decreasingly portrayed as neutral, umpire-like arbiters of law. They are policymakers whose penchant for ideological excess is exposed by the new media, challenged by interest groups, curbed by legislation, thwarted in confirmation proceedings, and punished in judicial elections. And while public confidence in the courts has traditionally remained relatively stable and strong, it is at least worth noting that in 2014 Gallup reported that those surveyed who expressed a "great deal" or "quite a lot" of confidence in the Supreme Court had dipped to 30%: an all-time low in the history of the survey question.[33]

I am not suggesting that the rule of law paradigm is on the brink of collapse. As the introduction took pains to emphasize, crisis claims are overstated. Survey data do not show that the judiciary's legitimacy is in peril, even if support for the Supreme Court is declining. Independence norms are centuries in development and will not perish easily. There are no concerted efforts by the public or their elected representatives to defy unpopular rulings (although pockets of defiance by state officials in the wake of the Supreme Courts' 2015 decision invalidating state laws banning same-sex marriage are noteworthy). Isolated rulings provoke outcry from various quarters, but public opinion is sharply divided as to whether the ideological orientation of the Supreme Court is too liberal, too conservative, or about right.[34] Whether that is because the justices' ideological center of gravity tends not to drift too far from that of the public or the popularly elected president who nominated them, or because justices sometimes vote strategically to avoid unnecessary confrontations, the net effect is to avert brinksmanship that invites crises.

What we see instead is a paradigm eroded by escalating challenges to the assumptions on which it rests. The bench is thereby placed in a seemingly untenable position: It can cling tenaciously to the rule of law paradigm, pledge allegiance to the paradigm's counterfactual premise that independent judges impartially follow facts and law alone, and suffer lingering death by a thousand cuts at the hands of an ever more disbelieving public. Or it can acknowledge the hypocrisy of the paradigm, concede that independence liberates judges to do more and less than follow the law, and invite the judiciary's detractors to rise up and sever judicial independence at the neck with a single blow.

The problem is not that "we are all legal realists now."[35] As chapter 4 showed, we have been legal realists of a sort for centuries. The problem is that maintaining the pretense of an independent judiciary that is impervious to extralegal influence in the teeth of long-standing realist suspicions to the contrary is gradually becoming unacceptable in the wake of persistent and proliferating challenges.

REORIENTING TO A LEGAL CULTURE PARADIGM

In chapter 2, I characterized sociolegal paradigms as models of interaction between law, society, and culture, to which affected communities adhere. Affected communities within the rule of law paradigm include scholars, media, judges, lawyers, interest groups, political parties, the public, and their elected representatives. The long-term peril for the rule of law paradigm is that it is losing adherents in several of those communities: Scholars have exposed the paradigm as counterfactual, and the media, interest groups, political parties, the public, and its elected representatives have challenged the paradigm's premises across a growing array of venues, to the end of isolating and discrediting the unyielding views of bench and bar. Absent intervening developments, continued erosion and eventual collapse of the rule of law paradigm seem inevitable. If those operating within the paradigm conclude that impartiality is a fiction, and that independence creates a safe harbor for partiality that undermines the rule of law that independence is ostensibly there to promote, the rule of law paradigm has lost its raison d'être. The paradigm will likely exit not with a bang, but a whimper, as political and popular controls eclipse the judiciary's independence incrementally and the lines separating the oversight of judges from other public officials gradually blur and dissolve.

If judicial independence can only be explained and justified with recourse to a paradigm that embraces a hypocrisy widely regarded as unacceptable, then the paradigm will (and should) crumble along with the independent judiciary that the failed paradigm cultivated. But that begs a critical question: Can judicial independence only be explained and justified with recourse to the discredited rule of law paradigm?

As splashy as it would be to roll out a paradigm shift with trumpets and fanfare, I propose more of a paradigm tweak that retools judicial independence and accountability for a judiciary that is subject to legal and extralegal influences. In so doing, my objective is to develop a "legal culture paradigm" premised on a positive theory of judicial decision-making that scholars, the media, the public, and their elected representatives can accept, and that the bench and bar can embrace and defend.

I begin with the modest proposition that the legal community has a distinct culture, of which judges are a part. I say "modest" because the term "legal culture" implicates a potentially sprawling array of profound and often controversial questions about the nature of law, its relationship to human culture, and the extent to which law itself is a form of culture.[36] My objective here is more limited and less provocative.

The definition of culture itself is a contested issue. As Austin Sarat has warned: "To talk about culture, in the first instance, is to venture into a field where there are almost as many definitions of the term as there are discussions of it."[37] Rather than pursue the definitional conundrum down a rabbit hole, I defer to the expansive but useful formulation of Naomi Mezey, a contributor to Sarat's edited volume on law and culture, who defines culture as "a set of shared, signifying practices—practices by which meaning is produced, performed, contested and transformed."[38]

Within the legal community, signifying practices that produce and transform meaning are introduced in law school. These practices assume three basic forms: (1) structures that signal a break from other disciplines and a transition to life in the law; (2) teaching methods aimed at educating students to "think like a lawyer"; and (3) a curriculum focused on legal doctrine. In the discussion that follows, I rely heavily on a lengthy article by Professor Judith Wegner,[39] a coauthor of the influential 2007 Carnegie Report on legal education,[40] because her article describes the architecture of legal education with extensive quotations from student and faculty interviews conducted at sixteen representative law schools—interviews that are not publicly available.

Law schools subject aspiring lawyers to an array of structures that introduce them to a distinct legal culture, beginning the week they arrive. Legal education is positioned as an intensive immersion program that is all law, all the time, in which students typically spend long hours in the same building, attending the same classes in the same rooms with the same classmates and the same professors, studying from the same texts in the same library, and relaxing in the same lounge.[41] Students are exposed to a new vocabulary that only those with legal training understand.[42] They are subjected to ritual trials by fire: participating in conscripted Socratic dialogues with faculty in large classes; drafting briefs and making oral arguments that serve as capstones to first-year research and writing programs; and taking lengthy, comprehensive finals.[43] They are subject to an ethos of competition for the best grades, the best co-curricular credentials (such as law review or moot court), and the best jobs, which motivates students to embrace and conform to institutional norms.[44]

Law school likewise employs an array of teaching methods aimed at training students to "think like a lawyer." First, teaching students to think like lawyers means showing them how to learn the law for themselves, as lawyers do: They are not told what the rules of law are but are taught how to read cases, statutes, and rules from which they are expected (with guidance from faculty) to derive applicable rules of law for themselves.[45] Second, teaching students to think like lawyers means training them in the art of legal reasoning. Legal reasoning includes a grab bag of skills, one being organized thinking: understanding and applying templates for resolving legal problems by isolating key issues from operative facts, identifying applicable legal rules, analyzing how to interpret the rules to resolve the legal issues, and coming to appropriate conclusions.[46] Another such skill is critical thinking: deriving legal conclusions from factual premises by means of logical deduction; reasoning by analogy, so that analogous problems are resolved in similar ways; and sorting wheat from chaff, so as to focus on the facts, issues, and rules that matter and discard those that do not.[47] Third, teaching students to think like lawyers means preparing them to manage and manipulate indeterminacy. Law schools teach law through difficult cases and problems. What makes those cases and problems difficult is uncertainty over what the pertinent facts are, what broadly or imprecisely phrased rules of law require, and how preexisting law should apply in new factual settings. Because these cases and problems arise in an adversarial context, indeterminate scenarios yield competing answers, which require students to understand and argue "both sides" of disputed issues.[48] In such cases, faculty guide students in developing the best policy arguments each side can make in support of the proposition that the judge should rule in that side's favor.[49] Fourth, because students learn law in adversarial settings, learning to think like lawyers means placing students in the role of agent and advocate for their clients.[50] Critical to being an effective advocate is setting one's personal feelings aside, stepping into the client's shoes, and making the best argument possible on the client's behalf, given the constraints of applicable facts and law.[51]

Finally, the law school curriculum focuses on doctrinal law—procedural and substantive. Recent waves of reform have undertaken to expand clinical education, and devote more class time to ethics, professional self-identity, and practice-oriented competencies. But doctrinal law remains a mainstay of the curriculum.[52] In substantive law courses, students learn the law of torts, contracts, property, the Constitution, intellectual property, corporations, and so on. In procedural law courses, students learn the law of civil procedure, evidence, criminal procedure, federal jurisdiction, administrative law, conflicts of law, and complex litigation. And the essay and multiple-choice examinations that determine student grades test their ability to apply rules of substantive and procedural law that students derive from the cases and problems studied in those doctrinal courses.

Returning to the working definition of culture, these "practices" produce and transform meaning for aspiring lawyers by infusing what the practices emphasize with importance. Three conclusions that this transformative process encourages law students to draw are of particular importance here: (1) law matters; (2) indeterminacy is pervasive; and (3) policy considerations fill gaps that legal indeterminacy creates. First, the structure, method, and curriculum of legal education all but bellow the message that law matters. Substantive and procedural law matter: They would not dominate the law school curriculum otherwise. The structure and logic of legal reasoning divorced from personal feelings matter. The process of sifting through pertinent facts, law, and policy options to the end of furnishing judges with the information they need to reach the best result in a given case is conceptualized as the method by which lawyers pursue justice for their clients. Second, the culture of legal education signals that legal indeterminacy is pervasive. It is at the core of every thorny legal problem in every law school course. And exploiting that indeterminacy for the client's benefit is a critical component of what it means to think like a lawyer. Third, policy matters to law students because they know it matters to judges. Law students develop competing policy arguments to resolve indeterminate cases because judges exercise discretion and judgment that is influenced by policy considerations, or, more accurately, the policy considerations that judges prefer.

These three points of emphasis inculcated into aspiring lawyers during law school, are reinforced later by cultural practices of the bar. Law still matters: Induction into the fraternity of lawyers is signaled by passing a bar exam that limits the anointed (and the competition) to those who exhibit a basic command of substantive and procedural law. Continuing legal education requirements, malpractice standards, and rules of professional conduct that make ongoing competence in law an ethical responsibility, convey the unremarkable message that good lawyers know the law and that bringing applicable law to bear is relevant to resolving client problems in (and out of) court. Rules of professional conduct have been construed to forbid lawyers from accusing judges of disregarding the law and substituting their personal political agendas.[53] Indeterminacy remains pervasive. When indeterminacy is lacking – in other words, when applicable law and facts point to outcomes so clear that alternative conclusions are frivolous –clients are sent home or their matters settled. Exploiting indeterminacy thus remains the lawyer's bread and butter, so much so that the Model Rules of Professional Conduct devote a cluster of rules to prohibiting lawyers from manufacturing indeterminacy that does not exist, or eliminating indeterminacy that does, by filing frivolous claims, making false statements, offering false evidence, failing to cite controlling law, enabling false testimony, or seeking to influence judges, jurors, or the public in inappropriate ways.[54]

With few exceptions, judges are lawyers: State law demands it; and in the federal system, no nominee for an Article III judgeship could survive the confirmation gauntlet without a law degree.[55] Hence, by the time judges ascend the bench, they have been immersed in the legal culture for

years—first as law students and later as practitioners. As judges, they un-
dergo an added layer of acculturation on the job: in "baby judges school,"
when they first arrive; in continuing judicial education programs throughout their careers; from codes of judicial conduct;[56] and most important,
from fellow judges and personal experience.

Core to that acculturation are collegiality norms. Circuit Judge and
former Harvard Law Professor Harry Edwards has written at length about
the role collegiality plays in keeping ideological excesses in check on intermediate appellate courts. For judges who take law seriously, the desire
to earn and preserve the respect of like-minded colleagues operates as an
additional brake on conscious pursuit of private, extralegal agendas. Edwards's argument is corroborated in a backhanded way by data showing that
appellate court panels comprised of judges appointed by presidents from
both political parties are likeliest to produce moderated results compatible
with preexisting legal doctrine.[57] Trial judges, in contrast, operate in comparative solitude, but data suggest that they prize the respect and validation
of their appellate court colleagues reflected in high affirmance rates.[58]

Conversely, the experience of the Wisconsin Supreme Court illustrates
how the collapse of collegiality norms can contribute to paralyzing personal and ideological divides. Wisconsin was a politically polarized state
that elected or reelected five justices (in nominally nonpartisan races) on
its seven-member court between 2007 and 2013. Several of those campaigns were bruising affairs, in which ideologically aligned interests threw
their financial support behind their favored candidates amid charges that
big money was buying influence.[59] Allegations of ethical lapses followed:
Justice Ziegler was reprimanded for presiding over cases (as a court of
appeals judge) in which her husband had an interest;[60] an ethics complaint against Justice Gableman's charged him with running misleading
campaign commercials;[61] and Justice Prosser was investigated for a phys-
ical altercation with Justice Bradley during a meeting of the justices in
chambers.[62] On a related front, the campaign support that the justices
received,[63] the alleged bias manifested in Justice Gableman's campaign
commercials,[64] and other purported conflicts, formed the basis for a flurry
of disqualification requests over succeeding years, all of which the members of the court denied.[65]

With this series of events came a debilitating and divisive devolution
of collegiality. Justice Prosser called Chief Justice Abrahamson a "bitch"
amid deliberations over the Gableman ethics complaint, and later accused his colleagues of leaking the incident to embarrass him.[66] When
Justice Bradley dissented from the court's revised disqualification rule,
it drew a sharp rebuke from the majority for being announced prema-
turely.[67] The press reported that Justices Abrahamson and Bradley were

fearful of Justice Prosser and had received additional security, while Justice Roggensack dismissed such reports, and the underlying concerns, as unfounded.[68] Resolution of the disciplinary action arising out of the Prosser-Bradley bout was thwarted by mass-recusals that left the court without a quorum.[69] As collegiality norms collapsed, members of the court retreated to ideologically aligned camps, and split along ideological lines over: the Court's disqualification standards;[70] whether Justice Gableman's campaign commercials warranted court action;[71] whether Justice Prosser put Justice Bradley in a chokehold or was defending himself when Bradley charged him with her fists balled;[72] and whether the court should seek professional help to overcome its dysfunction.[73] In short, Wisconsin's example is an aberrational exception that helps to prove the more common rule that collegiality norms, when cultivated and preserved, contribute to the judiciary's legal culture.

The proposition that the bench and bar have a distinct legal culture is hardly novel. Preeminent scholars have made such observations for years.[74] Insofar as the practices of the legal community give that community meaning, such practices contribute to the development of norms that influence community behavior. Political scientist Rogers Smith made a related argument that explains political behavior through an institutional lens, when he wrote that institutions such as the judiciary "influence the self-conception of those who occupy roles defined by them in ways that can give those persons distinctively 'institutional' perspectives. Hence such institutions can play a part in affecting the political behavior that reshapes them in turn."[75] Lief Carter and Thomas Burke, among others, have since added to a growing literature base that analyzes the relevance of legal reasoning to judicial decision-making from a cultural, neo-institutional perspective.[76]

Consistent with the conclusion that legal training influences norm formation, the data show that law students and lawyers are oriented more toward thinking than feeling.[77] They show that legal education improves students' reasoning skills.[78] They show that law students exhibit allegiance to legal norms. As Eileen Braman found in an important empirical study of legal reasoning:

> We . . . saw the influence of legal norms in participants' justifications and responses to closed-ended questions. Law students reported being significantly more confident in their judgments in conditions where there was controlling legal authority. They were also more likely to cite specific authority when it was controlling. Moreover, findings demonstrate that participants felt the need to acknowledge opposing evidence in their justifications, consistent with norms suggesting that they should consider arguments raised by opposing litigants in the context of adversarial decision-making.[79]

Braman also found that law students are likelier to resolve legal problems with reference to policy arguments when law is indeterminate, and that students preferred legal policy arguments that corresponded to their ideological predilections.[80] It is a short step from there to Braman's finding that ideological predilections influence legal reasoning among law students in significant ways. Thus, Braman's findings are consistent with the thrust of research summarized in chapter 3, which showed that judges are subject to legal and extralegal influences. The essential point for purposes here, however, is that aspiring lawyers with legal training internalize legal norms.

In a similar vein, Mark Graber found that people with legal backgrounds analyze constitutional issues differently than those with political backgrounds.[81] Those with legal backgrounds, for example, are more concerned with the due process rights of criminals than elected officials.[82] Like Braman, however, Graber does not suggest that extralegal influences are irrelevant to lawyers and judges—only that for those with legal education and experience, law is a factor that matters in constitutional decisions, decisions that are products of complex interactions among constitutional texts, precedents, values, and policy preferences.[83]

The foregoing analysis leads to a series of propositions core to a legal culture paradigm that the legal community would likely regard as too obvious to be interesting. First, members of the legal community are acculturated to take substantive and procedural law seriously. For them, the rule of law is real, and to the extent it is diluted by extralegal influences, it remains an objective or ideal. The suspicion entertained by strident devotees of the attitudinal model, that lawyers shed the law like an ill-fitting suit and transform themselves into politicians in robes when they ascend the bench, pays insufficient heed to the power of cultural context. The legal community's mantra that judges bracket out extralegal influences and uphold the law does not capture the complexity of the judicial role and is widely and rightly perceived as exaggerated by a skeptical public. It nonetheless embodies a deeply entrenched norm that articulates core aspirations for the bench. And to concede that judges do not and cannot always live up to the mantra's ideal is not to concede its irrelevance. As chapter 3 took pains to show, recent social science research reveals the continuing significance of law as an influence on judicial decision-making, particularly outside of the U.S. Supreme Court. The legal culture deserves at least some of the credit here: Law will exert greater influence in a community that pledges its allegiance to resolving disputes with exclusive reference to applicable law than one that does not.[84]

Second, from the perspective of law students, lawyers, and ultimately judges, indeterminacy is inherent in the nature of an adversarial system and core to their understanding of law itself. For some social scientists who seek to measure the impact of law on judicial decision-making, the vacuum that indeterminacy creates and extralegal influences fill demonstrates law's irrelevance. But this view is shortsighted in several respects. Pervasive indeterminacy in hard cases does not belie the more or less predictable application of settled law in easy cases. Moreover, in hard cases, when an indeterminate outcome turns on which of two competing legal policies the judge finds more persuasive, the likelihood that the judge's ideological preferences will affect her choice of legal policy does not make the matter any less one of legal policy: It simply underscores the complicated interplay between law, policy, and ideology. Finally, the indeterminate issues on which outcomes turn are nonetheless limited and channeled by settled law.

Take, for example, a hypothetical, so-called "§1983" civil rights case (named after the statutory section that authorizes the cause of action): The plaintiff alleges that two city police officers, while acting under color of state law, deprived her of her Fourth Amendment rights by undertaking an unauthorized search of her trailer and requests money damages. The defendants assert that their conduct was excused by a court-recognized "good faith" exception to liability: Although conceding that a recent Supreme Court decision invalidated searches of this kind, that decision postdated the trailer search here, for which reason defendants argue that they conducted the search in good faith, on the reasonable assumption that it was lawful. The plaintiff disagrees, arguing that preexisting precedent forbade the search when conducted. Liberal judges may interpret the good faith exception more parsimoniously than their conservative colleagues, which could influence how they construe precedent in effect at the time of the search. But to characterize this as a clear win for ideology over law overlooks the multitude of issues that law has quietly resolved: that the plaintiff is an aggrieved party under the statute; that the defendants were "acting under color of state law" when they conducted the search; that the search violated the Fourth Amendment as currently interpreted by the Supreme Court; that liability is subject to a good faith exception; and that the statute authorizes the plaintiff to seek money damages for her injury.

Third, all of the foregoing said, no straight-thinking law student, let alone lawyer, believes that ideology and other extralegal factors do not influence judicial decision-making in difficult cases. That begs the critical question of why, when they are speaking in the public square, the legal community in general and judges in particular cling so tenaciously to the view that judges follow the law and nothing else.

There are four explanations, two of which have previously been explored. The first, as alluded to at the outset of this chapter, is fear of public backlash. If judges are candid about extralegal influences on their decision-making with a public that prefers its judges to chant the rule of law paradigm mantra, the consequences could be adverse. The second explanation, as discussed in chapter 3, is motivated reasoning: Judges sincerely believe that they set extralegal influences aside and follow the law. That is because, when the law is indeterminate and the judge is confronted with two credible, competing arguments in support of opposite conclusions, the judge is subconsciously predisposed to favor the argument more closely aligned with her ideological or other extralegal predilections.

A third explanation for why judges do not credit arguments that they are influenced by extralegal factors lies in the cognitive theory of naive realism. Naive realism begins with the banal proposition that people think others perceive the world subjectively, through their own interpretive lenses. But people also tend to operate under the naive misapprehension that they themselves see the world as it is and assume that they make decisions on the basis of this "objective reality."[85] Hence, studies reveal that people generally are poor at self-assessment and tend to be overly optimistic judges of their own abilities.[86] Inflated preconceptions of their abilities, in turn, lead subjects to overestimate their competence in performing specific tasks.[87] Unsurprisingly, then, test subjects "report being less susceptible than their peers to various cognitive and motivational biases."[88] They tend to exhibit a blind spot to their own biases, take their perception of the world as objective reality, and attribute contradictory perspectives to bias in others, rather than themselves.[89] For judges and their audiences, this creates a circle of reciprocal naiveté. Court critics, convinced that their interpretation of applicable law is objective and reasonable, excoriate judges as biased rogues or activists who make decisions at odds with critics' views. Judges, conversely, who think that their decisions reflect an objective assessment of applicable facts and law, are predisposed to dismiss detractors' arguments to the contrary as the product of subjective bias. As a consequence, in the public policy debate, judges are loath to credit arguments of those who claim that judges are subject to extralegal influences, contrary to judges' own perceptions.

Fourth, and finally, is "gravitational pull." In a legal community acculturated to taking law seriously, the peril of acknowledging the ubiquity of extralegal influences is that it can weaken the rule of law norms around which the bench and bar have galvanized. The rule of law ideal can be more nearly realized by a community of true believers who strive to follow the facts and law alone. They may privately concede the inevitability of extralegal influence, but trumpeting those concessions risks transforming the devout into doubters who are less committed to minimizing the impact of extralegal influences, thereby diminishing law's gravitational pull within the legal community.

These explanations for why the judiciary sticks to its rule of law script are mutually compatible. Motivated reasoning explains why judges sincerely believe that they set extralegal influences to one side and follow the law. Naive realism reaffirms the objective rightness of that assessment in judges' minds and leads them to marginalize contrary conclusions (including conclusions drawn from social science data) as wrongheaded and biased. In academic and other, less visible settings, judges sometimes credit (if grudgingly) the thrust of social science data, and discuss the ways in which different factors influence the discretion and judgment that judges exercise. But giving extralegal influences public credit jeopardizes the gravitational pull of law within a legal community that is devoted to minimizing such influences and risks backlash from outsiders for whom the perceived appeal of rule of law rhetoric remains strong.

THE ROLE OF JUDICIAL INDEPENDENCE IN A LEGAL CULTURE PARADIGM

We come now to a critical juncture for the legal culture paradigm. The influences to which the judiciary is subject have been described in terms consistent with the results of social science research and public perception. By virtue of their immersion in a distinct legal culture, judges take law seriously but make decisions that can be influenced, often subconsciously, by their policy preferences and other extralegal factors. Hence, judges are "policymakers" in some meaningful sense of the term. The rule of law paradigm defends an independent judiciary on the grounds that independent judges do no more or less than follow the law. But in a legal culture paradigm, can one defend the independence of judicial "policymakers," when policymakers in the legislative and executive branches of government enjoy no comparable freedom from popular or political control?

As an initial matter, it will be recalled from chapter 4, that "good" judges have long been regarded as possessed of four qualities. They are honest; they are capable; they are impartial; and they are independent. But independence is unique among these qualities for two reasons. First, independence has a weaker historical pedigree. Until the eighteenth century, judges were traditionally subject to the pleasure of the monarch. Second, and more important, it is difficult to imagine how a judge could be too honest, capable, or impartial, but the same is not true of independence. Independence in appropriate measure can shield judges from external threats that undermine their capacity to uphold the law, but independence in excess can enable judges to act on their internal biases or predilections and disregard the law.

Notwithstanding the unique ambivalence reserved for independence among the qualities traditionally attributed to a good judge, there are at least three reasons why judges arguably need a measure of judicial independence from political control, despite the policymaking component of their role. Chapter 4's foray into popular understandings of the judicial role over time showed how the four attributes of a good judge have traditionally been portrayed as instrumental values that further three goals: upholding law, implementing fair process, and administering justice. Those same three goals justify a quantum of judicial independence in a legal culture paradigm.

Upholding the Law

The legal culture paradigm does not abandon allegiance to the law. To the contrary, it posits that law students, lawyers, and ultimately judges are acculturated to take law seriously. What distinguishes the paradigm I propose from its predecessor is the extent to which the legal culture paradigm acknowledges the part that an array of influences can play in judicial decision-making at the margins. Hence, within a legal culture paradigm, judicial independence promotes law and the rule of law, but in more qualified ways.

In easy cases, where the law and facts are so clear they leave little room for discretion or judgment, independence insulates judges from political pressure to contort the rule of law that judges are acculturated to follow. Although law students, law professors, and the media tend to dwell on difficult, hotly contested cases, Richard Posner notes that "most cases are routine . . . rather than residing in that uncomfortable open region in which judges are at large," and that "the routine case is dispatched with the least fuss by legalist methods."[90]

In difficult cases, where the outcome is uncertain (and so more subject to extralegal influences) law still limits what the contestable legal questions are, what the range of acceptable outcomes is, and what the appropriate method of analysis should be. Independence helps to ensure that judges are not pressured by interested participants or observers to exceed those limits.

Further, the indeterminate nature of law may give law itself a degree of elasticity that incorporates extralegal influences. Those considering a controversial legal question may interpret the applicable law in different ways, but the "rule of law" often allows for a range of proper answers. This flexible understanding of the law allows judges to exercise their best judgment, so long as they are buffered from external interference with that judgment. While such a construction may frustrate social scientists intent on defining law precisely enough to differentiate its impact from other influences,[91] a more capacious definition of law better captures its meaning for the legal community. As Stephen Burbank has written, "I prefer the messiness of lived experience to the tidiness of unrealistically parsimonious models."[92]

Implementing Fair Process

The legal culture paradigm's premise that judges are acculturated to take law seriously includes procedural as well as substantive law. Thus, independent judges who are predisposed to respect procedural rights promote procedural fairness.[93] Judicial proceedings include myriad safeguards that regulate how information is gathered and decisions are made. Parties are entitled to notice and a hearing, where they are afforded access to counsel and given an opportunity to question witnesses subject to rules of evidence; and they are guaranteed the right to an impartial judge who must disqualify himself for bias and must not discuss the case with others ex parte.[94] Such procedural safeguards assume that judges will make decisions on the basis of information so obtained and constrained, which in turn assumes that the judge is independent enough to do so—meaning, that she can resist pressure from outsiders who would make a nullity of procedural safeguards by bending the judge to their will. Thus, as Martin Redish and Laurence Marshall have written, "[n]one of the core values of due process can be fulfilled without the participation of an independent adjudicator."[95]

To say that judicial independence promotes due process by enabling judges to conform their decision-making to a process that follows procedural safeguards is not to say that the decisions judges make are or should be impervious to extralegal influences. Judges who are insulated enough from external pressure to respect litigants' due process rights still exercise discretion when evaluating the information they receive and make decisions subject to a range of influences, as Edward Rubin has explained:

> [D]ue process does not demand that decisions exclude public policy considerations or that they flow logically or definitively from the applicable rules. But it does demand a certain type of decision-making, specifically decision-making that is constrained by the established procedural protections.[96]

Moreover, judicial independence not only enables judges to adhere to established procedural safeguards, but is itself a procedural safeguard that promotes public confidence in the administration of justice and the legitimacy of government. Tom Tyler and others have shown, across a range of contexts, that litigants who "fare poorly at trial will not denigrate the judge or the system as long as they believe their outcomes are fair ones reached by fair procedures."[97] A report of the National Center for State Courts echoes that "perceptions that courts use fair procedures and treat groups equally are the strongest predictors of favorable evaluations of court performance."[98] Judicial independence, by ensuring that the choices judges make are not dictated by interested observers intent on intimidating judges into reaching desired outcomes, may thus be viewed as a procedural protection that enhances due process and governmental legitimacy—even if the decisions that independent judges make are influenced by legal and extralegal considerations.[99]

Administering Justice

Even those who argue that judges are politicians in robes must acknowledge an elemental difference between judges and legislators. Without disputing that judges, like legislators, can be "policymakers" in some sense of the term, judges, unlike legislators, adjudicate cases between parties. In adjudicating cases, judges find facts and reach conclusions of law, to the ultimate end of administering justice. As a practical matter, when applicable law is clear and binding on a court, the judicial role is circumscribed. The rule of law ideal dictates that judges follow the law—philosophical disquisitions on unjust laws notwithstanding—and judges are subject to discipline if they deliberately do otherwise.[100] When, however, applicable law is ambiguous, justice, of necessity, requires judges to bring other considerations to bear in interpreting the law to reach results that the judge deems best or most just in that case. Returning to the premises of the legal culture paradigm, judges are trained from their first days of law school to resolve such indeterminacy with reference to policy considerations.

"Justice" is a polymorphous term that means different things to different people. Now is not the time to develop and defend a preferred theory of justice. As a purely descriptive matter, however, it is enough to say that judges make decisions they regard as best, and chapter 3 tells us that when doing so they are influenced by a range of factors, including legal texts, their conceptions of good public policy (as derived from their educations, life experiences, and worldview), the strategic consequences of their decisions, the audiences they are seeking to reach, and self-interest, among other factors. In this regard, judges are "pragmatists" in the most banal sense of the term.[101] By its nature, pragmatism takes an eclectic approach to the appropriate influences on judicial decision-making that is compatible with the legal culture paradigm. As Thomas Grey has written, "the pragmatist tendency is to promote trade rather than warfare between normative and descriptive theorists, storytellers and model-builders, interpreters and causal explainers."[102] Writing in 1991, Richard Rorty observed that "[p]ragmatism was reasonably shocking seventy years ago, but in the ensuing decades it has gradually been absorbed into American common sense."[103] Richard Posner and others are thus probably not exaggerating when they conclude that the term "pragmatist"—as embodied in a penchant for deciding difficult cases with reference to public policy, the purposes underlying relevant rules, and the social and institutional consequences of their rulings against the backdrop of applicable law—"best describes the average American judge at all levels of our judicial hierarchies and yields the greatest insight into his behavior."[104] Judge Posner sometimes pits the "legalist" in opposition to this conception of pragmatic justice[105] (although "justice" is not the term Posner uses), but that seems largely unnecessary. The enlightened legalist embraces the gravitational force of law, but should recognize the role of discretion and judgment in divining applicable law, and the need to exercise that discretion and judgment with recourse to the tools of the pragmatist. To that extent, pragmatism truly is ubiquitous.

The kind of pragmatic justice that a legal culture paradigm facilitates is not limited to judges who serve as "umpires" (whatever that means) at trial or on appeal. Without celebrating or decrying the gradual disappearance of trials, as discussed in chapter 2, the need for independence in a legal culture paradigm logically extends to judges who are case managers, settlers, or problem solvers. The need for judges to broker dispute resolutions with an eye toward achieving best results in the context of case sensitive facts and law remains regardless of whether such disputes culminate in trial. Dependence can contort this case-sensitive administration of justice in the context of a mediated settlement to no less an extent than in a trial. Pragmatism as a proxy for justice in this all-encompassing form is susceptible to the criticism that it is too true to be good because it characterizes what judges do in terms so broad as to lose descriptive, predictive, and prescriptive force.[106] That critique might be fatal were I bringing universal pragmatism to bear for the purpose of analyzing how pragmatists collectively would or should resolve particular legal problems. My point here, however, is more limited: Insofar as pragmatism writ large describes the justice that most judges administer, judicial independence is an essential ingredient for the effective administration of pragmatic justice in all its variations. Ascertaining how the law should be applied in a given context to yield the best, fairest, or most reasonable or just results (pick your preferred adjective) necessarily requires a familiarity with and an appreciation for the details of the case at hand. A judge is uniquely situated to acquire the detailed information needed to make pragmatic choices in the cases over which she presides. Rendering that judge subservient to the wishes of interested observers who lack familiarity with (or concern for) context-specific facts, or context-applicable law undermines the ability of the judge to arrive at just or fair outcomes.

Framing the justice-seeking goals of judicial independence in a pragmatic, content-neutral way, without imposing a unified theory of justice, implies that the independence tent is large enough to accommodate differing theories of justice. While that is so, it does not mean that independence requires us to endure outlier theories that yield intolerable results. Independence affords judges the flexibility to reach just results on a case-by-case basis, but that flexibility is circumscribed by applicable law. Applicable law can be amended to constrain the indeterminate spaces where differing theories of justice hold sway, so that the range of possible outcomes is limited to variations of the acceptable. This does not foreclose the possibility that a judge will disregard the constraints of applicable law and impose her idiosyncratic theory of justice, but that is where accountability-promoting mechanisms come into play, as elaborated upon in the next section. The same may be said for the judge who is perceived to impose her partisan political predilections in the guise of "justice." Public anger is directed less at judges who bring extralegal factors to bear in the pursuit of justice, than at judges who bring such factors to bear to advance personal agendas. Where justice ends and agendas begin is another place to draw the line between independence and accountability.

Repackaging the justifications for an independent judiciary in the legal culture paradigm enables the legal community to defend the judiciary's autonomy without recourse to otherworldly claims that judges are apolitical or that law, formalistically defined, is all that matters in judicial decision-making. The default position of the rule of law paradigm is that competent, principled, impartial, and independent judges will set extralegal influences to one side and uphold the law—a position that has proved counterfactual and increasingly difficult to defend. The default position of the legal culture paradigm, in contrast, is that competent, honorable, impartial and independent judges, though subject to extralegal influences, will uphold the law as they construe it to be written, respect procedural fairness and pursue justice.

THE ROLE OF JUDICIAL ACCOUNTABILITY
AND OVERSIGHT IN A LEGAL CULTURE PARADIGM

The default position of the legal culture paradigm is that a measure of independence from external pressures and blandishments enables judges to do what they are acculturated to do, which is take the law seriously, follow established legal process, and seek just outcomes within the limits of applicable law, even if the decisions they make can be colored by their ideological (and other) predilections. By the same token, unchecked independence can liberate judges to stray from the default position and pursue political agendas at the expense of objectives that independence in the new paradigm aims to further. Hence, a measure of accountability is needed to ensure that independence furthers, rather than thwarts, the purposes it aims to serve.

The legal community's defense of the rule of law paradigm makes room for accountability to guard against the possibility that judges will abuse their independence. Indeed, "independence versus accountability" debates in judicial oversight rival debates over "law versus politics" in judicial decision-making for their intensity and ubiquity. But it is a limited, if not parsimonious, form of accountability that the rule of law paradigm tolerates—one that relies largely on the judiciary to regulate its own excesses and sharply limits the role that "political" processes should play in curbing judicial excesses; hence, the legal community's century-old campaign has been to "depoliticize" the courts. If, however, we concede the inevitability that judicial decision-making is subject to certain kinds of "political" influences, then the time has come for the legal community to abandon its crusade to "depoliticize" the judiciary, to appreciate the need for a more robust form of accountability or oversight, and for a revised paradigm to emerge that seeks to manage rather than exterminate judicial politics.

Managing judicial politics is a line-drawing exercise: The goal is to delineate where independence should end and accountability begin in order to optimize the objectives judicial independence serves. But where that line should be drawn will vary, depending on whom one asks and why they care. That is because oversight of the judiciary—and regulation of its independence and accountability—must be evaluated from three distinct perspectives introduced in chapter 4: (1) that of parties in an adjudicative dimension of judicial oversight; (2) that of the public in a political dimension of judicial oversight; and (3) that of judges, in an ethical dimension of judicial oversight.

The Adjudicative Dimension of Oversight

At an elemental level, judges resolve disputes for the benefit of parties to those disputes. Psychologist Tom Tyler has found that parties are more apt to accept adverse outcomes in litigation when they felt that they had their "day in court" because they appeared before a judge who treated them fairly.[107] For parties, then, their interest in judicial conduct is personal to them, acutely felt, case-specific, and shaped by first-hand experience. The focus of their attention is on the process employed to litigate their cases, and whether that process protects them adequately from the excesses of judges, on the one hand, and the excesses of those in a position to control judges, on the other. This, then, is the adjudicative dimension of judicial oversight.

The Political Dimension of Oversight

Judges may adjudicate disputes between private parties, but they are more than private dispute resolution specialists. They are public officials who together comprise a separate and independent branch of government. As such, their institutional legitimacy logically depends on the continuing support of the public that the judges serve, which in turn depends on whether the public regards its judges as fulfilling their constitutional roles. If the decisions judges make lead the public to worry that judges are abusing their authority, the judiciary's institutional legitimacy may suffer. Relative to the parties, the public's interest in judicial oversight is less personal than philosophical or ideological, more diffuse than acute, systemic rather than case-specific (although highly publicized cases can breed systemic concerns) and shaped less by first-hand experience than by impressions gleaned from public discussions on the acceptability of judges to the body politic. In other words, the focus of the public's attention is on judges in relation to the role they play in the administration of government, which is "political" in the original sense of the term. This is the political dimension of judicial oversight.

The Ethical Dimension of Oversight

Two thousand years ago, Plato, quoting Socrates, wrote that "four things belong to a judge." What those things were (to "to hear courteously, to answer wisely, to consider soberly, and to decide impartially"[108]) matters less than that those things were qualities characterized as belonging to one who assumes the role of a judge: qualities that embody a Platonic ideal to which judges aspire. In this way, the judge offers a third perspective on judicial oversight. As arbiters of disputes over the rights of parties in litigation, judges have an interest in the adjudicative dimension of judicial oversight; and as representatives of the third branch of government, judges are desirous of institutional legitimacy and hence have an interest in the political dimension too. But as women and men whose self-identity as "good" judges is tethered to an institutional culture that prizes the qualities discussed in this chapter as virtues, judges bring a distinct ethical dimension to judicial oversight.

In the adjudicative dimension, we balance accountability and independence to ensure parties a fair hearing. That goal is compromised if judges lack either the independence to be fair or the accountability to deter their prejudices. In the political dimension, we balance independence and accountability to ensure the public a judiciary it supports. That goal is thwarted if the public perceives judges as unaccountable, rogue politicians, or dependent marionettes manipulated by elected officials, parties, or interest groups. In the ethical dimension, we balance independence and accountability a third way to cultivate good and virtuous judges who are committed to law, fair process, and justice. That goal is stymied if good judges are subject to retaliation for pursuing systemic objectives, or if bad judges are unaccountable for their indifference to those objectives.

In other words, the goal of the legal culture paradigm is to craft an independence-accountability blend that manages judicial politics to best promote the rule of law, procedural fairness, and justice, but the optimal mix can vary by dimension. The independence-accountability blend needed to ensure parties a fair hearing in the adjudicative dimension may differ from that that needed to provide the public with judges it trusts in the political dimension, which may differ from that needed to ensure that judges behave honorably in the ethical dimension.

Two examples will illustrate the point. First, consider the judicial selection debate. In the political dimension, holding judges accountable to the electorate in contested elections may be just the thing to reassure the public that judges will pursue justice and the rule of law in ways the public understands and approves. But in the adjudicative dimension, parties with unpopular causes may reasonably worry that judges whose continuation in office depends on voter support lack the requisite independence to decide their case fairly, according to law. In the ethical dimension the analysis is more mixed. Electoral accountability may put strain on a judge's duty to honor her oath and live up to the Platonic ideal of a good judge, in situations where following the law as she understands it to be written could jeopardize her tenure. On the other hand, for judges acclimated to electoral accountability, subjecting themselves to periodic elections to ensure that they are acceptable to the people they serve is not incompatible with the nature of their roles.

Second, consider ethics rules that forbid judges from publicly commenting on pending and impending cases. In the adjudicative dimension, parties to adjudication should logically favor such restrictions. Indeed, ABA Model Code Rule 2.10 reflects adjudicative dimension concerns, by forbidding judges from making public statements "that might reasonably be expected to affect the outcome or impair the fairness of a matter pending or impending in any court."[109] In the ethical dimension, judges often take an even more exacting view, and regard a near absolute bar on public comments on pending cases as more in keeping with the dignity and integrity of the judicial role. As Judith Kaye, former Chief Judge of New York's high court explained:

> To secure an impartial forum . . . and to assure the dignity of the judicial process, judges by and large must stay out of the fray. They do not duel with public officials about the correctness of their decisions. They do not conduct press conferences about cases; and they have no call in radio and television shows to explain their rulings. They rely on their decisions, whether written or oral, to speak for themselves.[110]

Hence, disciplinary bodies charged with enforcing Rule 2.10 have erred on the side of presuming that public comments are prejudicial.[111] But in the political dimension, such a rule may be unnecessary, if not counterproductive, because knowing more about a judge's views on important issues in the cases she decides can reassure the public that judges are upholding the law and administering justice in politically acceptable ways.

These examples demonstrate that independence-accountability debates are destined to be frustrating, fruitless affairs, if the task is seen as being to make the correct choice from a menu of two options. What these examples suggest instead is that the operative task is to engage in a perpetual balancing act across three dimensions, the implications of which are explored in the last two chapters.

CONCLUSION

The legal culture paradigm proposed here, is grounded in five essential propositions: First, judges are immersed in a legal culture that takes law seriously. Second, pervasive legal indeterminacy requires judges to exercise judgment and discretion with reference to policy considerations that bring legal and extralegal considerations to bear. Third, judicial independence buffers judges from external interference with their acculturated predisposition to follow the law as they construe it to be written, respect procedural safeguards, and administer justice. Fourth, because unfettered autonomy can liberate judges to flout the objectives independence seeks to further and pursue their own agendas, the legal culture paradigm contemplates a robust role for judicial accountability and oversight, relative to the rule of law paradigm. Fifth, accountability and oversight in the legal culture paradigm operates in three distinct dimensions: (1) an adjudicative dimension that protects the rights of parties in litigation; (2) a political dimension, that promotes public confidence in the courts; and (3) an ethical dimension, that preserves the integrity of the judge's role. It is now possible to map the legal culture paradigm I describe here, onto existing mechanisms of judicial oversight, to the end of reconceptualizing the transformation of the American judiciary summarized in chapter 2, as a generations-long movement toward heightened oversight in the political dimension.

CHAPTER 6

Conceptualizing the Dimensions of Judicial Oversight

Preceding chapters convey the deeply entrenched and widely shared view that "good" judges are capable, honest, impartial, and independent. Although judges and lawyers sometimes tout these qualities as ends in themselves, they are better understood as instrumental values that enable judges (despite being subject to extralegal influences) to uphold the law, follow the strictures of fair process, and administer justice. The legal culture paradigm, as I have constructed it, accepts the ubiquitous understanding embedded in centuries of popular culture that judges are not perfectly capable, honest, impartial, or independent. Nor need they be; rather, they need only be capable, honest, impartial, and independent enough to further law, process, and justice objectives.

Oversight aims to ensure that judges are good enough to further these objectives. Oversight mechanisms are thus accountability-promoting devices that manage the autonomy of judges to the extent necessary to ensure that systemic objectives are furthered. Assessing whether a judge is good enough can vary by perspective or dimension. In the political dimension, a judge's conduct may be good enough to further law, process, and justice objectives from the perspective of the public interested in a politically acceptable judge. But that same judge may or may not be good enough to further those objectives in the adjudicative dimension, from the perspective of a litigant interested in a fair hearing, or the ethical dimension, from the perspective of a judge interested in living up to the platonic ideal of her role.

Independence occupies a unique niche in this scheme. It can be a help: an instrumental value that furthers law, process, and justice objectives by insulating judges from external interference with their acculturated predisposition to pursue such objectives. But in excess, independence can also be a hindrance that liberates judges to act on their internal biases and flout the law, process, and justice objectives that independence aims to further. Hence, oversight seeks to strike an appropriate balance between independence and accountability in each dimension.

This chapter begins by reorganizing systems of judicial oversight with reference to their appropriate dimensions, to the end of showing how oversight mechanisms in each dimension regulate judicial conduct and the independence-accountability balance to further legal culture paradigm objectives. The chapter also highlights constraints on those mechanisms that limit their application in ways that allow for expeditious judicial administration while still ensuring that judges are good enough to promote law, process, and justice objectives in each dimension. It is then possible to revisit the changing landscape of the courts discussed in chapter 2, for the purpose of showing that decades of crisis rhetoric decrying heightened politicization of the judiciary can be understood as heralding a gradual shift in control of judicial oversight from mechanisms in the adjudicative and ethical dimensions to the political.

ORGANIZING JUDICIAL OVERSIGHT MECHANISMS BY DIMENSION

Reconceptualizing judicial oversight in terms of three distinct but overlapping dimensions begins with a core question: What is a given oversight mechanism's primary objective? Answers fall into one of three possible clusters: (1) to ensure that the adjudicative process serves the needs of litigants in the adjudicative dimension; (2) to ensure that judges conduct themselves in a manner consistent with the essential nature and requirements of the judicial role in the ethical dimension; or (3) to ensure that judges and the judiciary conduct themselves in ways acceptable to the general public in the political dimension. The distinct means by which regulatory schemes manage judges and courts can, for the most part, be explained with reference to the varying goals of promoting judicial oversight in these three dimensions.

I elaborate here on the primary mechanisms that regulate oversight in each dimension: (1) due process, disqualification, and rules of litigation procedure in the adjudicative dimension; (2) oaths of office and codes of judicial conduct and their accompanying disciplinary processes in the ethical dimension; and (3) judicial removal, selection, and legislative oversight in the political dimension. In so doing, I do not mean to imply that the compartmentalization of judicial oversight is tidy.[1] Mechanisms that I have assigned to one dimension can serve the interests of another.

For example, disqualification rules that parties exploit to protect their rights to an impartial judge in the adjudicative dimension also serve as standards of good judicial conduct in the ethical dimension; and those same rules, by subjecting a judge to disqualification if an objective outside observer might question the judge's impartiality, seek to protect public confidence in the political dimension.[2] Codes of judicial conduct, while centered in the ethical dimension, include rules oriented toward ensuring a fair process for parties[3] and promoting public confidence in the courts,[4] which overlap with the adjudicative and political dimensions, respectively. Impeachment, while a remedy for judges whose partiality violates the public trust in the political dimension, also delineates standards of judicial conduct that inform the ethical dimension and, by subjecting judges to removal for bribery and other offenses, protects the integrity of the judicial process for litigants in the adjudicative dimension.[5] Notwithstanding such messiness at the margins, thinking about mechanisms of judicial oversight in relation to the dimensions they occupy is worth the trouble because it elucidates the complexities of judicial oversight, reveals recent trends, and, as discussed in chapter 7, ultimately illuminates the path to reform.

Regulating Oversight in the Adjudicative Dimension

There are three basic procedural mechanisms that regulate judges to the end of preserving the rights of parties in the adjudicative dimension of oversight: (1) the due process clauses of the federal and state constitutions; (2) disqualification processes; and (3) rules of litigation procedure (including appellate review).

The Due Process Clauses

The Fifth and Fourteenth Amendments of the U.S. Constitution prohibit the national and state governments, respectively, from depriving persons of their life, liberty, or property without due process of law. In addition, many state constitutions have a due process clause of their own.[6] The Supreme Court has opined that "a fair trial in a fair tribunal is a basic requirement of due process."[7] Insofar as the due process rights at stake in court proceedings are those of parties, enforcement of those rights falls logically within the adjudicative dimension of judicial oversight.

A fair trial before a fair tribunal implicates all four qualities of a good judge: impartiality, independence, integrity, and competence. The

Supreme Court has declared that the due process clause guarantees parties the "right to have an impartial judge."[8] As to independence, whether a judge's fairness is compromised by partiality in the form of internal bias, or dependence in the form of external pressure, the result is the same: Hence, "[n]one of the core values of due process . . . can be fulfilled without the participation of an independent adjudicator."[9] Impartiality is likewise intertwined with basic honesty and integrity. In *Tumey v. Ohio*, for example, the Court used the due process clause to invalidate a state court scheme in which judges were paid from fines they assessed against defendants—a conflict of interest that would tempt less than forthright judges to impose unwarranted fines to line their pocketbooks.[10] Finally, for reasons that should be self-evident, scholars have included basic competence to the list of due process requirements for a fair tribunal.[11]

The due process clauses articulate broad principles but are of only modest practical importance to judicial oversight in the adjudicative dimension. That is because the circumstances in which the Court has actually held that a judge has deprived a party of its right to a fair hearing in a fair tribunal are few. Such limited applications are attributable to historical, pragmatic, and prudential constraints.

Historically, civil and common law systems each afforded parties ample opportunity to challenge their respective fact-finders—judges under civil law and jurors under common law.[12] English common law judges, however, were entitled to an almost ironclad presumption of impartiality, subject to a lone exception for cases in which they had an economic interest in the outcome.[13] Two and a half centuries later, the four dissenting justices in *Caperton v. Massey* pointed to this ancient presumption in support of their argument that a probability of judicial bias should not violate due process,[14] a point that the majority deflected by emphasizing how exceptional and extreme the facts of *Caperton* were.[15] In other words, the ancient presumption of impartiality limits the application of the due process clause to deeply rooted exceptions and truly outrageous circumstances.

Pragmatically, some forms of unfairness are more manageable to regulate than others. For example, personal conflicts of interest can be delineated by clear(ish) rules triggered whenever a conflict arises. Divining judicial bias, in contrast, requires an assessment of the judge's subjective state of mind—a difficult task that courts have long been reluctant to undertake.[16] In *Caperton*, the majority sought to make such assessments more manageable by crafting an objective, "probability" of bias standard for assessing due process claims.[17] Chief Justice Roberts, writing on behalf of the four dissenters, was unconvinced, and itemized forty questions that the new standard left unanswered, leading him to the conclusion that regulating probable bias was unworkable.[18] The majority's rejoinder was to emphasize repeatedly how rarely its probable bias standard would be triggered.[19]

Prudentially, the due process clause is a backstop, or last resort constrained by respect for separation of powers and federalism concerns that "demarks only the outer boundaries of judicial disqualifications."[20] While the Fifth Amendment's due process clause presumably guarantees litigants the right to an impartial judge in federal court, federal courts have long avoided constitutional questions when cases can be resolved on non-constitutional grounds.[21] Given the availability of disqualification under federal statute,[22] which triggers a duty to recuse long before less exacting due process standards are violated, recourse to the Fifth Amendment is unnecessary. The need for state courts to ameliorate judicial partiality through resort to the Fourteenth Amendment or the due process clauses of their own constitutions is similarly obviated by the availability of state disqualification rules, which entitle parties to secure the disqualification of judges whose impartiality might reasonably be questioned.[23] Although the Fourteenth Amendment affords federal courts the opportunity to address the qualifications of state judges, principles of comity and federalism have restricted the reach of Fourteenth Amendment claims.[24]

Disqualification

Like due process, disqualification rules seek to ensure parties a fair hearing in the adjudicative dimension by affording them an opportunity to challenge the impartiality of their assigned judge. Hence, parties may request the removal of their judge if the judge's impartiality might reasonably be questioned, which is presumptively so if she is biased or encumbered by conflicts of interest that the disqualification rule specifies.[25] Although disqualification rules focus on impartiality, independence and integrity are likewise in play. For example, when a judge knowingly presides over the case of a close relative and decides the case in that relative's favor, non-disqualification calls the judge's integrity as well as her impartiality into question.[26] And when a judge does not recuse herself from a case in which she owes money to the party or the party's lawyer, it raises issues of dependence as well as partiality.[27]

Disqualification is subject to some of the same constraints that shape the scope of due process. Historically, judges have enjoyed the same presumption of impartiality that limits the application of due process analysis.[28] Pragmatically, the subjective nature of judicial bias has limited its reach as a traditional ground for disqualification.[29]

More fundamentally, perhaps, the same judges who administer disqualification rules self-identify collectively as impartial and have done so for millennia: To concede bias under such circumstances can be seen as a concession of failure.[30] To offset these constraints, the Model Code calls for disqualification when the judge's "impartiality might reasonably be questioned," which seeks to avoid problematic inquiries into the judge's subjective state of mind, and to lessen the stigma of disqualification by focusing on perceived partiality, rather than partiality in fact.[31] However, because judges are already under a separate ethical directive to avoid perceived partiality as a subset of the duty to avoid the appearance of impropriety, reassuring judges that their ethical transgression is limited to creating an appearance of impropriety can be cold comfort that does not eliminate judicial ambivalence.[32] One multistate study showed that judges are least troubled by disqualification for traditional conflicts of interest,[33] where the rules are relatively clear, and disqualification is automatic when facts giving rise to a conflict are present (for example, when the judge holds stock in the defendant corporation, or the judge's brother is the plaintiff). Conversely, ambivalence rises with more discretionary inquiries into the judge's biases or personal relationships with case participants.[34] Simply put, because disqualification rules require judges to rule on the partiality of their brethren (and often themselves), judicial construction of those rules can be expected to err on the side of the presumption of impartiality.

Rules of Litigation Procedure

Rules of litigation procedure include rules governing pretrial litigation, trials, and appeals. They constrain judges in ways that promote the instrumental values of judicial competence, integrity, impartiality, and independence as well as the law, process, and justice goals that those values further, for the benefit of parties in the adjudicative dimension.

Litigants are afforded a right to appellate review in the federal courts and virtually every state system.[35] Appellate review is commonly justified in terms of the need to correct lower court errors.[36] But "error" includes not only the honest mistakes of conscientious judges but also the erroneous rulings of incompetent, dishonest, partial, or dependent adjudicators.[37] And correcting errors of fact, law, or process—whatever their cause—furthers the core objectives of promoting law, fair process, and the administration of justice. In mandamus proceedings, when errors are so egregious as to constitute usurpations of judicial power, circuit courts have sometimes admonished district judges for their lack of candor or impartiality.[38] In addition to reversing erroneous rulings that may have been the product of incompetence, dishonesty, partiality, or dependence, federal circuit and Supreme Courts are authorized by statute to remand actions and "require such further proceedings to be had as may be just under the circumstances." Circuit courts have construed this statute to permit remand to a different district judge, when the circuit court is concerned about the fitness of the judge to whom the case was originally assigned.[39]

More generally, the law governing litigation procedure implements an adversarial system by means of rules that manage judicial excesses in subtler ways. In the 1930s, the Federal Rules of Civil Procedure (FRCP) abandoned the complex formalities of common law pleading that had thwarted litigants from getting their cases heard on the merits, by, among other things, reducing the multiplicity of common law causes of action to a single civil action,[40] and reducing the plaintiff's burden of initial pleading to supplying a "short and plain statement of the claim showing that the pleader is entitled to relief."[41] While the FRCP affords judges opportunities to decide cases on the merits prior to trial, those opportunities are carefully circumscribed to reduce the risk of premature judgments that could be colored (consciously or not) by ignorance or prejudice. Thus, for example, in defendants' motions to dismiss for failure to state a claim, the judge must accept as true all facts alleged in the complaint, and must err on the side of non-dismissal by construing the complaint liberally and drawing all reasonable inferences in the plaintiff's favor.[42] And at the summary judgment stage, the judge must let the case proceed to trial unless there is "no genuine dispute as to any material fact."[43]

At an elemental level then, the FRCP, and the adversarial process they regulate, restricts the authority of judges to act upon their predispositions, prejudices, and personal biases by sharply limiting their opportunities to end cases before the necessary facts can be adduced and merits explored. Judith Resnik described the underlying problem as one of prejudgment:

> Deciding at one point in time versus another is not intrinsically faulty unless the assumption is that prejudgment is based upon incomplete or inaccurate information. Prejudgment is suspect in the context of a system that assumes an increase in information over time and designates specific points in time when the act of judging becomes legitimate.[44]

By necessary implication, prejudgment is illegitimate because judges who lack the information needed to make reasoned determinations on the merits must ground their decisions in under-informed speculation that is the product of less than competent or less than impartial decision-making. Lon Fuller credited the adversarial process with imposing a structure that controls the judge's propensity toward premature decisions grounded in ill-informed personal predilections:

> An adversary presentation seems the only effective means for combatting this natural human tendency to judge too swiftly in terms of the familiar that which is not yet fully known. The arguments of counsel hold the case, as it were, in suspension between two opposing interpretations of it. While the proper classification of the case is thus kept unresolved, there is time to explore all of its peculiarities and nuances.[45]

Rules of litigation procedure thus structure adjudication to reduce the risk of errors caused by honest mistake, incompetence, dishonesty, partiality, dependence, or excessive independence to the end of promoting law, process, and justice objectives.

As with due process and disqualification, rules of litigation procedure operate under constraints. Procedures that afford meticulous judicial review, or defer resolution of cases on the merits pending discovery or trial, reduce the risk of error at the expense of increasing litigation costs and delays that can thwart access to justice. Hence, the first rule in the FRCP declares that the rules should be construed to secure not only the "just" determination of judicial proceedings, but the "speedy and inexpensive determination" as well[46]—which limits oversight of judges in the adjudicative dimension.

Regulating Oversight in the Ethical Dimension

In the ethical dimension of judicial oversight, the focus is on the intrinsic qualities that a good judge should possess and how a judge in possession of those qualities should conduct herself. Oversight in the ethical dimension is oriented toward ensuring that judges adhere to high standards of conduct because that is what good judges do. In the ethical dimension, regulatory mechanisms include oaths of office, and codes of conduct, together with the disciplinary processes that implement the codes or otherwise enforce standards of conduct.

Oaths of Office

The U.S. Constitution requires all state and federal legislators, and executive and judicial branch officers to "be bound by oath or affirmation, to support this Constitution."[47] With respect to judges, a federal statute directs incoming justices and judges to swear or affirm that they will "administer justice without respect to persons, and do equal right to the poor and to the rich," and that they will "faithfully and impartially discharge and perform" their duties "under the Constitution and laws of the United States. [So help me God]."[48] States require comparable oaths of office.[49]

The judicial oath of office falls within the ethical dimension of judicial oversight in two respects. First, the oath reduces to their essence the defining duties of a good judge. Second, the oath renders those duties a matter of moral and sometimes religious obligation. It is not as though judges would be free to disregard their duties in the absence of an oath requirement. Those duties are separately regulated by constitutions, statutes, and codes of conduct that judges ignore on pain of reversal, discipline, or removal. But the oath seeks to enhance compliance with those duties by making them the subject of a solemn promise to God or man— the deepest of ethical obligations that constitution writers can conjure. As William Blackstone explained, "[t]he sanction of an oath . . . does not increase the civil obligation to loyalty; it only strengthens the social tie by uniting it with that of religion."[50] To the extent that the religious dimension of the oath has gradually become largely ceremonial, it nonetheless punctuates the depth of commitment that the oath seeks to engender.

Judges often identify the oath of office as a relevant constraint on their conduct. Some have spoken of their oaths as a form of accountability that constrains their independence. For example, Missouri's chief justice observed that "'Independence'. . . should not be interpreted . . . to mean that a judge is free to do as he or she sees fit," because "[s]uch behavior runs counter to our oaths to uphold the law."[51] A federal judge made the related point that "[t]he Framers believed in judicial independence but not in the literal sense of the word 'independent,'" in part because "[j]udges would be bound by oath or affirmation to support the Constitution."[52] Other judges have characterized their oaths as constraining them to act independently in the teeth of efforts to hold them accountable inappropriately. One federal judge commented that "[i]n our oath of office, we swear to administer justice without respect to persons and without fear or favor. If we are to be true to our oath, we can not [*sic*] live in fear of political or personal reprisals."[53] And an Ohio Supreme Court justice argued that elected judges "although accountable to the public, still swear an oath of office that agrees to uphold the rule of law 'without respect to persons,'" which limits the influence such accountability exerts.[54]

Codes of Conduct and Disciplinary Processes

Elaborating on the ways codes of conduct operate in the ethical dimension is simplified by the fact that the Code of Conduct for United States Judges and the Codes of judicial conduct for every state judiciary are derived to varying degrees from the American Bar Association's Model Code of Judicial Conduct.[55] These Codes operate in ways that implicate a distinct ethical dimension of oversight. The preamble to the 2007 Model Code of Judicial Conduct seeks to "assist judges in maintaining the highest standards of judicial and personal conduct"[56] because, as the preamble to the original 1924 Canons of Judicial Ethics explained, "the character and conduct of a judge should never be objects of indifference, and . . . declared ethical standards tend to become habits of life."[57]

At their core, the "high standards of conduct" that the Code seeks to inculcate into those who occupy judicial roles implicate independence, impartiality, integrity, and competence[58]—the instrumental values that cut across all three dimensions of oversight. As the reporters to the most recent Code revision project explained, "the importance of judicial independence, integrity, and impartiality is underscored by the recurrence of the phrase throughout the Rules."[59] The Code preamble adds "competence" to the "three I's" as a fourth core value;[60] Canon 2 generally and Rules 2.5 and 2.12 specifically impose ethical duties of competence and diligence on judicial officers in their judicial, administrative, and supervisory capacities. As in the adjudicative dimension, in the ethical dimension the Code positions independence, impartiality, integrity, and competence as instrumental values that enable the judiciary to play a "central role in preserving the principles of justice and the rule of law."[61] The Code is replete with rules and admonishments directing judges, imbued with these core values, to uphold the law,[62] respect procedural rights,[63] and promote access to justice.[64]

In state systems, there is a direct relationship between codes of conduct and processes for judicial discipline. The preamble to the Model Code of Judicial Conduct states that, in addition to serving as a guide to "assist" judges in maintaining high standards of conduct, the Code is "intended . . . to provide a basis for regulating [judges'] conduct through disciplinary agencies."[65] Thus, states promote the virtues of good judging via hortatory exhortations for judges to embrace the Code as a way of life, paired with disciplinary action for judges who violate the Code's letter.

In the federal system, the Code of Conduct for United States Judges is based on the same American Bar Association model followed by each of the fifty states. Judges are subject to discipline, however, not for violating the Code per se, but pursuant to a federal statute, for conduct "prejudicial to the effective administration of the business of the courts."[66] As to the relationship between the Code and the statute, the Judicial Conference has opined that "[a]lthough the Code of Conduct for United States Judges may be informative, its main precepts are highly general; the Code is in many potential applications aspirational rather than a set of disciplinary rules.[67] The Code of Conduct for United States judges is no more "general" (or aspirational) in its terms than the Codes that operate as disciplinary rules in all fifty states and is significantly less general in its terms than the disciplinary statute itself. By divorcing the Code of Conduct from discipline under the statute, however, the federal judiciary affords itself significantly more discretion over when to administer discipline—or not. In the federal system, then, the Code of Conduct encourages judges to behave ethically, while the disciplinary process sanctions judges for behaving unethically, but does so along parallel tracks that do not intersect to the same extent as in state systems.

As noted at the outset of this chapter, regulatory mechanisms in the adjudicative and ethical dimensions undeniably overlap. Such areas notwithstanding, judicial conduct is regarded and regulated differently in the two dimensions.

Some conduct that is deemed problematic in the ethical dimension of oversight is not necessarily problematic in the adjudicative dimension. For example, the Code directs judges not to "initiate, permit, or consider ex parte communications"[68] because private communications between the judge and one party in the absence of another "suggest bias or partiality"; impair judicial competence by increasing the "risk of an erroneous ruling"; and invite "improper influence if not outright corruption" to the detriment of judicial integrity.[69] Another Rule admonishes judges to avoid making "any public statement that might reasonably be expected to affect the outcome or impair the fairness of a matter pending or impending," and which an accompanying comment explains is "essential to the maintenance of the independence, integrity, and impartiality of the judiciary."[70] Sometimes, judges who make improper ex parte communications or public statements on pending cases are ordered to disqualify themselves[71]—but not always. As one treatise has summarized the state of the law, "[o]ut-of-court comments about a pending case, like ex parte conversations, are prohibited for other reasons, but they will not be considered disqualifying on the basis of impermissible bias unless they go too far."[72]

In the ethical dimension, then, ex parte communications (with enumerated exceptions) are categorically improper because of the threat they pose to the judge's real or perceived impartiality, competence, and integrity, but in the adjudicative dimension, such communications do not justify the comparably categorical conclusion that the judge's impartiality might reasonably be questioned for purposes of disqualification. Rather, in the adjudicative dimension, the communications must be evaluated case by case to see if they go "too far." Similarly, public comments on pending cases that are improper in the ethical dimension do not trigger automatic disqualification in the adjudicative dimension: Disqualification is largely limited to bias emanating from an extrajudicial source, because it is expected that judges will form views about claims and parties during judicial proceedings; unless a judge's public comments reveal extrajudicial bias or an utter incapacity to be fair, disqualification is unwarranted.[73] Looked at another way, in the ethical dimension, when judges adopt and enforce codes of conduct, they apply prophylactic standards to guide good judges away from conduct that could impugn their impartiality, independence, and integrity. In the adjudicative dimension, where judges are subject to the added constraint of having dockets to manage efficiently for the benefit of parties interested in timely access to justice, it counsels against the application of disqualification rules that are any broader than necessary to assure parties a fair hearing in the case in question.

Conversely, some conduct that is deemed problematic in the adjudicative dimension of oversight is not problematic in the ethical dimension. As previously noted, across state and federal systems, disqualification is a matter of ethics and procedure. Even though procedural and ethical disqualification directives are essentially the same,[74] the application of those directives is not: Whereas a judge is subject to disqualification in the adjudicative dimension when her impartiality might reasonably be questioned, irrespective of the judge's state of mind, she is typically subject to discipline in the ethical dimension only when non-disqualification is willful (i.e., when she knew or should have known that disqualification was necessary).[75] In the adjudicative dimension, parties are entitled to a fair process featuring an impartial judge, which is a goal that is compromised when the disqualification standard is met. A good judge in the ethical dimension likewise disqualifies herself when the disqualification standard is met. Good judges, however, make honest mistakes—mistakes made all the more understandable by a separate ethical directive that admonishes judges to decide the cases they are assigned unless disqualification is required, out of respect for the administrative burdens that unnecessary disqualifications pose.[76]

The conclusion that erroneous non-disqualification sometimes spells trouble in the adjudicative dimension before it does so in the ethical dimension is consonant with the more general principle that when judges make honest mistakes, the appropriate remedy is appeal, not discipline.[77] To reverse judges for honest mistakes is salutary; to punish judges for honest mistakes threatens their decisional independence.[78] Although state judges have an ethical duty to "uphold and apply the law,"[79] errors are subject to reversal in the adjudicative dimension, not discipline in the ethical dimension, unless the errors are so egregious or chronic as to manifest bad faith or incompetence.[80]

In the ethical dimension, codes often regulate judicial conduct by restricting judicial speech; contrast the adjudicative dimension, where a judge's speech is rarely restricted per se, but where the baleful effects of that speech on the parties' rights to a fair hearing can be ameliorated by the judicial process, thereby regulating judicial speech less directly. A core constraint on the administration of judicial oversight through codes of judicial conduct and disciplinary processes, then, is constitutional: Codes of conduct seek to preserve impartiality, independence, integrity, and competence by restricting judicial speech and expressive conduct, which judges and judicial candidates have sometimes challenged as a violation of their First Amendment rights.[81] In *Republican Party of Minnesota v. White*, a clause in the Minnesota Code of Judicial Conduct (derived from the 1972 Model Code) forbade judicial candidates from announcing their views on issues that could come before them as judges. In a 5 to 4 opinion, the Court invalidated the clause on First Amendment grounds and rejected the state's argument that the clause furthered the goal of promoting judicial impartiality.[82] More recently, in *Williams-Yulee v. The Florida State Bar*, in another 5 to 4 opinion, the Supreme Court upheld a rule that directed judicial candidates to solicit campaign contributions through their campaign committees and forbade them from doing so themselves, reasoning that the rule was narrowly tailored to further the compelling state interest of preserving judicial integrity.[83] In the aftermath of *White* and *Williams-Yulee*, uncertainty persists over the extent to which codes of judicial conduct may restrict campaign and other speech without running afoul of the First Amendment.[84]

Regulatory structures in the adjudicative and ethical dimensions are routinely brought to bear in this case or that disciplinary proceeding, but are ill-equipped to tackle more pervasive problems the public regards as systemic. Part of the difficulty lies in the piecemeal orientation of these mechanisms. Granting an isolated litigant's request for disqualification or disciplining a judge for an appearance of impropriety does little to ameliorate entrenched suspicions that judges categorically are under the thrall of their political ideology, socioeconomic status, gender, race, or other extralegal influence. Rules of ethics categorically prohibit judges from becoming so enthralled,[85] and rules of procedure subject individual judges to disqualification when it occurs.[86] But rules of ethics and procedure are enforced against judges by other judges, which skeptical observers may regard as so many foxes guarding the henhouse. To address these more diffuse and systemic concerns for the benefit of the public whose confidence in the courts swings in the balance, regulatory mechanisms in the adjudicative and ethical dimensions of oversight are supplemented by an array of devices in the political dimension.

Regulating Judicial Oversight in the Political Dimension

The unifying feature of structures that regulate oversight in the political dimension is that they are implemented by the public, or the public's elected representatives, for the purpose of promoting the judiciary's institutional legitimacy with the body politic. Such structures are logically subdivided into three categories: (1) mechanisms for judicial removal; (2) mechanisms for judicial selection; and (3) mechanisms for oversight of the judiciary.

The political dimension is uniquely equipped to address two kinds of problems: (1) problems that citizens or their representatives regard as troublesome, but which judges—who oversee regulation in the adjudicative and ethical dimensions—do not; and (2) problems that are otherwise ill-suited for remediation outside of the political dimension because of constraints under which regulation in other dimensions operates. Of particular relevance here are suspicions that broad segments of the judiciary are captured by their biases or political interests, which, despite being concerns of long-standing, go largely unaddressed in litigation and disciplinary settings. With respect to the most publicized and pervasive of these public suspicions—that judges allow their ideological interests to subvert the rule of law—regulation in the political dimension manifests an inherent tension. In effect, public and political branch oversight discourages judges from acting on their internally generated political preferences in ways that could undermine competent, honest, impartial, and independent decision-making; but such oversight simultaneously incentivizes judges to act on externally imposed political preferences in ways that could undermine competent, honest, impartial, and independent decision-making. Insofar as regulation in this arena is intra-dimensional and seeks to balance the burdens and benefits of oversight on core instrumental values, to the end of optimizing public confidence in the courts, delegating the task of striking the preferred balance to the public and its elected representatives has intuitive appeal.

Mechanisms for Judicial Removal

Removal mechanisms serve as a bridge between the ethical and political dimensions of oversight. In the federal system, the sole mechanism for judicial removal is the impeachment process.[87] Impeachment is situated in the political dimension, as I have defined it, by virtue of being a power within the sole authority of Congress to exercise, for the redress of "treason, bribery or other high crimes and misdemeanors"[88]—offenses that Alexander Hamilton characterized as "political" in nature and constituting an "abuse or violation of some public trust."[89] But impeachment is linked to the ethical dimension too, insofar as conduct that the judiciary deems bad enough to warrant discipline can be bad enough to undermine public trust and warrant impeachment. Accordingly, the ultimate disciplinary sanction that federal statute authorizes the judiciary to impose in the ethical dimension is to refer a matter to the House of Representatives for a possible impeachment inquiry in the political dimension.[90]

Impeachable offenses have included conduct compromising each of the four instrumental values of good judging and each of the three objectives those values seek to further. Competence was at issue in the nation's first impeachment, when Judge John Pickering was removed for (among other things) insanity.[91] Impartiality, integrity, and independence are implicated in an array of removals loosely organized under the heading of "corruption." In those cases, judges received money or other benefits from people interested in the business of the courts, which rendered the judges dependent on their benefactors, compromised their impartiality, and impugned their integrity.[92] The sanctity of law, the fairness of the process, and the pursuit of justice are laid to waste by quid pro quos, or the equivalent, in which judges exploit their offices for benefits.

In state systems, the primary mechanism for judicial removal is the disciplinary process.[93] I have previously situated judicial discipline in the ethical dimension because it is the means by which judicial systems enforce codes of conduct to the end of taking judges to task for ethical departures from their appropriate roles. Self-policing in this way can simultaneously promote public confidence in the courts, but other mechanisms for judicial removal are more clearly denominated political because they are controlled by nonjudicial actors. In addition to impeachment processes, various states employ additional removal mechanisms: (1) the legislative address, which authorizes the legislature to seek the removal of a judge by petitioning the governor; (2) automatic removal of a judge upon conviction of specified crimes, which gives the executive branch a role to play in judicial removal through criminal prosecution; and (3) judicial recall, in which the electorate is enabled to seek the removal of a judge in special elections.[94]

Mechanisms for judicial removal in the political dimension operate under the constraint of being cumbrous by constitutional design; these mechanisms authorize political branch encroachments on the tenure, and hence the autonomy, of the judiciary and their unwieldiness operates as a check against overuse.[95] For example, removal by impeachment in the federal system and most states requires impeachment upon a majority vote by one chamber of the legislature followed by a trial and conviction upon a supermajority vote in the other chamber.[96]

The role these removal mechanisms play in policing judicial conduct and promoting public confidence in the impartiality of the judiciary, however, is not necessarily limited to those few cases in which judges are removed by such mechanisms. When a judge is threatened with impeachment, recall, or removal by legislative address, it underscores the seriousness of the speaker's concern and calls public attention to the underlying problem with the judge's conduct.[97] Moreover, the threat itself can chasten the judge in subtle and sometimes not so subtle ways. For example, in 1996, U.S. District Judge Harold Baer reversed a ruling to suppress evidence in a drug case after congressional leaders threatened him with impeachment.[98] In 2003, a Massachusetts Superior Court judge resigned after a bill of legislative address was filed in response to a sentence she imposed in a kidnapping case.[99] That same year, the Nevada Chief Justice survived a recall election over her unpopular decision in a tax case, but resigned at the end of her term.[100] Finally, recourse to these mechanisms, even if they do not remove or chasten, gives court critics a platform to rally support for systemic concerns in the political dimension. At the beginning of the nineteenth century, for example, Jeffersonian Republicans called public attention to what they regarded as excessively partisan judges appointed by the predecessor Federalist regime, with a campaign to remove them.[101] And in the 1990s, Republican congressional leaders did the same, proposing to impeach "liberal activist" judges appointed by prior administrations.[102]

Mechanisms for Judicial Selection

In state systems, judges are selected by at least five different means, involving various combinations of governors, commissions, legislatures, and voters.[103] Each of these participants can have a role to play in evaluating judicial candidates' past or prospective competence, integrity, impartiality, and independence, and their relative commitment to law, process, and justice. As a practical matter, however, the choices that governors and commissions make to exclude particular judicial candidates are largely inscrutable, and legislatures have primary responsibility for judicial selection in only two states. That leaves voters, and because over 80% of state judges stand for judicial elections of some sort,[104] the role that elections play in policing judicial impartiality is the focus here.

Elections have one foot in judicial selection and the other in judicial removal: In states with contested elections, the net effect of selecting a challenger over an incumbent is to remove the incumbent from office; and in states with retention elections, the public's role in judicial selection is limited to deciding whether an incumbent should be removed to make way for a new appointment. Either way, in the political dimension of oversight, elections serve as a means to police the same instrumental values and systemic objectives regulated in the adjudicative and ethical dimensions. Judicial candidates have been called to task for their competence,[105] their integrity,[106] their impartiality,[107] and their independence.[108] Perhaps the most salient issue in recent judicial campaigns, however, concerns claims that candidates have ideological agendas that compromise their integrity, impartiality, and independence (from their own biases) that trump their commitment to law and justice. Examples abound in which judicial candidates have been portrayed by their opponents as activists whose commitment to law and justice is compromised by their ideological biases on such matters as same-sex marriage, the death penalty, abortion, water rights, and tort reform.[109]

The primary constraint on elections as an oversight mechanism in the political dimension concerns the tension alluded to earlier: Electoral accountability can pressure judges to disregard the law, process, and justice objectives that elections aim to encourage. While worries about unaccountable judges run amok have stalled a mid-twentieth-century movement among the states to end contested judicial elections,[110] worries about elections run amok have thwarted any movement in the opposite direction.[111] Arguably, a secondary constraint concerns limits on voter capacity—measured in terms of competence and interest—to regulate judicial performance at the ballot box in a meaningful way.[112] While the debate over whether such impediments can be overcome rages on, the fact remains that voters tend to regard elections as legitimacy enhancing—which is the relevant data point for purposes here.[113]

In the federal system, Supreme Court nominees have likewise been rejected or withdrawn over competence, integrity, impartiality, or independence concerns. In the modern era, the Senate blocked President Johnson's nomination of Abe Fortas to replace Earl Warren as Chief Justice partly over concerns that Fortas had served as a political advisor to the president while on the Court and had accepted exorbitant speaking fees, raising questions about his independence and integrity.[114] The Senate rejected President Nixon's nomination of Judge Clement Haynesworth in part because he presided over cases in which he held stock in corporate parties,[115] creating doubts as to his integrity and impartiality. The Senate also rejected Nixon's nomination of Harold Carswell, on the grounds that he was a racist and a mediocre intellect, implicating his impartiality and competence.[116] President Ronald Reagan's nominee, Douglas Ginsburg, withdrew after his recent marijuana use was revealed, which (for an administration committed to cracking down on illicit drugs) impugned the nominee's integrity at least as far as his respect for drug laws was concerned.[117] And George W. Bush's nominee, Harriet Miers, withdrew after she was criticized as an under-qualified crony of the president, which flagged competence and independence concerns. [118]

As recounted in chapter 2, however, the alligator in the bathtub of modern Senate confirmation proceedings has been nominee ideology. Beginning in the late nineteenth century, the ideological bent of a nominee's prospective decision-making became an increasingly prominent issue in Supreme Court confirmation proceedings (including nominations ostensibly rejected on other grounds) that culminated in the 1987 Senate rejection of Robert Bork on ideological grounds alone. Post-Bork, inquiries into nominee ideology have spilled over into circuit, and sometimes district, court confirmation proceedings. As with state judicial election campaigns, the fixation on ideology in confirmation proceedings ostensibly seeks to purge the judiciary of "activists" or "extremists" who lack the integrity, impartiality, and independence needed to put law, process, and justice ahead of their political preferences.

From the perspective of social science, the "judicial activist" bogeyman is a cartoonish distortion of reality. The adversarial process presupposes that there is always more than one way to look at difficult legal and factual questions. When the answers to such questions are unclear, honorable judges must, of necessity, exercise judgment—judgment informed by their life experience. And the data show that such judgment can be influenced by a variety of factors including ideology, race, gender, and others.[119] Campaigns to purge judicial decision-making of ideological influences are thus misinformed or disingenuous. More reasonably conceived, such campaigns seek to ensure that ideological influences on the exercise of judicial judgment or discretion will fall within a politically acceptable range. To that extent, selection processes are aimed at producing judges who will be good enough to retain public support in the political dimension of judicial oversight.

In the federal system, constraints on the confirmation process are strategic and logistical. Strategically, in the aftermath of the Bork rejection, nominees have learned to be less forthcoming in confirmation hearings.[120] That has made it more difficult for opposition campaigns to expose nominees as politically unacceptable. And so, despite concerted efforts to portray nominees as ideologues or extremists, after Bork, no Supreme Court nominee has been rejected, blocked, or withdrawn on such grounds alone. Moreover, as a strategic matter, the president has the upper hand in Supreme Court appointments showdowns. Senate antagonists must wage one exhausting opposition campaign after another to overcome the "presumption of confirmation" created by the Constitution's lower threshold of a simple Senate majority needed for appointment.[121] For the president, in contrast, a Senate rejection may be embarrassing and cost him political capital, but it is less trouble for him to go to the next name on his short list than for the Senate to organize sequential oppositions.[122]

Mechanisms for Legislative Supervision

In state and federal systems, legislatures have varying degrees of regulatory authority over judicial pay raises and court structure, jurisdiction, budgets, administration, and procedure.[123] These tools can give the political branches a role to play in the adjudicative and ethical dimensions of oversight. For example, in the federal system, Congress has enacted legislation governing disqualification and procedural rulemaking, which structures the manner in which courts regulate oversight in the adjudicative dimension.[124] Congress has also enacted the Judicial Conduct and Disability Act, which is a means by which the federal judiciary manages oversight in the ethical dimension.[125]

At their core, however, mechanisms for legislative oversight of the courts are centered in the political dimension. By virtue of its power to establish (and by negative implication, disestablish) inferior courts, Congress has broad regulatory authority over the lower courts,[126] including their subject matter jurisdiction, organization, budgets, salary increases, practice, procedure, and administration. These mechanisms can be used to promote by now familiar instrumental values and systemic objectives to the intended satisfaction of the public and their elected representatives. For example, Congress has established[127] and expanded[128] federal court jurisdiction over suits between citizens of different states to afford out-of-state litigants a refuge from state courts that were arguably partial to their own citizens. Congress has established circuit courts of appeals to control what its committee reports characterized as district court "despotism"— arbitrary abuses of power that purportedly enabled district judges to abuse their independence to the detriment of their integrity, impartiality, and competence.[129] Congress has enacted legislation limiting sentencing discretion (statutory minimums, maximums, and sentencing guidelines) in a putative effort to constrain judicial biases.[130] And congressional efforts to curb the judiciary's perceived ideological excesses (excesses that arguably threaten judicial competence, integrity, and impartiality values and the law, process, and justice objectives those values further) have included proposals to: (1) disestablish or cut the budgets of uncooperative courts; (2) freeze judicial salaries; and (3) deprive judges of jurisdiction to hear controversial cases.[131] Many state legislatures have undertaken to regulate their respective judiciaries in similar ways toward similar ends, by manipulating judicial salaries and budgets and proposing to curtail subject matter jurisdiction and judicial review.[132]

The authority of legislatures to oversee the courts is subject to constitutional and normative constraints. As to constitutional constraints, Article III limits legislative control over judicial tenure and salaries, and the judiciary's exclusive constitutional authority to exercise judicial power bars Congress from overturning judgments by legislation.[133] Congress's authority to establish and disestablish the lower courts does not extend to the Supreme Court, where congressional authority is limited to making regulations and exceptions incident to the Court's appellate jurisdiction, and exercising whatever additional powers are implied by the "necessary and proper" clause.[134] Many state constitutions grant their judicial systems greater institutional separation and independence than their federal counterparts, which can further limit legislatures' regulatory authority over state court operations.[135] As to normative constraints, I have argued elsewhere that over the course of the nineteenth century, Congress gradually internalized judicial independence norms that constrained its political will to control judges and their decision-making to the full extent authorized by the Constitution.[136] The net effect was to render less viable, tools seemingly at Congress's disposal to chasten judges whose internal political interests in the outcomes of cases they decided compromised their impartiality, integrity, competence, and independence.[137]

TRACKING MOVEMENT BETWEEN DIMENSIONS

Professors Stephen Burbank and Barry Friedman have reconceptualized judicial independence with the insight that the judiciary's independence is not monolithic—it has different forms, different meanings, and different applications in different contexts.[138] The same may be said of judicial oversight generally. Describing judicial oversight in terms of its adjudicative, ethical, and political dimensions—each with distinct schemas for regulation that vary across and within jurisdictions—illuminates the relationship between judicial process, ethics, and politics and reveals an architecture for conceptualizing oversight that illuminates some important trends.

The critical trend for purposes here is toward more aggressive oversight in the political dimension relative to the adjudicative and ethical dimensions. In some instances, there has been a transfer of power from the adjudicative or ethical dimensions to the political. In other instances, an upsurge of activity in the political dimension has operated by default to supplant regulation in the adjudicative or ethical dimensions.

In the political dimension itself, oversight of judicial selection has ramped up in ways that have intruded on judicial prerogatives traditionally relegated to judges in the adjudicative dimension. The new politics of state judicial elections have morphed supreme court races into well financed referenda on judicial decisions—a weapon in the arsenal of the political dimension that rose to prominence in the latter third of the twentieth century.[139] Isolated statutory overrides and constitutional amendments aside, ameliorating bad judicial decisions has traditionally been the province of judicial reversal and reinterpretation by judges in the adjudicative dimension. The changing nature of judicial races—the role of big money and the specter of defeat at the ballot box—effectively insinuates an additional measure of political dimension influence by voters into the adjudication of hot-button issues.

The same may be said for Senate confirmation of federal judges. The appointments process has always been "political": Presidents have almost always chosen nominees from the ranks of the president's political party and Senate opposition to judicial nominees has always been subject to partisan, political influences independent of the candidate's capabilities or credentials. But evaluating Supreme Court nominees with reference to the ideology of their future decision-making is essentially a twentieth-century innovation—an innovation that expanded to include circuit (and sometimes district) judges beginning in the 1980s.[140] The net effect is to afford Senators in the political dimension an additional measure of prospective influence over judicial decision-making that previously would have been relegated by default to judges in the adjudicative dimension, who would be called upon to reverse or revisit erroneous decisions of ideologically overzealous judges.

In the adjudicative dimension, several developments have reoriented the focus of oversight from judicial self-administration toward heightened legislative supervision in the political dimension. When it enacted the Rules Enabling Act in the 1930s, Congress transferred some of its rulemaking authority in the political dimension to the judiciary in the adjudicative dimension so that the judiciary might bring its special expertise as adjudicators to bear in devising uniform rules of practice and procedure for parties appearing before the federal courts.[141] As discussed in chapter 2, beginning in earnest in the 1970s, procedural rulemaking has become ever more ideologically charged. Rule-makers have infused the process with opportunities for majoritarian influence, and Congress has exhibited heightened interest in supervisory control over practice and procedure in the political dimension on such issues as litigation expense and delay, class actions, and litigation misconduct standards.

In *Twombly* and *Iqbal*, the Supreme Court bypassed formal procedural rulemaking by reinterpreting an existing rule. There, the Court eased dismissal standards in the adjudicative dimension by directing judges to dismiss complaints that strike them as "implausible," in light of their common sense and experience.[142] In so doing, the Court sought to bring an operative constraint in the adjudicative dimension to bear by alleviating judges of the burden to devote scarce judicial resources to claims they regard as marginal. Insofar as "common sense" is subject to ideological and other extralegal influences, the expanded zone of discretion that *Twombly* and *Iqbal* created has left a regulatory vacuum rife with policy implications that actors within the political dimension are keen to fill. Hence, the question of pleading standards has moved to Congress, where it has become a hotly contested issue.[143] Moreover, increasing the discretion of judges to dismiss cases at the preliminary pleading stage of litigation in light of predilections travelling in the name of "common sense," invites more sustained inquiry into the politics of "common sense" during confirmation proceedings. To date, district judges have largely avoided the highly politicized confirmation showdowns that have beset Supreme and circuit court nominees.[144] To the extent that "plausibility" is in the eye of the beholder, however, it may be only a matter of time before the "common sense" of district court nominees is tested in the appointments crucible.

With respect to due process and disqualification, the Supreme Court's decision in *Caperton* arguably revitalized impartiality in the adjudicative dimension by concluding that non-disqualification in the teeth of probable bias was a due process violation.[145] The impact of *Caperton*, however, is sharply limited by the constraints under which the due process clause regulates judicial disqualification. As previously explained, such constraints relegate due process challenges to the status of a last resort reserved for nippy days in hell.[146] The *Caperton* majority emphasized that non-disqualification will violate due process only in outlier cases when judges exhibit a flagrant probability of bias that inexplicably manages to evade capture by standard disqualification rules.[147]

Caperton could still be read as a backhanded invitation for state judiciaries to avoid due process challenges by implementing meaningful disqualification regimes in the adjudicative dimension—regimes that require recusal whenever a judge's impartiality might reasonably be questioned. An ironic impediment to regulating oversight through rigorous enforcement of disqualification rules in the adjudicative dimension, though, is that the procedures many courts follow to implement those rules compromise the perceived impartiality that disqualification rules seek to promote. In most federal circuits and many states, judges whose disqualification is sought decide the matter for themselves.[148] Appellate review is available, but with rare exception, appellate courts employ a highly deferential standard of review,[149] which proceeds from the dubious premise that when deciding whether a judge is or appears to be too biased to hear a matter, we should defer to the assessment of the judge who allegedly is or appears to be too biased to hear the matter. Moreover, on courts of last resort, judges typically have the first and final word on their own qualifications to sit, and may err on the side of non-disqualification if there is no means to replace them when they withdraw.[150] Insofar as being impartial is a defining feature of a good judge across dimensions, judges who implement disqualification rules in the adjudicative dimension would seem predisposed to reject petitions impugning their own impartiality. As a consequence, many lawyers have long been reluctant to seek disqualification of judges, who are unlikely to second-guess their own impartiality and who may take umbrage at the suggestion that their impartiality is in doubt.[151]

For their part, judges have pushed back against efforts to reform disqualification procedure, by arguing that such reforms are unnecessary and burdensome—core efficiency concerns that constrain the regulation of impartiality in the adjudicative dimension. In 2007, the American Bar Association launched the Judicial Disqualification Project, which was aimed at "taking judicial disqualification seriously."[152] The Project's 2009 preliminary report proposed six specific reforms to "diminish or eliminate the need for targeted judges to rule on motions for their own disqualification."[153] Two draft resolutions followed, which sought to implement the recommendations of the draft report,[154] but were withdrawn following objections from the American Bar Association's judicial division (among other American Bar Association entities).[155] A third resolution proposed simply that "each state should have in place clearly articulated procedures . . . for the handling of disqualification determinations" that "should be designed to produce resolutions of disqualification issues that are both prompt and meaningful."[156] Even that, however, drew Judicial Division fire,[157] and the call for prompt and meaningful determinations was replaced by a fourth resolution the American Bar Association ultimately adopted, for "prompt review by another judge or tribunal, or as otherwise provided by law or rule of court, of denials of requests to disqualify a judge"[158]—which, given the universal availability of appellate review, could fairly be characterized as endorsing the status quo. Similarly, in the aftermath of *Caperton*, American Bar Association resolutions to address disqualification when campaign supporters appear before the judge have been proposed, diluted, and withdrawn.

With efforts to reinvigorate the administration of disqualification in the adjudicative dimension languishing, activity in the political dimension has filled the void. The House Judiciary Committee held hearings on judicial disqualification in 2009 that focused on disqualification procedure.[159] A 2009 survey found that over 80% of the public thought that disqualification requests should be decided by a different judge than the one whose disqualification was sought.[160] Interest groups and the media have tapped into the public's skepticism of judicial self-disqualification with several highly publicized campaigns to pressure Supreme Court justices into recusing themselves in high-profile cases. Justice Scalia's non-disqualification in the duck-hunting imbroglio of 2004 has been followed by campaigns to disqualify Justices Thomas and Kagan from participating in an impending case challenging the constitutionality of health care legislation. Finally, events of recent generations show gradual movement away from oversight in the ethical dimension and toward heightened interest in the political dimension. A primary constraint on the robust operation of disciplinary mechanisms in the ethical dimension is that those mechanisms are implemented by and for judges. In the federal system, that constraint has rendered the lower courts susceptible to criticism that the disciplinary process is under-enforced and that the Code is under-utilized.[161] Such criticism has piqued congressional interest, thereby shifting the focus of attention to the political dimension. Thus, in response to the latest wave of concern, the House held oversight hearings on the disciplinary process.[162] Members of Congress investigated the conduct of judges whose disciplinary proceedings have stalled,[163] with an eye toward possible impeachment. The Chair of the House Judiciary Committee introduced legislation to establish an inspector general to investigate disciplinary complaints against judges.[164] And senators frustrated by the Judicial Conference's failure to regulate the ethics of judges attending educational seminars at vacation resorts underwritten by corporations interested in the outcomes of cases those judges decided, introduced bills to ban "junkets for judges."[165]

The Supreme Court, in contrast to the "inferior courts," is not subject to any disciplinary process (other than impeachment) and has no code of conduct to which it has bound itself.[166] Chief Justice Roberts has explained that justices on the Court do in fact consult the Code but that is not to say they treat it as binding.[167] Thus, for example, Justices Scalia and Thomas were featured speakers at the 2012 annual meeting of the Federalist Society, which arguably violated the Code of Conduct as construed by the Judicial Conference (which bars judges from being guest speakers at fundraising events).[168] The vacuum created by the absence of a code to regulate the Court in the ethical dimension has been filled in the political dimension with proposed legislation and a campaign launched by the media and interest groups questioning the ethics and perceived impartiality of individual justices, decrying the absence of a code that applies to the Supreme Court, and calling for reform. At the same time, a group of preeminent scholars has called attention to the under-regulation of the Supreme Court in the adjudicative and ethical dimensions and proposed reform.[169]

Among the states, *Republican Party of Minnesota v. White* diminished the constitutional authority of state Supreme Courts and judicial conduct organizations to regulate the political speech of judges and judicial candidates in the ethical dimension. More recently, in *Williams-Yulee v. The Florida State Bar*, the Supreme Court upheld a state rule that barred judicial candidates from soliciting contributions directly, but took pains to characterize it as "one of those rare cases where a speech restriction withstands strict scrutiny."[170] Insofar as the ethical propriety of judges taking positions on future cases from the campaign stump remains an issue, it is an issue relegated by default to the political dimension.[171] And so, in the post-*White* era, judicial campaigns have featured an awkward ballet in which interest groups have asked judges to state their views on issues they may decide; when judges demur, citing impartiality concerns, the groups have sought to make a campaign issue of the judges' intransigence.[172]

CONCLUSION

Regulatory mechanisms for oversight of the courts can be organized or conceptualized in terms of whether a given mechanism aims primarily to promote fair hearings for parties in an adjudicatory dimension of oversight; public confidence in the courts in a political dimension of oversight; or virtuous conduct by judges in an ethical dimension of oversight. The changing landscape of American courts, which the bench and bar have attributed to "politicization," is better understood in terms of a shift in emphasis and influence from the adjudicative and ethical dimensions of judicial oversight to the political. What remains to be decided is whether this development is salutary or deleterious, and if the latter, what can and should be done about it.

CHAPTER 7

Explanations and Prescriptions

The weakest link in the chain of claims this book makes is arguably the first: that the landscape of the American courts is undergoing a political transformation. The issue is not whether chapter 2 misdescribed or exaggerated this development or that. The issue is whether these developments, taken together, represent something new that is worth worrying about. I stop short of making the crisis claims that have dominated recent discourse within the legal community, but my central thesis—that the rule of law paradigm is under stress and needs to be retooled—nonetheless turns on a showing that recent events in the life and times of the American judiciary go beyond business as usual.

The challenge has been to show that developments of the past hundred years have affected the courts in ways that transcend the cyclical assaults the rule of law paradigm has weathered throughout the nation's history and jeopardize its long-term well-being. To that end, chapter 2 isolated emerging trends cutting across cycles that are changing America's courts and eroding a foundational premise of the rule of law paradigm: that independent judges who preside over trials and hear appeals can be counted on to set ideological and other extralegal influences aside and follow the law. The list of emerging trends is long:

- Trial rates have declined to the point where the "trial judge" is a contradiction in terms, for which reason, traditional justifications for the independence of umpire-like adjudicators who officiate disputes at trial cease to apply.
- Federal judicial confirmation proceedings have transformed the nominee's political ideology into a pivotal qualification for judicial office.
- State judicial election campaigns have become interest group funded referenda on candidate ideology and how candidates should decide ideologically charged issues.

- The substantive implications of ostensibly "procedural" rules have spawned partisan disputes over the limits of judicial discretion and how best to manage judges, by means of procedural rule-making and disqualification.
- Ideologically freighted cable news punditry and internet "citizen journalism" have changed how courts are critiqued and perceived.
- Codes of conduct and disciplinary processes have created new systems of judicial oversight and new forums for the critique of judges and judicial systems by interest groups and individuals with political agendas.
- Concerns relating to racial bias in the administration of justice have become persistent and pressing.
- Establishing intermediate appellate courts and making high court review discretionary has limited supreme court dockets in the federal and many state systems to fewer, policy-laden questions of first impression where courts must effectively make new law.

The takeaway from the political transformation that these developments embody is not that America has abandoned its faith in the rule of law paradigm and embraced nihilistic legal realism. General support for judges and the rule of law shows no signs of impending collapse, and the ubiquitous inkling that independent judges do more and less than follow the law predates the legal realists by millennia. There has been a long, relatively stable state of cognitive dissonance, in which strong support for the proposition that independent judges disregard extralegal influences and follow the law has coexisted with a pervasive suspicion that independent judges are subject to a host of extralegal influences.

Rather, the message this book seeks to convey is that these enumerated developments comprise a transformation that has destabilized this state of cognitive dissonance. Across a snowballing aggregation of venues spanning a century, the premises underlying the rule of law paradigm have been tested, challenged, and contradicted, in ways that cast doubt on the paradigm's long-term future.

The legal culture paradigm that I have proposed retools its rule of law predecessor by accommodating a measure of judicial independence in the context of courts whose judges—consistent with public perception and social science research—are subject to extralegal influences. It proceeds from the premise that judges are immersed in a legal culture that enshrines the rule of law ideal, but that pervasive legal indeterminacy renders extralegal influences inevitable. To manage extralegal influences while accommodating rule of law norms, the legal culture paradigm embraces four instrumental values that serve three systemic objectives. Good judges should be capable, honest, impartial, and independent.

These four instrumental values enable judges to promote law, process, and justice objectives. Judges can uphold the law as they construe it to be written, respect established legal process, and administer justice, despite (and sometimes because of) extralegal influences made inevitable by legal indeterminacy that requires judges to exercise judgment and discretion.

The rule of law paradigm is under attack because its premise—that independent judges are influenced by law alone—is increasingly perceived as unacceptably counterfactual by several affected communities, including scholars, the media, the public, and their elected representatives. The legal culture paradigm, in contrast, rests on a factual premise those communities can more readily accept: Judges are acculturated to take law, process, and justice seriously, but must resolve indeterminate legal questions with recourse to policy considerations that implicate factors fairly denominated extralegal even if those considerations are inextricably intertwined with and extensions of operative law.

How much freedom judges should have to bring extralegal influences into play when filling spaces created by legal indeterminacy is a critical question for the legal culture paradigm that the rule of law paradigm avoids by positing extralegal influences out of existence. Because capability, integrity, impartiality, and independence are instrumental values, good judges need not be perfectly capable, forthright, impartial, and independent. They need only be capable, forthright, impartial, and independent enough to uphold the law, respect established process, and administer justice. Mechanisms for holding judges accountable to fellow judges, the public, and their elected representatives, aim to ensure that judges are indeed "good enough," by constraining their freedom to bring extralegal influences to bear when the result would be detrimental to systemic objectives.

As discussed in chapter 5, independence is unique among the instrumental values, in that a judge cannot be too capable, honest, or impartial, but can be too independent. The legal culture paradigm thus seeks judges who are independent enough to further law, process, and justice objectives without being susceptible to inappropriate external pressures, but not so independent that they are free to disregard systemic objectives and pursue private agendas. Oversight of judicial independence thus poses a special challenge, as evidenced by long-standing and ultimately unproductive squabbles over where independence should end and accountability begin.

The legal culture paradigm gets past these squabbles with the insight that the optimal independence-accountability balance varies by perspective or dimension. Parties seeking a fair hearing in the adjudicative dimension may have a preferred independence-accountability blend that is different from that favored by members of the public seeking a judiciary they will support in the political dimension. The public, in turn, may draw the independence-accountability line in a different place than judges who seek to fulfill the responsibilities of their role in the ethical dimension.

There is no guarantee that moving in the direction of a legal culture paradigm would lead the American judiciary out of the woods. The paradigm offers a conceptual justification for why judges who are subject to ideological and other extralegal influences need a measure of independence to promote law, process, and justice objectives. But court critics (and the new media they exploit), who are less interested in conceptual justifications than preferred policy outcomes, can be counted upon to continue accusing judges of exceeding the appropriate limits of their independence and undermining systemic objectives whenever judges reach conclusions with which the critics disapprove. In the parlance of our times, "haters gonna hate."

While the legal culture paradigm cannot prevent attempted manipulation by the fringe, it can better equip paradigm caretakers within the legal community to counter those attempts. It has proved difficult to defend judges against encroachments on their independence with the other-worldly claim that independent judges follow the law and nothing else, when scholars and public alike know better. It is quite defensible, however, to claim that a measure of independence furthers law, process, and justice objectives because that claim proceeds from the supportable premise that independent judges are subject to legal and extralegal influences.

The strength of the legal culture paradigm transcends service as a model that affected communities can better support than its ailing, rule of law predecessor. It helps to reveal movements between dimensions. As chapter 6 showed, when issues of independence and accountability are viewed through a three-dimensional lens that analyzes those issues from the perspectives of parties, public, and judges, the developments contributing to the political transformation I have described reveal a generations-long trend. This trend reflects movement away from oversight of the courts by judges and the judiciary in the adjudicative and ethical dimensions, and toward greater oversight by the public and their representatives in the political dimension.

The capacity of the legal culture paradigm to reveal this trend suggests two possibilities that this final chapter explores. First, the three-dimensional orientation of the legal culture paradigm has unique explanatory force—not only in spotting trends, as chapter 6 showed, but in explicating other conceptual impasses. Second, if one can show that the adjudicative, political, and ethical dimensions of judicial oversight each protect core values, then the legal culture paradigm has prescriptive strength too, that justifies efforts to reverse trends toward increased oversight in one dimension that threaten the viability of oversight in the others.

THE LEGAL CULTURE PARADIGM
AS AN EXPLANATORY DEVICE

Paradigms are explanatory by nature—as models, they explain the world they conceptualize. Chapter 5 elaborates on how, relative to the rule of law paradigm, a legal culture paradigm can better explain judicial decision-making and the means and ends of good judging to the satisfaction of communities operating within the paradigm. Chapter 6 explains how, within the legal culture paradigm, regulatory oversight seeks to promote good judging by striking a balance between independence and accountability that is best analyzed from three distinct perspectives or dimensions. This section, in turn, explores some of the conceptual thickets surrounding judicial oversight to the end of showing how a three-dimensional analysis, and the constraints under which the dimensions operate, illuminate pathways through those thickets.

It is easier to appreciate the explanatory force of a three-dimensional analysis in context. Consider the following examples, the puzzles they present, and the conceptual challenges they pose for regulatory oversight.

In 1974, Lillian Hellman wrote that "[n]obody outside of a baby carriage or a judge's chamber can believe in an unprejudiced point of view."[1] As jaded as she may have meant to sound at the time, in a skeptical age when social science research has rejected the notion that judges entertain an "unprejudiced point of view," the distinction she drew between judges and the general population seems almost naive. "Prejudice" adversely affects judicial impartiality, independence, integrity, and competence: impartiality, by implicating judicial bias; independence, insofar as judges are prejudiced by the views of those upon whom judges are dependent; integrity, by leading judges to knowingly to subvert facts and law to gratify their prejudices; and competence for judges whose prejudices stem from ignorance. If the realm of the unprejudiced is now peopled only with infants, are the vaunted values of impartiality, independence, integrity, and competence a fiction, or worse, a scam? Are systems of oversight that respect the judiciary's autonomy missing the point?

Vaughn Walker was a gay district judge who invalidated California Proposition 8, which outlawed same-sex marriage.[2] Under the federal disqualification statute, Walker's sexual orientation did not furnish a reasonable basis to question his impartiality.[3] On the other hand, if Judge

Walker owned a single share of stock in a corporation that intervened to defend Proposition 8, he would have had to disqualify himself immediately.[4] Yet, it seems much less likely that Walker's nominal shareholding would incline him to uphold Proposition 8, than that a lifetime as a gay man would incline him to invalidate it. Have systems of oversight gotten it backward?

In 2003, the U.S. Senate blocked President George W. Bush's nomination of District Judge Charles Pickering to the circuit court, on the grounds that his ideologically conservative views fueled doubts among interest groups and Senate Democrats that he, as an independent circuit judge, would impartially uphold the law;[5] and yet, upon returning to his duties as an independent district judge, it would have been frivolous for parties to seek Judge Pickering's disqualification on the grounds that his impartiality might reasonably be questioned.[6] Why do systems of oversight employ a double standard?

Minnesota's Code of Judicial Conduct (and the 1972 Model Code of Judicial Conduct) included an ethics rule that forbade judicial candidates from announcing their views on issues that they would likely decide as judges—a rule the state defended as necessary to preserve judicial impartiality.[7] Justice Scalia, writing for the Supreme Court in 2002, emphatically rejected the view that impartiality meant a "lack of preconception in favor of or against a particular legal view," on his way to invalidating the rule on First Amendment grounds.[8] Yet sixteen years earlier, then nominee Judge Scalia refused to announce his legal views to the Senate Judiciary Committee, explaining that "the only way to be sure that I am not impairing my ability to be impartial in future cases . . . is simply to respectfully decline to give an opinion on whether any of the existing law on the Supreme Court is right or wrong,"[9] adding:

> I think it is quite a thing to be arguing to somebody who you know has made a representation in the course of confirmation hearings, and that is, by way of condition to his being confirmed, that he will do this or do that. I think I would be in a very bad position to adjudicate the case without being accused of having a less than impartial view of the matter.[10]

Both Scalias fixated on impartiality, but independence and integrity were implicated too: Do judges compromise their independence from voters or Senators by making representations to those audiences that they "will do this or do that" as a condition of being selected? Do a judge's subsequent departures from such representations cast doubt on her integrity by implying that, as a candidate, she misrepresented her views to gain office? Which Scalia was right?

In the seventeenth century, Sir Matthew Hale devised a code of judicial conduct for his own use, which included a rule that stated: "I never engage myself in the beginning of any cause, but reserve myself unprejudiced till the whole be heard."[11] More recently, however, the Supreme Court has directed judges to dismiss complaints at the beginning of any case that judges deem "implausible" in light of their "common sense" and "experience," to avoid the resulting expense of discovery if judgment were postponed.[12] Is impartiality becoming expendable?

Returning to the first of these imponderables, the Hellman problem is a stage-setter: It frames the debate that this book has engaged. Consistent with Hellman's observation that no one believes in an unprejudiced point of view outside of a judge's chamber, judges "believe" themselves unprejudiced. After all, judges "persistently and adamantly deny that their fact-finding or legal interpretations are motivated by their personal . . . preferences."[13] Cognitive psychology offers an explanation (traveling under the name "motivated reasoning") for why judges are sincere in their belief that they are not so influenced: The impact of ideology is subconscious in cases where facts or law are indeterminate and judges choose the argument they find more persuasive.[14] After two millennia of evidence to the contrary, however, it is too late in the day to make categorical claims that judges are literally unprejudiced in the sense of being impervious to extralegal influences.

Hellman made her observation in a book review: Unlike fiction writers, she explained, "the historian or biographer . . . must make sure . . . that the people he is writing about are not the victims of his loving or unloving heart."[15] Thus, even if it is impossible to have an unprejudiced point of view, she concluded, "simply in self-interest, the biographer must try for one."[16] The same may be said of judges in a legal culture paradigm: Even if a perfectly impartial perspective is unattainable, we still insist that judges—aided by those who oversee judicial systems—"try for one."

In a legal culture paradigm, perfection remains the aspiration for judges acculturated to respect the law and marginalize extralegal influences. For the paradigm to work, however, judges need not be perfect; they need only be "good enough," which is to say capable, forthright, impartial, and independent enough to further law, process, and justice objectives. And being good enough is perspective or dimension-dependent: What is good enough to provide parties with a fair judge in adjudication may or may not be good enough to provide the public with a politically acceptable judge, or good enough to afford the judiciary an ethical judge.

Once the inevitability of imperfection is acknowledged, it becomes possible to unpack the quandary presented by Judge Walker and the same-sex marriage case. Insofar as Judge Walker's perspective is informed by his experience as a homosexual, the same can be said of the heterosexual judge. To the extent that these differences in perspective are characterized as forms of bias that can influence a judge's interpretation of the equal protection clause in the context of a gay marriage case, they are ubiquitous. And in the adjudicative dimension of impartiality, which is constrained by the need for an ample supply of judges to decide cases, universal disqualification would be impracticable.

Whether a judge is gay or straight, Christian or Jew, man or woman, black or white, may well exert a more significant extralegal influence on judicial decision-making in certain kinds of cases than, say, whether the judge owns a few shares of stock in a corporate party. But from the practical perspective that constrains the adjudicative dimension, the disqualification procedure depends on more or less bright lines and limited applications. Hence, disqualification for stock ownership presents a manageable disqualification rule, while disqualification for affiliation with a given race, gender, ethnicity, or sexual orientation—absent specific statements or conduct indicative of bias in a particular case—does not. Moreover, absent such particularized evidence of bias, the right of parties to an impartial hearing in the adjudicative dimension is not compromised but arguably furthered by the diversity of perspective that comes from judges with varying backgrounds. If one accepts the premise that there is often no "correct" answer in spaces created by legal indeterminacy, then as long as a judge's race, gender, ethnicity, or sexual orientation informs her discretion without overriding her commitment to follow the law, respect process, and administer justice, diversity of perspective can help to keep the implicit biases of different perspectives in check.

Judge Pickering's scenario addresses the flip side of the same coin. A judge's political ideology can influence her decision-making to an even greater extent than her race or gender, but like the influence of gender or race, ideology furnishes neither a necessary nor manageable basis for disqualification in the adjudicative dimension.[17] The political dimension, in contrast, is unencumbered by the same constraints and is less concerned with ensuring litigants a fair hearing, than with preserving the public's confidence in the judiciary. Hence, the Senate may challenge the fitness of nominees in light of racial, gender, or ideological biases that would not call the judge's fitness into question in disqualification proceedings. For example, it is difficult to imagine that Justice Sotomayor would be disqualified from race and gender discrimination cases on the grounds that her impartiality might reasonably be questioned because she once said that her status as a Latina woman influences her decision-making.[18] And yet, in confirmation proceedings, the Senate devoted considerable attention to whether that very statement would undermine public confidence in her impartiality to an unacceptable degree.[19] The same point can be made of Judge Pickering: Ideological predilections that would have little bearing Pickering's impartiality in a disqualification setting, nonetheless called his impartiality into question during his Senate confirmation proceedings.

The Senate's rejection of Judge Pickering's nomination to the circuit court underscores how much ideological orientation has to do with whether a judge is "good enough" in the political dimension, where a nominee's fitness is measured with reference to whether the judge's views on legal issues are politically acceptable. In that setting, the judge who shares her views risks undermining her acceptability with the public and being rejected by the Senate for that reason. It is thus understandable that nominee Scalia declined to take public positions on issues he was likely to decide as a justice.

This is not to imply that in the political dimension of judicial oversight, the public is averse to judges sharing their views in principle. To the contrary, in state systems, surveys show that the public welcomes such information; and in the federal system, Senators relentlessly seek such information from the nominees. Moreover, the Court's bottom line in *White* is that in the context of judicial elections—the ultimate political dimension forum—there is no place for an "announce clause" barring judicial candidates from announcing their views, which is what candidates for elective office are expected to do. Rather, judicial candidates—like nominee Scalia—deflect inquiries into their views on issues likely to come before them for two reasons: (1) as a matter of strategy, because announcing one's views can antagonize ideological opponents in the political dimension; and (2) as a matter of principle, because judges are concerned that announcing their views could undermine a fair hearing for parties in the adjudicative dimension or undermine the appropriate role of a judge in the ethical dimension.

White can be faulted, not for its political dimension critique of the announce clause, but for its failure to appreciate that when judicial aspirants announce their views amid campaigns, it can have significant ripple effects in the adjudicative and ethical dimensions that ought to be weighed in the balance. Nominee Scalia was acutely sensitive to those ripple effects: An ethical judge should not announce his views in confirmation proceedings, he declared, because those views would be taken as a "condition" of his selection, to the detriment of his perceived impartiality with litigants. Because American judges are acculturated to view their roles from the perspective of the ethical and adjudicative dimensions, they continue to decline overtures to announce their views in judicial campaigns, notwithstanding their First Amendment right to do otherwise, which simultaneously avoids potentially tenure-threatening elaborations on their views in the political dimension. Perhaps as a consequence, the impact of *White* on judicial campaigns in the years since it was decided has been limited.[20]

Which brings us to the problem presented by *Twombly* and *Iqbal* (together *Twiqbal*) where the Supreme Court has infused the pleading process with new clout by enabling judges to dismiss complaints as soon as they are filed, if they do not allege a plausible claim—an assessment that the Court has instructed judges to make with reference to their "common sense" and "judicial experience."[21] By encouraging judges to make plausibility assessments prior to discovery, the Court has weakened a procedural impediment to premature judgment. Insofar as "plausibility is in the eye of the beholder,"[22] the new standard invites judges to act on their predispositions, and one recent study has confirmed that in race discrimination cases, there has been a statistically significant change in dismissal rates between black and white judges post-*Twiqbal*.[23]

The debate over pleading standards turns on the question of whether the need to curb the costs and delays of discovery (constraints under which the judiciary is subject in the adjudicative dimension) trump the benefits of protracting the litigation process to better guard against prejudgment and the perils of judges bringing their prejudices into play at the outset of the litigation. In *Twombly* and *Iqbal*, the Court answered that question in the affirmative. The implication underlying these decisions is not that impartiality is expendable, but that it is expensive, and that a pleading standard which tolerates a bit more prejudgment in exchange for a bit less cost and delay, yields a balance that is "good enough" for the adjudicative dimension.

The Supreme Court's conclusions in *Twiqbal* have generated significant intra-dimensional disagreement, with noted judges expressing concern that a plausibility standard invites premature decisions that undermine plaintiffs' right to a fair hearing in the adjudicative dimension. However, even to the extent that the independence-accountability balance *Twiqbal* strikes, by affording district judges greater discretion to act upon their "common sense" with reduced concern for circuit court reversal, is deemed acceptable in the adjudicative dimension, the political dimension is another story. As chapter 6 detailed, various legislators, interest groups, and pundits in the legal media have moved the fight to Congress, where they have sought to turn political dimension sentiment against *Twiqbal*.

Chapter 6 characterized *Twiqbal* as one in a series of developments in the political transformation of the American judiciary that comprise a generations-long trend toward intensified oversight of the courts in the political dimension. The bench and bar have decried "politicization" of the courts as deleterious to the rule of law paradigm it defends. But the legal culture paradigm I have proposed acknowledges the inevitability of extralegal influences on judicial decision-making—including "political" ones. To that extent, it recognizes the need for a more robust political dimension of oversight to manage judicial politics. This begs the ultimate question: Is the trend toward political dimension hegemony a good thing, or a bad thing?

THE LEGAL CULTURE PARADIGM
AS A PRESCRIPTIVE DEVICE

To this point in the book, the three-dimensional analysis of court oversight developed in preceding chapters has been descriptive or explanatory in its orientation. It has rationalized the perennial debate between judicial independence and accountability in terms of a tension in the oversight of the courts from the sometimes-competing perspectives of parties in an adjudicative dimension, public in a political dimension, and judges in an ethical dimension. Viewing oversight of the courts through that lens reveals long-term trends toward heightened activity in the political dimension that lies at the center of the political transformation I have described in this book.

This three-dimensional analysis, however, is not merely descriptive. It has normative underpinnings that can and should guide the course of court oversight in a legal culture paradigm. The starting point is with the three dimensions and their normative foundations.

The political dimension of oversight preserves and promotes the judiciary's institutional legitimacy within the ranks of the governed, or body politic. A representative democracy derives its authority to govern from the consent of the governed. As John Locke theorized, such consent is expressly given by those who form a new government and tacitly given by those in later generations who acquiesce to the government's authority in return for the benefits they derive.[24] Locke noted, however, that such consent is properly withdrawn when the institutions of government "act contrary to their trust," which will be so when they make themselves "masters or arbitrary disposers of the lives, liberties or fortunes of the people."[25] For Locke, this turn of events would trigger the people's right to rebel and form a new government.[26]

While Locke's body politic was confined to the propertied classes, Thomas Paine advocated a more egalitarian strain of representative democracy: "When a people agree to form themselves into a republic . . . it is understood that they mutually resolve and pledge themselves to each other, rich and poor alike, to support this rule of equal justice among them.[27]" Paine likewise emphasized that the legitimacy of a republic hinged on the public's continuing consent: "[T]here never can exist ... any generation of men, in any country, possessed of the right or the power of binding and controlling posterity to the *'end of time'*. . . . Every generation must be as free to act for itself, *in all cases*, as the ages and generation which preceded it."[28]

Paine's reboot of Locke exerted a profound influence on the framers of the US Constitution. James Madison characterized the Constitution as a "compact, express or implied," that "must be executed according to the forms and provisions specified in the compact" as long as it "remains undissolved."[29] But that compact is subject to dissolution: Madison explicitly acknowledged "the right of seceding from intolerable oppression," which "is another name only for revolution, about which there is no theoretic controversy."[30]

In a system of government that depends for its success and survival on the continuing consent of the governed, flagging public support for the institutions of government is a mark of dysfunction. Oversight of the courts in the political dimension can correct or avoid such dysfunction by striking an independence-accountability balance aimed at preserving the judiciary's legitimacy with the public. In that way, subjecting the judiciary to a system of political dimension oversight is democracy-enhancing. Moreover, preserving the courts' legitimacy with the body politic promotes a more efficacious administration of justice, insofar as the public is likelier to acquiesce peacefully to the adverse rulings of a judiciary it respects.[31]

Within the ethical dimension of judicial oversight, it is easy work to get from the descriptive to the normative. The ethical dimension regulates the instrumental values of good judging—capability, integrity, impartiality, and independence—from the perspective of judges who aspire to standards of conduct consistent with the Platonic ideal of their role. Those standards of conduct are tightly tethered to virtues widely shared and deeply embedded in western culture dating back to Aristotle— virtues that the ethical dimension seeks to promote. Lawrence Solum's virtue-centered theory of judging maps nicely onto the ethical dimension of oversight in ways that underscore the dimension's normative foundation. Solum identifies "thin" judicial virtues that correlate closely to the instrumental values of good judging that I have identified.[32] He contrasts "thick," justice-oriented virtues that correspond closely to the objectives of good judging that the instrumental values promote.[33] Hence, the ethical dimension does more than explain how judges and the judiciary regulate judicial conduct with reference to the norms of their roles—it furthers the good of virtuous judging.

The adjudicative dimension and its party-centric perspective aimed at affording litigants a fair hearing are imbued with due process values. I have previously identified fair process as an "objective" of good judging (together with upholding the law and the administration of justice). As an objective of good judging, affording litigants a fair process can be evaluated and regulated from the perspectives of the public (in the political dimension), judges (in the ethical dimension), or the parties themselves (in the adjudicative dimension). It is in the adjudicative dimension, however, where core due process values are implicated most directly, because due process rights are invoked by persons at risk of losing their life, liberty, or property to the state or federal governments. The persons at risk of losing their life, liberty, or property in judicial proceedings are parties to adjudication. And the normative significance of affording parties due process in judicial proceedings is entrenched in western culture dating back at least as far as the Magna Carta.[34]

In short, the political, ethical, and adjudicative dimensions of judicial oversight are imbued with normative significance. They embrace the values of institutional legitimacy, civic virtue, and due process, respectively, and I make no claim to priority among them. For the most part, systems of regulation in each dimension are mutually compatible. For example, judges who fix cases in exchange for bribes threaten all three core values and may be impeached in the political dimension, disciplined in the ethical dimension, and reversed (and their orders voided) in the adjudicative dimension, without cross-dimensional stress.

As elaborated in chapter 6, however, oversight that promotes core values in one dimension can be in tension with core values in another. To the extent that the core values each dimension promotes are values worth preserving, maintaining a balance between dimensions that protects each from unwarranted encroachment or diminution by the others is desirable. Whether a given dimension's oversight is insufficient, appropriate, or excessive, should be assessed in relation to that dimension's oversight objectives and its impact on oversight in the other dimensions.

Viewed in this light, the political transformation of the American judiciary, in which oversight in the political dimension has sometimes supplanted oversight in the adjudicative and ethical dimensions, is troubling to the extent it seeks to promote legitimacy values at the expense of virtue and process values. Insofar as political dimension hegemony is undesirable, the question becomes how to restore inter-dimensional balance.

I propose three strategies to restore such balance—education, reclamation, and moderation. I do so with a mindset that is both hopelessly pessimistic and irrepressibly optimistic. Chapter 2 ended by linking the political transformation of the American judiciary it described to powerful sociopolitical currents that have polarized American law and politics, and cultivated in the public a burgeoning, generations-long antipathy toward the role of government in American life. To the extent that arresting or reversing trends within the judiciary turns on arresting or reversing these deeper sociopolitical currents, the strategies I recommend may well be futile. At the same time, an understated but recurring theme of this book is that the judiciary is different from the other branches of government. It is different because the judiciary is peopled with lawyers whose partisan political impulses are tempered by an acculturated respect for legal norms. It is different because good judges strive to preserve their impartiality by disregarding (or at least distancing themselves from) the public's polarized political preferences. It is different because legislatures and the people they serve have afforded judges a traditional measure of independence from partisan political control that they have not extended to public officials in the executive and legislative branches. And it is different because the judiciary enjoys significantly more public support than the "political" branches, despite signs that such support is weakening. Because of these differences, there is room for optimism that the public and its elected representatives will be receptive to arguments that we can return some self-regulatory control to the judiciary in the adjudicative and ethical dimensions of oversight, provided that oversight in the political dimension remains vigilant.

Education

Restoring balance across the adjudicative, ethical, and political dimensions of oversight begins with making the transition from a rule of law paradigm to a legal culture paradigm. Excessive oversight in the political dimension is attributable in large part to the rule of law paradigm and its counterfactual premise that independent judges disregard extralegal influences and follow the law. If good judges are impervious to extralegal influences, as the rule of law paradigm posits, then evidence of such influences (e.g., data showing the correlation between justice ideology and case outcomes) can be interpreted as evidence of independent judges gone rogue—a legitimate cause for public concern that the political dimension of oversight is uniquely suited to address.

The legal culture paradigm, in contrast, proceeds from the premise that judicial independence furthers law, process, and justice objectives that judges are acculturated to take seriously, notwithstanding extralegal influences made inevitable by legal indeterminacy. Because independence can liberate judges to disregard law, process, and justice objectives, the legal culture paradigm contemplates a political dimension of oversight that will curb such excesses and preserve the judiciary's institutional legitimacy with the public that judges serve. But the presence of extralegal influences, by themselves, neither undermines the justification for judicial independence (as it does under the rule of law paradigm) nor triggers a need for heightened oversight in the political dimension.

Hence, transitioning from a rule of law paradigm to a legal culture paradigm will move the inevitability of extralegal influence on judicial decision-making in difficult cases from cause for alarm to business as usual, and so diminish the perceived need for an aggressive political dimension response. Making that transition, however, will require re-education within and without the legal community.

Making the jump to a legal culture paradigm logically begins in law schools, where future lawyers, judges, and (many) lawmakers are first exposed to the way lawyers and judges think. Policy analysis, in which students are called upon to resolve difficult legal questions with reference to competing policy concerns—is already a fixture of legal education.[35] No thoughtful law professor or student thinks that judges can or do decide indeterminate questions of law with exclusive recourse to legal texts, unaided by reference to underling legal policy.

Legal education's fixation on teaching students to "think like a lawyer," however, tends to constrain how policy analysis is taught. Students learn to make competing policy arguments grounded in law and legal policy while cast in roles as lawyers for their respective clients. Judith Wegner, relying on comprehensive survey and interview data from seventeen law schools, reported that many law professors exhibit a "reticence to engage with value judgments and norms that are embedded deeply in the fabric of law."[36] Hence, "[s]trikingly, few faculty spoke of 'justice' and the need to discuss it."[37] As one faculty respondent explained, students "must see the strength and weaknesses of cases versus morality, yet, in practice, litigation pushes them away from this objectivity toward adopting a role as the client's agent."[38] Another respondent added that "some students give just political analysis. They get a lower grade. They need to do legal analysis."[39] Although the policy-laden nature of judicial decision-making "open[s] the way for conversation about values associated with judicial decisions," Wegner concludes that "faculty often seem to gloss over" that conversation, which "leave[s] the impression that students' values should be checked at the door."[40]

In short, law students are trained to make policy arguments to courts and are acculturated to accept that judges are influenced by such arguments. Aspiring lawyers are not stupid. They know that competing values underlie those policy arguments, and that legal and extralegal factors influence which values and corresponding policy arguments a given judge will find most persuasive. In other words, the legal culture paradigm's core premise—that judges have been trained to follow the law, respect applicable process, and do justice—is intuitive to anyone who has survived law school, as is the complementary premise that extralegal factors (including, but not limited to, public policy considerations) can influence the outcomes of indeterminate cases. That said, law school classes rarely discuss what social science teaches about the factors that actually influence judicial decision-making, or how those factors relate to the trifold mission of the courts to uphold the law, adhere to legal process, and administer justice. As a consequence, law school has a left a gap in students' legal education on the goals and empirics of judging that under-prepares them to assume the role of good judges committed to law, process, and justice.

I do not propose to revolutionize legal education. Rather, I recommend a modest addendum to traditional lines of inquiry in the ubiquitous, quasi-Socratic dialogues that dominate law school pedagogy. In law school classes, students are routinely called upon to unpack the cases they read by summarizing the pertinent facts, isolating the relevant legal issue, and identifying the applicable legal rule before analyzing how the court applies that rule to resolve the underlying legal issue. To that end, faculty typically adduce competing arguments and their policy implications. Professors often invite students to comment on which argument they find more persuasive, and whether the court's legal conclusion was right. To this ritualized dance, I would add a final step: How should the judge decide which choice to make when the law's application to a given set of facts is unclear and she is called upon to exercise discretion or judgment? Within the confines of a legal culture paradigm, this inquiry should elicit a conversation about the interplay between law and justice, and what justice requires in the context of a given case (which opens the door to discussing different theories of justice and decision-making). And it can elucidate the legal and extralegal influences, informed by social science, to which a judge's case-specific conceptions of law and justice are subject, when such influences are salutary, when they are tolerable, and when they are undesirable.

Exposing law students to social science data detailing the legal and extralegal influences on judicial decision-making, as a smaller part of the policy-analysis training that law students receive every day, would be a modest but important reform. From a purely practical standpoint, this additional component would equip students more systematically with information that good litigators gain haphazardly from experience. Recall the Supreme Court forecasting project, discussed in chapter 3.[41] The authors there reported that experienced Supreme Court litigators bested academics and the computer model in predicting case outcomes, which at least suggests that the litigators involved had become quite adept at identifying the legal and extralegal factors likely to influence the Justices' decisions.[42] The sampling of litigators was too small for the researchers to draw firm conclusions as to their performance vis-à-vis other forecasters in the study, but it is at least suggestive. In short, aspiring lawyers are trained to make policy arguments designed to influence judges in close cases; knowing what social science tells us about which judges are likely to find what policy arguments more persuasive, promotes effective lawyering.

More broadly, incorporating a small social science component into the law school curriculum provides the next generation of the legal community with a way of looking at what judges do that better equips it to manage judicial politics more effectively and to push back against unwarranted political dimension incursions on judicial autonomy. By tethering a conversation about legal and extralegal influences to varying conceptions of law and justice, the proposed reform reinforces a core tenet of the legal culture paradigm: that independence enables judges to further law, process, and justice objectives despite—and sometimes because of—extralegal influences. It furnishes aspiring lawyers with the analytical tools to differentiate between acceptable influences that further law, process, and justice objectives, and unacceptable influences that do not. And to the extent that influences traditionally characterized as extralegal are integral to divining just answers to indeterminate legal questions, it illuminates a relationship between the legal and extralegal, between law and policy, that diminishes the sharpness of this often-false dichotomy— a result compatible with the ethos of the legal culture paradigm.

One quick example: Consider the role of race and gender in judicial decision-making. On the one hand, a judge's race and gender contribute to his or her life experience that can inform judicial discretion in salutary ways, by enabling judges to better understand the circumstances of parties with common experience and convey that understanding to fellow judges, to the ultimate end of promoting just decision-making. On the other hand, a judge's race and gender can bias his or her judgment in deleterious ways, as the social science of implicit bias shows. Moreover, when it comes to implicit bias, forewarned is, to no small extent, forearmed: Future judges who are predisposed to embrace the comfortable default position that race and gender are irrelevant to them and their decision-making are better equipped to counteract their own implicit biases if they are made aware of such biases and familiarized with the corresponding coping strategies.[43] A classroom conversation about the relationship between race, gender, judicial decision-making, and justice, informed by the operative social science, can thus promote a deeper understanding of how to manage legal indeterminacy in a legal culture paradigm.

When court defenders advocate education about judges and courts, they usually mean educating the general public, not themselves. A widely shared sentiment, spoken as a kind of mantra, is that ignorance is to blame for the rule of law paradigm's failure to gain traction with average Americans, who do not understand or respect the courts' counter-majoritarian role. "When I was a sprat," the aging lawyer creaks, "they taught civics in public schools!"—*shakes fist.* To support the claim that the public is woefully under-informed, speakers often allude to surveys, showing that high percentages of the public cannot identify justices on the Supreme Court, the three branches of government, and so on.[44] Some scholars have pushed back, showing that such surveys are methodologically flawed, and presenting survey data of their own, finding that the public is not as badly informed as the legal community claims.[45]

Far be it from me to fling myself in the way of proposals to reinvigorate civics education in elementary and secondary schools. Advocating more education is like endorsing puppies, pie, or the eradication of disfiguring disease, where opposition, if any, will be limited to misanthropes and trolls. When it comes to the public's suspicion that independent judges often do more and less than follow the law when deciding cases, however, the "problem" is not that the public is ignorant. To the contrary, the public's suspicion is corroborated by social science data. The problem is that the legal community is marketing a paradigm that disavows extralegal influences—influences it characterizes as anathema to the rule of law. In recent generations, the public shows signs of growing impatient with such counterfactual claims and has turned to the political dimension of judicial oversight to control extralegal influences.

Regardless of whether reformers revitalize civics education, judges have other opportunities for public education and interaction: School children visit courthouses, and judges visit schools. Judges meet with legislators and testify before legislative committees. They address civic, charitable, and fraternal organizations. They speak with jurors about the role of judges and courts before jurors are impaneled and often speak with them again after they have reached a verdict. In addition, the virtual world generally and social media, in particular, offer vast, if uncertain opportunities for public interaction.

Codes of judicial conduct actively encourage judges to engage in outreach,[46] which affords judges ample opportunity to speak with the public about what judges do, in terms that can ease the transition to a legal culture paradigm. At a program where I suggested that judges be more open about the discretion and judgment they exercise in their conversations with the public, one judge commented afterward that that was like "asking Lenin to embrace capitalism." I do not, however, propose that judges describe themselves as policymakers, discuss the role ideology plays in their decision-making, or talk about how their race, ethnicity, gender, socioeconomic status, emotions, or other extralegal factors influence their choices in specific ways. In a legal culture paradigm, judges are acculturated to take law, process, and justice so seriously that such influences do not usually insinuate themselves consciously, and calling upon judges to discuss their subconscious influences seems destined to end badly for all but the few who are immersed in the social science data themselves.

Rather, the revised talking points that I propose for judges who engage in community outreach are neither controversial nor problematic:

- Discuss the qualities a good judge should possess—being capable, honest, impartial, and independent—and the relationship of those qualities to the objectives of good judging: giving parties their day in court, following the facts and law, and rendering justice.
- Explain how it works in easy cases, when the facts and law are clear, the correct result is clear, and the need for judges to be buffered from outside influences that could contort that result is obvious.
- Explain how it works in hard cases, when the facts or law are unclear, as is the "right" result, which requires judges to exercise judgment or discretion to determine the outcome that is best or just under the circumstances. Such explanations need not be confined to extrajudicial settings. For example, one scholar has recommended that judges limit recourse to the "rhetoric of constitutional absolutism" in difficult cases and strike a more conciliatory tone with dissenting arguments, thereby dispensing with the implausible pretense of legal certitude that only diminishes the judiciary's legitimacy.[47]
- Discuss how judges decide questions where the exercise of judgment or discretion is necessary, for example, when they: impose a sentence on a convicted criminal defendant; decide which parent will receive custody of the children in a divorce proceeding; grant a new trial in a civil action; or parse the meaning of an ambiguous statute or ordinance.
- Illustrate how judges use their discretion and judgment to achieve just results in such cases. For example, when deciding what the appropriate sentence should be for defendant X in a difficult criminal case, what constraints were imposed by law? By sentencing guidelines? By past practice? Within those constraints, what factors struck the judge as mitigating? Aggravating? A careful listener might detect an ideological orientation to the factors the judge identifies. For example, liberal judges may be more

concerned about the defendant's background; conservatives may be more attentive to victim impact. But the overriding point is that despite such differences, both judges are seeking to administer justice under law.

- Emphasize why it is important to insulate judges from outside threats, blandishments, or political pressures that could subvert case-sensitive discretion and judgment that judges are uniquely positioned to exercise by virtue of their familiarity with the applicable facts and law that outsiders lack.
- Explain why this makes judges different from other public officials, like legislators, who are not expected to be impartial or independent in the same way and are not called upon to divine and apply existing law on a fact-driven, case-by-case basis.
- Talk about the institutional safeguards against independence run amok: a judge's acculturation to law and the judicial process; her oath of office; juries; appellate review; lawmaking processes (including constitutional amendments and statutory overrides); codes of conduct; judicial discipline; and removal mechanisms.

Candid conversations that follow this template quietly reveal the ways in which judges bring their backgrounds and experience to bear in making "judgment calls" to the end of showing how judges administer justice worth protecting against excessive political dimension incursions. At the same time, those conversations reveal how the adjudicatory, ethical, and political dimensions keep judicial excesses in check, in ways that justify continued public support.

Reclamation

The tri-dimensional analysis I have provided proceeds from the premise that the same problems may be viewed and regulated in different ways. Education, as described in the preceding section, encourages judges to enter the political dimension themselves, for the purpose of engaging the public in conversations about the complexities of good judging. One piece of that mission is to explain how judges oversee themselves and the judicial process in the ethical and adjudicative dimensions, and why such oversight deserves public support and confidence. Moreover, such outreach enables judges to highlight circumstances in which oversight in the adjudicative and ethical dimensions is preferable to regulation in the political dimension, which will be so when unnecessarily heavy-handed political dimension controls jeopardize values (virtuous judging and due process) that the other dimensions promote.

Ongoing outreach and education can then be paired with more aggressive oversight in the adjudicative and ethical dimensions aimed at
reclaiming turf ceded to the political. This is not a novel strategy. The Judicial Conference of the United States has proved itself adept at thwarting
what it regards as unduly aggressive congressional incursions, through
heightened self-regulation.

In 1990, for example, the Judicial Conference avoided a showdown
with Congress over the judiciary's long-standing opposition to permitting
cameras in federal courtrooms, by instituting a three-year pilot project.[48]
The pilot project gambit rendered the judiciary's proceedings more trans-
parent to the public, thus giving Congress a political dimension "win." But
the judiciary retained control over the project's scope, implementation,
and duration, thereby enabling it to regulate its adjudicative dimension
concerns over the impact of televised proceedings on parties, witnesses,
jurors, and court decorum.

In 2000, bills were introduced in Congress to prohibit judges from
participating in expense-paid educational seminars sponsored by corporations with business before the courts.[49] Federal judges and the
Judicial Conference opposed such legislation as an affront to the separation of powers, their freedom of speech and association, and their
independence—but ultimately revised an ethical ruling to impose significant restrictions on judicial attendance at expense-paid seminars. In response, congressional sponsors discontinued their quest for legislation.[50]

In 2006, members of Congress, dissatisfied with what they perceived
as the judiciary's failure to discipline judges in high-profile cases, proposed to create an office of inspector general within the federal judiciary
and initiated an impeachment inquiry into the conduct of a judge whose
disciplinary proceeding was pending.[51] The Judicial Conference objected
to the inspector-general proposal as a threat to its independence[52] but re-
vamped its disciplinary process,[53] which it acknowledged could stand improvement in high-profile cases, and the bill was never adopted.[54]

The thrust in each of these three instances has been to blunt a political dimension initiative by substituting a proposal within the judiciary's
control in the ethical or procedural dimensions that addressed political
dimension problems, and effectively reclaimed regulatory control. When
such reclamation efforts have failed, it is because they have been perceived
as not taking political dimension concerns seriously enough. For example, in 1990, Congress enacted the Civil Justice Reform Act, which called
upon each federal judicial district to develop civil litigation expense and
delay reduction plans. It did so over the objections of the Judicial Conference, which proposed a fourteen-point, Conference-implemented
plan in its stead. Bill sponsor and Senate Judiciary Chairman Joseph

Biden explained what he regarded as the inadequacies of the Judicial Conference plan:

> We need this legislation to establish a statutory national policy for addressing the problems of litigation costs and delay, to set forth specific cost and delay reduction techniques, and to ensure the implementation of court-developed plans according to certain, yet reasonable, timetables. These things are all missing from the Conference's 14 Points, and as a result I find the Conference's proposal wholly inadequate.[55]

These comments followed negotiations between the Judicial Conference and the Senate Judiciary Committee, in which the Conference ultimately opposed the legislation on the recommendation of a different Conference Committee than the one with whom the Conference had asked the Senate Judiciary Committee to negotiate. The Senate Judiciary Committee perceived such tactics as dilatory and sharply rebuked the Conference in its Committee Report:

> Such actions only serve to undermine the cooperative relationship between Congress and the judicial branch that our citizens rightly expect and deserve. It is the committee's hope—and, indeed, its expectation—that this troubling process will not recur.[56]

Congress subsequently enacted the Civil Justice Reform Act over the Judicial Conference's objections.

The particular opportunities for the judiciary, operating within the adjudicative and ethical dimensions of oversight, to reclaim turf ceded to the political, will vary with the times and circumstances. Three illustrative possibilities of current relevance include: (1) pleading standards; (2) Supreme Court ethics; and (3) judicial disqualification.

Pleading Standards

When it comes to authority to create or amend Federal Rules of Civil Procedure generally and pleading rules, in particular, the Rules Enabling Act has awarded joint custody to Congress and the judiciary.[57] Congress remains free to enact rules of practice and procedure, but the Rules Enabling Act authorizes the federal judiciary to promulgate rules of its own, subject to congressional override.

In *Twombly* and *Iqbal* the Supreme Court revised its interpretation of an existing rule to require that complaints articulate a claim that the district judge deems plausible, if they are to survive a motion to dismiss.[58] The Court decided those cases in the adjudicative dimension, insofar as it was interpreting rules of procedure from the perspective of parties to litigation, and their respective rights and responsibilities. But the furor that followed threatens to bleed into the political dimension in two ways. First, members of Congress, mostly progressives, concerned that *Twiqbal* curtailed access to courts to the detriment of public confidence, introduced legislation to overturn *Twombly* and *Iqbal* by amending procedural rules directly, bypassing the Rules Enabling Act process that delegates primary responsibility for rule reform to the courts in the adjudicative dimension.[59] *Twiqbal* beneficiaries, mostly businesses with the support of political conservatives, like the National Association of Manufacturers, launched campaigns against the legislation.[60] Second, directing district judges to dismiss civil claims they regard as implausible before any facts have been adduced through discovery, creates a new avenue of inquiry in Senate district court confirmation proceedings, namely: the extralegal underpinnings of the nominee's "common sense" and "judicial experience," that *Twiqbal* directs judges to bring to bear when deciding whether a complaint is plausible.

A book of this kind is no place to discuss the minutia of draft legislation or proposed rule reforms. Suffice it to say that there are at least two ways in which courts might recapture the initiative. First, the Supreme and inferior courts could sand the edges of *Twiqbal* to moderate its impact in ways that address emerging political dimension concerns. *Twiqbal* is arguably in tension with a prior line of cases. In that prior line, the Supreme Court was asked to interpret a rule which requires the plaintiff's complaint to include a "short, plain statement showing that the pleader is entitled to relief" to survive a motion to dismiss. The Court adopted a literal reading of that rule, and rejected lower court attempts to require greater specificity in pleading such cases.[61] To the extent that the added specificity this line of cases rejects is what renders a short, plain statement of the claim more "plausible" under *Twiqbal*, the potential for friction is clear. A Court responsive to the access concerns that have piqued political dimension interest could blunt the thrust of *Twiqbal*'s plausibility requirement by diminishing or rejecting defendants' demands for particulars at odds with the "short, plain statement" requirement that plaintiffs often cannot supply prior to discovery (because such particulars are within the defendant's exclusive control).

Second, the Judicial Conference could ameliorate the access problems created by a plausibility requirement, through rulemaking. A rule overturning *Twiqbal* directly seems unlikely, insofar as the Rules Enabling Act provides that any rule the Conference promulgates is ultimately prescribed by the Supreme Court, which is to say the Court that issued *Twombly* and followed it with *Iqbal*.[62] But the Judicial Conference could explore alternative ways to address the underlying problem that animated the Court's decision in *Twombly*, namely, the infliction of high discovery costs on defendants in marginal cases. For example, when a complaint states a claim that the district judge deems possible (because it includes allegations that, if true, would give rise to a legal claim) but not plausible (because the judge regards an allegation as too conclusory to sustain the inference that plaintiff draws), a new rule could authorize a truncated period of discovery for the limited purpose of enabling the plaintiff to seek the information it needs to make its conclusory allegations sufficiently concrete.[63] If the plaintiff's efforts bear fruit, the motion to dismiss will be denied, the defendant will be directed to file its answer (possibly after the plaintiff files an amended complaint to substitute more concrete allegations), and the case will proceed to full discovery; if not, the motion to dismiss (possibly redesignated as a motion for summary judgment) will be granted. Existing electronic discovery rules take a similar approach, by enabling district judges to order a discovery "sampling" of applicable databases before deciding whether a more extensive and expensive search is warranted.[64] In this way, the plausibility standard could be retained without closing the courthouse doors on plaintiffs before giving them access to information within the defendant's control that is essential to fleshing out their claims.

Supreme Court Ethics

Ethics and the Supreme Court is another issue area where emerging political dimension interest and oversight can be reclaimed by the Court itself in the ethical dimension. In his 2011 annual report on the federal judiciary, Chief Justice Roberts rejected calls for the Supreme Court to adopt a code of conduct, in terms that seemed strangely insensitive to the political dimension concerns that animated them.[65] The Chief Justice explained that adopting a code was unnecessary because the Court's justices already "consult" the Code of Conduct applicable to lower federal court judges[66]—a point that is oddly sophistic, inasmuch as consulting a Code and agreeing to abide by it are two different things. The Chief Justice attributed calls for the Court to adopt the Judicial Conference's Code of Conduct to "common misconceptions" born of ignorance to the facts that the Court fell outside Conference jurisdiction, and that the Conference's Code did not address ethical questions unique to the Supreme Court.[67] Such a point begs the question of why the Supreme Court of the United States is loath to use an existing code as a model that it modifies to suit its needs and adopts as its own, as all fifty state supreme courts and the lower federal courts have done. Finally, the Chief Justice noted that the justices already acquiesce to ethics legislation imposing financial reporting requirements, limits on gifts and outside income, and disqualification standards, even though (a point he made twice, seemingly as a warning to the pushy) the "Court has never addressed whether Congress may impose these requirements."[68]

In addition to the issues raised by the Chief Justice, arguments over whether the Supreme Court should adopt a code of conduct can devolve into philosophical disquisitions on whether the Court can bind itself to an unenforceable code, given that code violations would not be subject to the disciplinary process, which is applicable only to judges in lower courts.[69] But all these arguments miss the point. When the highest court in the land is the only court in the land that is not subject to a code of conduct, adopting such a code can have symbolic significance for the body politic. Conversely, resisting calls to embrace a code through resort to defensive-seeming arguments has symbolic significance too. Unsurprisingly, perhaps, interest groups and legislators have made an issue of the Court's refusal to adopt a code and girded their loins for battle in the political dimension.[70]

It is understandable that the Court would not relent and adopt a code in the midst of active conflict, for fear of appearing to succumb to political pressure. But during an intervening period of calm, the Court could recapture the high ground in the ethical dimension, by quietly appointing a committee to study the Code and recommend changes for the Court to adopt. By tailoring a code to address the unique ethical landscape in which Supreme Court justices operate, the project could offer more concrete guidance to the justices and avoid unnecessary misunderstandings in the political dimension. For example, interest groups have criticized Justices Scalia and Thomas for serving as keynote speakers at events sponsored by the Federalist Society, because the Judicial Conference-promulgated Code prohibits such activities to the extent that the underlying events qualify as fundraisers.[71] Given the unique role of the Supreme Court in American government, there may be a reason to enable, if not encourage justices to speak on questions of law, the legal system, and the administration of justice, at events of this kind—a point not lost on the American Bar Association, whose 2007 Model Code of Judicial Conduct permits the practice.[72] Were the Supreme Court to adopt a code that cribbed from the American Bar Association Model on this particular, it could resolve uncertainty and quiet unnecessary criticism.

Disqualification

In the normal course, disqualification rules are brought to bear in the adjudicative dimension, for the benefit of parties who have reason to doubt the impartiality of their assigned judge, or in more egregious cases in the ethical dimension, where judges are called to task in disciplinary proceedings for willful failure to abide by disqualification rules. When disqualification issues spill over into the political dimension, it signals a matter of greater public concern. And as described in chapter 2, such spillover has become increasingly common. Disqualification (or non-disqualification) has been the focus of news stories, congressional hearings, protracted American Bar Association commission activity, and a widely publicized Supreme Court case.[73]

There are at least two illustrative avenues for judicial reclamation in the disqualification arena. First, in response to the flagship issue of judicial campaign finance, state supreme courts can promulgate rules that regulate judges who receive campaign support from lawyers, litigants, and their proxies. In *Caperton*, the Supreme Court all but invited the states to eliminate future Supreme Court intrusions upon state judicial disqualification, by formulating rules more rigorous than due process requires that disqualify judges from hearing cases in which they have received campaign support from lawyers or litigants who appear before them, in amounts sufficient to call their impartiality into question. Devising clear rules governing disqualification for campaign support signals the judiciary's attentiveness to the underlying problems that have piqued public interest and has the potential to diminish the frequency with which those problems recur.

Second, state supreme courts can develop procedures for judges within their jurisdictions that signal their intention to take disqualification more seriously. In the normal course of litigation, when a party makes a request to, say, dismiss a case, compel discovery, or impose sanctions for litigation misconduct, the requesting party files a motion, the opposing party files a memorandum in opposition to the motion, and the matter is scheduled for a hearing, after which the court issues a ruling accompanied by an explanation. With a request to disqualify, in contrast, such processes are not routinely applied: Opposing parties often remain silent, or detached; hearings are rarely scheduled; and rulings are usually unaccompanied by an explanation unless the request is denied. Judges often take umbrage at challenges to their impartiality, or marginalize them as strategically motivated; hence, such challenges are addressed quickly, quietly and less formally.

At least as problematic as truncated process is the practice of judges ruling on their own impartiality. English common law dating back to 1609 (and American constitutional law dating to 1927) has declared that no one may be a judge in his own case.[74] Oddly, however, the prevailing practice is to disregard this principle when it comes to the disqualification process: If a party alleges that his assigned judge is too conflicted or biased to be impartial, the issue is ordinarily decided by the judge who is allegedly too conflicted or biased to be impartial.

In a legal culture paradigm, imperfect impartiality is not an embarrassment to be ignored or trivialized, but a chronic condition to be managed. Subjecting disqualification proceedings to the standard rigors of the adversarial legal process seems an obvious way for the judiciary to retake the initiative in regulating an increasingly visible problem. In addition, courts can adopt procedures that reduce reliance on judicial self-assessment in disqualification proceedings (as many jurisdictions already do) by: providing for the transfer of disqualification petitions to a different judge; authorizing automatic, one-time requests for the substitution of a new judge; or adopting a less deferential standard of appellate review over non-disqualification rulings by the target judge.

Moderation

The Greek poet Hesiod is often credited as the first to advocate moderation in all things. Moderation is key to the art of compromise between extreme alternatives, but critics have faulted this kind of moderation when compromise is pursued at the expense of what is right. As presidential candidate (and Republican Senator) Barry Goldwater declared, "[E]xtremism in the defense of liberty is no vice! And . . . moderation in the pursuit of justice is no virtue!"[75]

Here, however, the moderation I advocate is not of this procedural strain but is more deeply substantive: Moderating cross-dimensional impacts is good because it is right. It is right for reasons previously explained: Each dimension of judicial oversight promotes a distinct value worth protecting, and protecting those values requires that no one value be pursued to an excess that disables the others. When aggressively promoting a given value in its corresponding dimension works no hardship upon other values promoted by other dimensions, all is well. When, however, one value is protected at the expense of another, the need for inter-dimensional moderation comes into play. Two problem areas, where moderation might fruitfully be brought to bear, are judicial selection and judicial speech.

Judicial Selection

The judicial selection debate is starkly binary. On one side are proponents of contested elections, who typically proceed from a simple premise: Judges are policymakers in robes who should be accountable to the people they serve.[76] From that premise, a syllogism follows: Unelected judges are unaccountable policymakers; unaccountable policymakers flout the rule of law and the will of the people; therefore, unelected judges flout the rule of law and the will of the people. Conclusion: Judges should be elected. Proponents of appointed judiciaries proceed from an opposing premise: Judges do not make the rules but apply them and should decide cases independently of those, including voters, who could interfere with their impartial judgment.[77] From there, the argument for an appointed judiciary is reducible to a competing syllogism: Judges must be independent of the electorate to uphold the rule of law and fulfill their constitutional role; elected judges are not independent of the electorate; therefore, elected judges do not uphold the rule of law and fulfill their constitutional role. Conclusion: Judges should be appointed.

As discussed in chapter 5, the argument in support of elected judiciaries is grounded primarily in the political dimension of judicial oversight: Elections are legitimacy-enhancing ways to hold judges accountable to the people they serve. The argument against elected judiciaries is grounded primarily in the adjudicative dimension: Judges who are accountable to voters lack the independence needed to ensure litigants a fair hearing.

Each argument seeks to further the value (institutional legitimacy or due process) that animates oversight in its corresponding dimension. At the same time, both arguments rest on exaggerated empirical premises. The truth reflected in the empirical work summarized in chapter 3 lies between claims that judges are policymakers in robes who are indifferent to law, and automatons who slavishly follow the law and nothing else. If we acknowledge that these competing arguments each seek to promote values that the legal culture paradigm holds dear, and that empirical truth lies between their competing premises, the virtue of a moderated approach becomes clear.

A moderated approach moves the debate away from one-size-fits-all arguments in which disputants assume that what is best for Massachusetts must be best for Mississippi. It moves the debate toward a middle position, in which the operative question focuses on what the optimal independence-accountability blend should be for a given jurisdiction at a given time. Jurisdictions where the public's first concern is with judges going rogue may favor robust, accountability-enhancing, legitimacy-promoting oversight via contested elections in the political dimension. Jurisdictions where the public's first concern is with judges under the thumb of legislatures, interest groups, campaign supporters, or the voters themselves, may favor independence-enhancing, due-process-promoting appointive systems that protect litigants from encroachments on their right to a fair hearing in the adjudicative dimension.

Such an approach explains why consensus across state systems is (and perhaps should be) unachievable, why occasional periods of sweeping transition from one selection system to another are inevitable when first concerns shift, and why, outside of those periods of transition, agitation for sweeping transition is fruitless. It likewise argues in favor of reform at the margins. During periods when the political will for system-changing reform is lacking, emerging concerns that oversight in one dimension has encroached on core values promoted by another dimension, can be addressed incrementally.

Insofar as the new politics of contested judicial elections in the political dimension are thought to encroach on the rights of parties to a fair hearing in the adjudicative dimension of a given jurisdiction, the perceived problem is threefold: (1) re-selection processes can punish judges for unpopular decisions; (2) privately financed judicial campaigns can render judicial candidates dependent on their supporters; and (3) candidate pre-commitments to decide future cases in specified ways can compromise future impartiality. Each of these three problems can be addressed incrementally:[78] Re-selection reforms could include lengthening judicial terms to diminish the frequency of the re-selection threat, or limiting judicial tenure to a single, lengthy term. Campaign finance reforms could include more stringent disclosure rules, contribution limits, and disqualification procedures.[79] Pre-commitment reforms could include enforcing existing ethics rules that prohibit pledges, promises, and commitments by judicial candidates, and promulgating rules that disqualify judges from cases in which they have made prior commitments.

Conversely, when appointive systems are thought to render judges insufficiently accountable, other incremental reforms are available. Some states prepare and publish detailed judicial performance evaluations.[80] While such evaluations are often prepared in anticipation of retention elections in "merit selection" systems, judges may wish to avoid the adverse publicity associated with a negative evaluation even when no election is impending.[81] Alternatively, states could do more to showcase disciplinary processes, which can include discipline imposed for abuses of judicial power.[82]

Judicial Speech

Codes of judicial conduct have prohibited judges (and judicial candidates) from announcing their views, making pledges, promises, or commitments in connection with cases likely to come before them, commenting publicly on pending and impending cases, and engaging in other forms of judicial, extrajudicial, and political speech and expressive activity deemed deleterious to judicial impartiality, independence, and integrity. Within the political dimension there has been agitation for more speech, rather than less, to the end of better informing the body politic, often on matters relevant to voters in judicial elections. Survey data suggest that the public welcomes judges and judicial candidates announcing their views, taking positions, and even making promises.[83] For its part, the Supreme Court has subjected code of conduct rules that restrict the speech of judicial candidates, to an unyielding strict scrutiny, and sometimes invalidated them on First Amendment grounds.[84]

Within the ethical dimension, however, self-censorship remains a defining quality of a good judge. Even though the Model Code of Judicial Conduct would seem to tolerate a judge's public comments on pending or impending cases if they cannot "reasonably be expected to affect the outcome or impair the fairness" of a pending or impending proceeding,[85] the ethical dimension ethos errs on the side of silence. As New York's Chief Judge Judith Kaye put it, judges must "stay out of the fray. . . . They rely on their decisions, whether written or oral, to speak for themselves."[86] In a similar vein, despite a 2002 Supreme Court holding that judges and judicial candidates have a First Amendment right to announce their views on issues that may come before them, judges have resisted calls for them to exercise that right, and the impact of that ruling on judicial campaigns has been negligible.[87]

A moderated view between these extremes would strike a balance consistent with the dominant themes of this book. For generations, if not centuries, judges have found safety in silence, but the political transformation I have described here renders the persistence of such an approach perilous. Transition from the eroding rule of law paradigm to the legal culture paradigm I propose requires judges to abdicate their vow of silence and explain themselves and their roles more fully to the body politic. Hence, my education recommendation is that judges get out there and speak more openly about what they do.

At the same time, speaking freely to the end of reassuring an inquiring public can extract a high toll on litigants whose cases judges adjudicate. To the extent judges make public statements that toxify juries in pending cases, or that pre-commit judges to reach conclusions in future cases they cannot reconsider in light of applicable facts and law without losing face or tenure, litigants' opportunity for a fair hearing in the adjudicative dimension is compromised.

Between unfiltered exposition in the political dimension, and taciturn retreat in the ethical dimension, lies a cautious middle position that allows for judges to speak more openly, subject to limitations dictated by the rights of litigants in the adjudicative dimension. Achieving this middle position will require judges in the ethical dimension to relax rules that restrict judicial speech in ways that are unnecessary to preserve a fair and impartial forum for litigants.[88] And it would be aided by the Supreme Court subjecting rules that restrict judge and judicial candidate speech in ways reasonably calculated to preserve an impartial forum for litigants to "exacting" scrutiny that is a bit more accommodating.[89]

CONCLUSION

The plethora of claims that the American judiciary is in a state of crisis is overblown. A capable and qualified judicial workforce continues to adjudicate cases filed in state and federal courts, without interruption. There are no signs that an angry public is poised to rise up and defy court rulings, strangle court budgets, or topple the administration of justice as we know it.

In short, the American judiciary is still standing, and the risk of impending face-plant is remote. It is, however, beginning to walk with a detectable limp. The political transformation that this book has chronicled calls into question the continuing vitality of the prevailing rule of law paradigm, which disavows the extralegal influences on judicial decision-making that the public, the media, public officials, and scholars take as a given. The ensuing skepticism, and sometimes cynicism, has eroded the rule of law paradigm as a unifying model of the courts in action. The legal culture paradigm that this book proposes in its stead proceeds from a different set of assumptions: that judges are acculturated to take law, process, and justice seriously, but that legal indeterminacy creates opportunities for extralegal influence upon decision-making that cannot be extinguished. Rather than pretend that such influences do not exist, the key is to manage them through systems of oversight in adjudicative, ethical, and political dimensions.

The crisis rhetoric of the bench and bar is animated in no small part by a fear that the judiciary has become too "politicized." To the extent that such rhetoric predicts the coming apocalypse, it is exaggerated; and to the extent it assumes the courts can be made a de-politicized place, it is naïve. But to the extent that it recognizes the concern that regulatory oversight in the political dimension has become overly pervasive and aggressive, it is well taken. Through education, reclamation, and moderation, I propose to restore balance between the dimensions of court oversight, to the end of establishing a legal culture paradigm that is stable and enduring.

CHAPTER 8

Conclusion

When all is said and done, this book seeks to make six basic points. First, the rule of law paradigm is premised on an understanding of what judges do and how they do it that has structured our conception of the American judiciary for centuries. That understanding begins with the notion that independent judges uphold and apply the law on a case-by-case basis. Independence ensures that judges will apply the law without fear or favor, free from extralegal influence. Judges, the rule of law paradigm posits, should be accountable to the law, in the limited sense that their decisions are subject to appellate review, constitutional amendment, and, in appropriate cases, legislative override, while the judges themselves can be removed via impeachment and (in state systems) disciplinary processes for gross misconduct. But accountability should be constrained so that judges are not beholden to the preferences of the public, their elected representatives, the parties, or others interested in the outcomes of cases the judges decide.

Second, the landscape of the American courts is changing in ways that render the traditional rule of law paradigm increasingly ill-equipped to continue serving as a template into the future. Social science—most notably political science and psychology—teaches us that, contrary to the rule of law paradigm, independent judges are subject to an array of extralegal influences, including ideology, race, gender, emotion, self-interest, desire for audience approval, strategic considerations, and others. The public has long understood that judges are subject to such influences, despite their claims to the contrary, but has embraced the rule of law paradigm, approved of judges who profess to do likewise, and as to judges' seeming hypocrisy, looked the other way. What has changed is that the public is no longer looking the other way. In recent generations the general public, their elected representatives, scholars, interest groups, and pundits have relentlessly challenged the premise that independent judges disregard extralegal influences and uphold the law, in the context of judicial confirmation hearings, judicial election campaigns, procedural rule reform, judicial disqualification proceedings, disciplinary actions, legislative oversight, and the new media. As a consequence, the galvanizing force of the rule of law paradigm has begun to erode.

Third, in this changing landscape, a legal culture paradigm reframes the role of judges and courts to better explain the need for judicial independence and accountability among judges whose decisions are subject to legal and extralegal influences. The legal culture paradigm posits that judges are immersed in a legal culture that takes law seriously, but that legal indeterminacy renders extralegal influence on judicial decision-making inevitable and necessary to the exercise of judgment. For judges who are subject to extralegal influence, judicial independence buffers them from external pressures that interfere with their acculturated predisposition to further three desirable objectives: (1) upholding the substantive law; (2) respecting the procedural rights of parties to a fair proceeding; and (3) reaching results they regard as just in light of case-specific facts and law. By acknowledging that independent judges are subject to extralegal influences, however, the legal culture paradigm recognizes that independence can liberate judges to pursue private agendas in derogation of the very objectives that independence aims to further; hence, the need for a more robust form of accountability or regulatory oversight of judges and courts than the rule of law paradigm envisions. How the appropriate balance between judicial independence and accountability should be struck in this new, legal culture paradigm is perspective or dimension-dependent. The balance needed to optimize judicial independence and accountability in the adjudicative dimension, where parties seek a judge who will afford them a fair hearing, can be different in the ethical dimension, where judges seek to acquit themselves honorably in accord with the norms of their calling, which can be different in the political dimension, where the general public seeks a judge it can trust.

Fourth, armed with this new, legal culture paradigm, it is possible to reconceive the changing landscape of the American courts in terms of a shift toward intensified regulation of judges in the political dimension of oversight and a corresponding de-emphasis on regulation in the adjudicative and ethical dimensions. The new politics of judicial selection, procedure, disqualification, discipline, legislative oversight, and race, as reported by the new media, signal a heightened interest in regulating judges and their decisions by the electorate, and the electorate's political representatives. Conversely, in the adjudicative and ethical dimensions, by sometimes managing judicial ethics and disqualification passively, limiting the authority of state courts to regulate judicial campaign speech, and affording trial judges the discretion to dismiss claims whenever their common sense tells them the claims are implausible, judges and courts have created a regulatory vacuum that the political dimension is eager to fill.

Fifth, the trend toward political dimension primacy is problematic because there is value to maintaining all three dimensions of oversight in constructive tension. Oversight in the adjudicative dimension promotes due process values; oversight in the ethical dimension promotes civic virtue; and oversight in the political dimension promotes the judiciary's institutional legitimacy. Hence, making courts and judges more responsive to public preferences by regulating judges in the political dimension in ways that jeopardize a fair hearing for litigants in the adjudicative dimension, or that compromise the integrity of the judicial role in the ethical dimension, can involve problematic trade-offs.

Sixth, needed balance between the dimensions of oversight can best be restored through education, reclamation, and moderation. With respect to education, small but significant changes in the ways law schools explain, discuss, and justify the choices judges make can go a long way toward reorienting future judges to the new, legal culture paradigm. And judges can acclimate the public to the new paradigm by speaking more candidly about the nature of judging and the judgment judges must exercise and its limits. Reclamation calls upon judges and judicial systems to recapture the initiative by taking proactive steps in the adjudicative and ethical dimensions—via rulemaking, institutional policy reform, and decision-making—to address the concerns that animate heightened activity in the political dimension. Moderation recognizes that preserving constructive tension across the adjudicative, ethical, and political dimensions of judicial oversight entails a perpetual search for a regulatory middle ground that respects and preserves the values each dimension furthers.

The informed skeptic may doubt whether the transition from the rule of law paradigm to a legal culture paradigm that I propose here, can happen, should happen, or will do any good. Traditionalists, who lionize the modern judge as the second coming of Solomon and huff at the claim that judges are subject to extralegal influences, can be counted upon to push back with indignation. Nihilists, who regard judges as politicians in robes and scoff at the suggestion that judges give a damn about the law, will do likewise. Among those who acknowledge that the legal culture paradigm better captures how judges think and what they do, some will worry that the public cannot handle the truth: Openly conceding that independent judges do more and less than follow the law is a dangerous gambit akin to pulling back the curtain on the Wizard of Oz that could do more to destroy public support for the judiciary than preserve it. Others will argue that transitioning to a legal culture paradigm, however reasonable the tenets of that paradigm may be, will do nothing to dissuade rabid court critics from prosecuting their strategically driven campaigns to control judges' decision-making via political processes in the name of thwarting putative usurpations of judicial power.

These concerns are overblown. Traditionalists, who cling to nineteenth-century formalism and deny the relevance of extralegal influences on judicial decision-making, are dinosaurs blinking in the aftermath of the asteroid impact. Nihilists among the ranks of social scientists who defeated anachronistic versions of the so-called legal model a generation ago are gradually being turned by data showing that law retains sway over judicial decision-making (to an increasing extent as one proceeds down the organizational chart from the US Supreme Court to courts of original jurisdiction)—how much sway being an appropriate subject of continuing disagreement.

Survey data show that the public thinks judges are subject to legal and extralegal influences, as the legal culture paradigm posits. Hence, the suggestion that the public cannot handle a truth they already accept as true seems a bit silly. That the public might nonetheless exaggerate or otherwise react badly to the implications of the legal establishment's concession that judges are subject to extralegal influences is a reasonable concern. But I am not suggesting that judges and lawyers stride to the podium, bellow that the emperor has no clothes, and drop the mike. I do not even advocate that they discuss the role that ideology, race, gender, strategic choice, or other extralegal factors play in judicial decision-making, in part because cognitive psychology tells us that such influences are largely subconscious, and in part because it would engender the misunderstandings of concern here. Rather, I simply advocate that when members of the bench and bar discuss the role of judges in the administration of justice, they put down the rule of law script and explain the art of judging in difficult cases. Listeners will understand that when judges apply disputed facts to ambiguous law in hard cases, the decisions they make will, of necessity, be informed by their backgrounds, educations, life experiences, and sense of justice, which is to say, extralegal factors. And that is okay.

Extremists will not be mollified. Those who cultivate a pathological distrust of judges or who entertain a conception of democracy so expansive as to advocate political dimension micromanagement of judicial decisions, will retain their antipathy to judicial independence and persist in their attacks. My target, however, is not the fringe but the center. The eroding rule of law paradigm, which clings to premises that the center no longer accepts, has its sights trained on where its target used to be. My ambition is to move with the target, by establishing a legal culture paradigm that the public will embrace, that social scientists will accept, and that the bench and bar can more credibly defend against perennial attacks from critics at the margins. A nation beset by polarized politics and diminished confidence in government generally may be reluctant to keep slack in the judiciary's leash. But the judiciary is different enough from the executive and legislative branches of government in perception and reality, to justify a measure of optimism for the future of an independence judiciary, if that future is guided by a more satisfactory legal culture paradigm.

This book began with a series of quotations from lawyers, judges, and scholars, who claimed that the American judiciary was in crisis. Others have responded with comparable certitude that the developments some have decried as crises are nothing more than the rough and tumble of business as usual in American judicial politics. I have argued that the truth lies between these extremes. No collapse of the constitutional order is imminent, but events generations in the making have rendered waiting on the precipice of a crumbling rule of law paradigm to see what happens next, a perilous long-term strategy.

Between the alarmists, who tell us that "the sky is falling," and the deniers, who would have us believe that "there is nothing new under the sun," is a third, comparably colorful metaphor, which I prefer because it better captures the American judiciary's current predicament: "frog in a simmering pot." The political transformation that I have described in this book has turned up the heat on the American judiciary in ways that render the time-honored rule of law paradigm increasingly anachronistic and indefensible. The transition to a legal culture paradigm, as I propose, will not take the pot off the burner: The role of the American judiciary as separate, co-equal branch of government, with power to review and invalidate decisions made by the other branches, ensures that the courts will always be on the stove. But it may keep the temperature below boiling.

NOTES

PRELIMS

1. Charles Gardner Geyh, *The Dimensions of Judicial Impartiality*, 65 FLA. L. REV. 493 (2013); Charles Gardner Geyh, *Can the Rule of Law Survive Judicial Politics*, 97 CORNELL L. REV. 191 (2012).

CHAPTER 1

1. Foreword to JAMES SAMPLE ET AL., THE NEW POLITICS OF JUDICIAL ELECTIONS, 2000–2009 (2010). In a like vein, Professor Jed Shugerman concludes his definitive history of judicial selection with the warning that "we face a new crisis in judicial politics and special interests." JED HANDELSMAN SHUGERMAN, THE PEOPLE'S COURTS: PURSUING JUDICIAL INDEPENDENCE IN AMERICA 273 (2012).
2. Paul D. Carrington,*Public Funding of Judicial Campaigns: The North Carolina Experience and the Activism of the Supreme Court*, 89 N.C. L. REV. 1965, 1966 (2011).
3. Eric J. Magnuson, *The State of the Judiciary*, BENCH & BAR MINN. 20, 23 (2008).
4. Michael M. Gallagher, *Disarming the Confirmation Process*, 50 CLEV. ST. L. REV. 513, 516–517 (2003).
5. Carl Tobias, *Filling the Judicial Vacancies in an Election Year*, 46 U. OF RICH. L. REV. 985, 986 (2012) (citing articles).
6. David Carlson, *Adapting Integer Programming Techniques to Circuit Restructuring*, 96 CORNELL L. REV. 583, 586–587 (2011) (discussing thirteen studies).
7. David Barron, *Judicial Independence and the State Court Funding Crisis*, 100 KY. L. REV. 755 (2011).
8. John G. Roberts Jr., 2006 Year-End Report on the Federal Judiciary, Third Branch (Admin. Office of the US Courts, Washington, DC), Jan. 2007, at 1,3, *available at* http://www.uscourts.gov/uscourts/news/ttb/archive/2007–01%20Jan.pdf.
9. Edward H. Pappas, *Judicial Independence in Crisis (Part 1)*, MICH. BAR J. 18 (2009) (quoting Massachusetts Chief Justice Margaret Marshall).
10. Margaret H. Marshall, *The Promise of Neutrality: Reflections on Judicial Independence*, 36 HUM. RTS. 3, 4 (2009) ("Fair and neutral judges, knowing that each written opinion may be scrutinized as a statement of political partisanship by interest groups, may feel tremendous pressure to look over their shoulders, to abandon the principles of judicial neutrality, when deciding cases"); *see also Law Day Speech by N.C. Superior Court Judge Thomas W. Ross*, N.C. LAW. WKLY., May 16, 2005 ("the constant, degrading and sometimes personal attacks on judges and the judiciary by political and other leaders are slowly eroding the credibility of the judiciary and will ultimately, I fear, undermine the rule of law.")

11. Martha Neil, *ABA Activism Survey Alarms Scholars*, 31 MONT. LAW 20, 21 (2005).
12. Neil Kinkopf, *The Progressive Dilemma*, 75 NOTRE DAME L. REV. 1493, 1493–1494 (2000).
13. Adam Steinman, *The Pleading Problem*, 62 STAN. L. REV. 1293, 1295 (2010).
14. Kevin Clermont & Stephen Yeazell, *Inventing Tests, Destabilizing Systems* 95 IA. L. REV. 821, 823 (2010).
15. *Id.* at 841.
16. Access to Justice Denied: Ashcroft v. Iqbal: Hearing Before the Subcomm. on the Constitution, Civil Rights, and Civil Liberties of the H. Comm. on the Judiciary, 111th Cong. 6–7 (2009) (statement of Professor Arthur Miller) ("The subjectivity at the heart of Twombly-Iqbal raises the concern that rulings on motions to dismiss may turn on individual ideology regarding the underlying substantive law").
17. CHRIS W. BONNEAU & MELINDA GANN HALL, IN DEFENSE OF JUDICIAL ELECTIONS 9 (2009) (challenging criticism of judicial elections as overstated); William P. Marshall, *Conservatives and the Seven Sins of Judicial Activism*, 73 U. COLO. L. REV 1217 (2012) (refuting claims of judicial activism); Marc Galanter, *The Day after the Litigation Explosion*, 46 U. MD. L. REV. 3 (1986) (questioning claims of caseload crisis); JAMES GIBSON: ELECTING JUDGES: THE SURPRISING EFFECTS OF CAMPAIGNING ON JUDICIAL LEGITIMACY (2012) (challenging claims that elections undermine public support for courts); William H. Pryor, *Not So Serious Threats to Judicial Independence*, 93 VA. L. REV. 1759 (2007) (arguing that perceived threats to judicial independence are overstated); MELINDA GANN HALL, ATTACKING JUDGES: HOW CAMPAIGN ADVERTISING INFLUENCES STATE SUPREME COURT ELECTIONS (2014) (arguing that attack advertising in judicial election campaigns encourages voter participation and engagement).
18. Charles Gardner Geyh, *Can the Rule of Law Survive Judicial Politics?* 97 CORNELL L. REV. 191, 192–193 (2012).
19. *Id.* at 197–214.
20. *Introduction: So What Does Law Have to Do with it? in* WHAT'S LAW GOT TO DO WITH IT? WHAT JUDGES DO, WHY THEY DO IT, AND WHAT'S AT STAKE? 3–6 (Charles Gardner Geyh ed., 2011).
21. KEITH J. BYBEE, ALL JUDGES ARE POLITICAL—EXCEPT WHEN THEY ARE NOT: ACCEPTABLE HYPOCRISIES AND THE RULE OF LAW (2010).
22. Joseph William Singer, *Legal Realism Now*, 76 CAL. L. REV. 465, 467 (1988).
23. Roy A. Schotland, *Comment*, 1998 LAW & CONTEMPORARY PROBLEMS, at 150 (1998).
24. Geyh, *supra* note 18 at 214–220.
25. Edward L. Rubin, *Independence as a Governance Mechanism, in* JUDICIAL INDEPENDENCE AT THE CROSSROADS 56, 70–71 (Stephen B. Burbank & Barry Friedman eds., 2002); Martin H. Redish, *Federal Judicial Independence: Constitutional and Political Perspectives*, 46 MERCER L. REV. 697, 708 (1995); Tom R. Tyler, *The Role of Perceived Injustice in Defendant's Evaluation of Their Courtroom Experience*, 18 LAW & SOC'Y REV. 51, 70 (1984).
26. MODEL CODE OF JUDICIAL CONDUCT R. 2.4(A) (2007).

CHAPTER 2

1. THOMAS S. KUHN, THE STRUCTURE OF SCIENTIFIC REVOLUTIONS 2–3 (1962).
2. *Id.* at 26–27.
3. *Id.* at 2–3.
4. ARISTOTLE, POLITICS BOOK III XVI (Ernest Barker, revised by Richard Stalley 1995).
5. *See* CICERO, *The Speech of M.T. Cicero in Defence of Aulus Cluentius Avitus* § 53, *in* 2 THE ORATIONS OF MARCUS TULLIUS CICERO 104, 164 (C.D. Yonge trans., 2008).

6. BRIAN Z. TAMANAHA, ON THE RULE OF LAW: HISTORY, POLITICS, THEORY 15 (2004).

7. *Id.* at 48–54.

8. THE FEDERALIST NO. 51 (James Madison) (Clinton Rossiter ed., 1961).

9. SCOTT DOUGLAS GERBER, A DISTINCT JUDICIAL POWER: THE ORIGINS OF AN INDEPENDENT JUDICIARY, 1606–1787 (2011); William Michael Treanor, *Judicial Review before Marbury*, 58 STAN. L. REV. 455 (2005).

10. Marbury v. Madison, 5 U.S. 137 (1803).

11. WILLIAM BLACKSTONE, COMMENTARIES ON THE LAWS OF ENGLAND 69 n. 1558 (1765).

12. THE FEDERALIST NO. 78 (Alexander Hamilton), *supra* note 8.

13. THE FEDERALIST NO. 81 (Alexander Hamilton), *supra* note 8.

14. TAMANAHA, *supra* note 6, 114–19 (2004); GEOFFREY DE Q. WALKER, THE RULE OF LAW: FOUNDATION OF A CONSTITUTIONAL DEMOCRACY 24–25 (1988).

15. TAMANAHA, *supra* note 6, at 119–22; WALKER, *supra* note 14, at 25–27.

16. TAMANAHA, *supra* note 6, at 122–26; WALKER, *supra* note 14, at 29–36.

17. Quoted in *New Dimensions of Citizenship*, LEWISTON DAILY SUN, May 27, 1963.

18. Gerhard Peters & John T. Woolley, The American Presidency Project, Ronald Reagan, *Address before a Joint Session of the Congress Reporting on the State of the Union*, Jan. 26, 1982, http://www.presidency.ucsb.edu/ws/?pid=42687.

19. Remarks by the President in Welcoming Senior Staff and Cabinet Secretaries to the White House, Jan. 21, 2009, http://www.whitehouse.gov/the-press-office/remarks-president-welcoming-senior-staff-and-cabinet-secretaries-white-house.

20. Alfred P. Carlton, *The American Judiciary Cornerstone of Society*, 41 JUDGES J. 22 (2002).

21. Michael Greco, *Address to the American Bar Association House of Delegates*, 2005 PROF. LAWYER 1.

22. U.S. CONST. art. VI.

23. 28 U.S.C. § 453 (1990).

24. MODEL CODE OF JUDICIAL CONDUCT R. 2.2 (2007).

25. Arthur S. Alarcon, *Political Appointments and Judicial Independence—an Unreasonable Expectation*, 16 LOY. L.A. L. REV. 9, 13 (1983).

26. Louis Lavorato, Chief Just., Iowa Sup. Ct., Chief Justice Reacts to Judicial Questionnaire (Aug. 9, 2006), http://www.iowacourts.gov/news_service/news_releases/NewsItem221/index.asp.

27. THE CONSTITUTION PROJECT, THE NEWSROOM GUIDE TO JUDICIAL INDEPENDENCE (2006), http://www.constitutionproject.org/wp-content/uploads/2012/10/37.pdf.

28. William G. Paul, *Remarks of the Outgoing President of the American Bar Association*, 31 N.M. L. REV. 55, 58, n. 25 (2001).

29. *Id.*

30. Charles Gardner Geyh, *The Elastic Nature of Judicial Independence, in* THE IMPROVEMENT OF THE ADMINISTRATION OF JUSTICE 167, 170 (Gordon M. Griller & E. Keith Stott eds., 7th ed. 2001).

31. *See* Kermit L. Hall, *The Judiciary on Trial: State Constitutional Reform and the Rise of an Elected Judiciary*, 45 THE HISTORIAN 337 (1983); Caleb Nelson, *A Re-Evaluation of Scholarly Explanations for the Rise of the Elective Judiciary in Antebellum America*, 37 AM. J. LEGAL HIST. 190 (1993); Roy A. Schotland, *Myth, Reality Past and Present, and Judicial Elections*, 35 IND. L. REV. 659, 661–62 (2002).

32. MODEL CODE OF JUDICIAL CONDUCT R. 2.4 (2007).

33. *Id.*

34. MODEL CODE OF JUDICIAL CONDUCT R. 1.2 (2007).

35. *See* U.S. CONST. amend V; U.S. CONST. amend XIV, § 1.

36. *See, e.g., In re* Murchinson, 349 U.S. 133, 136 (1955) ("A fair trial in a fair tribunal is a basic requirement of due process"); Tumey v. State of Ohio, 273 U.S. 510, 532 (1927) ("Every procedure which would offer a possible temptation to the average man as a judge to forget the burden of proof required to convict the defendant, or which might lead him not to hold the balance nice, clear, and true between the state and the accused denies the latter due process of law").

37. MODEL CODE OF JUDICIAL CONDUCT, Pmbl.

38. Stephen G. Breyer, *Judicial Independence in the United States*, 40 ST. LOUIS L. J. 989, 989 (1996).

39. Julie A. Robinson, *Judicial Independence: The Need for Education about the Role of the Judiciary*, 46 WASHBURN L. J. 535, 544 (2007).

40. Shirley Abrahamson, *Thorny Issues and Slippery Slopes: Perspectives on Judicial Independence*, 64 OH. ST. L. J. 3, 3 (2003).

41. Carlton, *supra* note 20.

42. John C. Trimble, *Without Fear or Favor: A Report by DRI's Judicial Task Force*, 10 (2007).

43. Sandra Day O'Connor, Forward, in CHARLES GARDNER GEYH, WHEN COURTS & CONGRESS COLLIDE: THE STRUGGLE FOR CONTROL OF AMERICA'S JUDICIAL SYSTEM (ppd ed. 2008).

44. *Kansas and Missouri Chief Justices Address Judicial Conferences*, 74 J. KAN B.A. 9 (2005) ("we are accountable to the law and not to the popular will") (quoting Missouri Chief Justice Michael Wolfe); James R. Pratt III, *Are We Being Fair to Our Judges and the Perception of Impartial Justice in Alabama by Having Partisan Elections for Judicial Office?* 72 ALA. LAW. 443 (2011) ("We all expect judges to be accountable to the law rather than political supporters or special interests") (quoting Justice Sandra Day O'Connor); H. Thomas Wells Jr., *ABA Decries Expensive State Judicial Races*, 34 MONT, LAW. 28 (2008) ("Judges should be accountable to the law and the Constitution, not the whims of the day or to popular public opinion") (Quote of American Bar Association president).

45. Jonathan Lippman, *William H. Rehnquist Award for Judicial Excellence Address*, 47 FAM. CT. REV. 199 (2009).

46. AM. BAR ASS'N, AN INDEPENDENT JUDICIARY: REPORT OF THE COMMISSION ON SEPARATION OF POWERS AND JUDICIAL INDEPENDENCE, 47–49, 55–56, 63 (1997); AM. BAR ASSN, JUSTICE IN JEOPARDY: REPORT OF THE COMM'N ON THE 21ST CENTURY JUDICIARY, 70–73, 84–85 (2003) ("JUSTICE IN JEOPARDY"). Members of the bench and bar who do not share the view that such threats jeopardize the judiciary's independence pit themselves in opposition to the majority. *See, e.g.,* William H. Pryor Jr., *Judicial Independence and the Lesson of History*, 68 ALA. LAW 389 (2007).

47. Roscoe Pound, *The Causes of Popular Dissatisfaction with the Administration of Justice*, 40 AM. L. REV. 729 (1906).

48. *Id.* at 734.

49. *Id.* at 749.

50. CHARLES GARDNER GEYH, WHEN COURTS & CONGRESS COLLIDE: THE STRUGGLE FOR CONTROL OF AMERICA'S JUDICIAL SYSTEM 53–54; 125–42 (2006).

51. *Quoted in* Barry Friedman, *The History of the Countermajoritarian Difficulty, Part I: The Road to Judicial Supremacy*, 73 N.Y.U. L. REV. 333, 401 (1998).

52. *Id.* at 399.

53. CONG. GLOBE, 39th Cong., 2d Sess. 501–02 (1867); *see generally,* Barry Friedman, *The History of the Countermajoritarian Difficulty (Part 2)*, 91 GEO. L. J. 1 (2002).

54. GEYH, *supra* note 50, at 66–70 (2006).

55. *See generally* WILLIAM ROSS, A MUTED FURY: POPULISTS, PROGRESSIVES, AND LABOR UNIONS CONFRONT THE COURTS 1890–1937 (1994).

56. Charles Gardner Geyh, *The American Judicature Society and Judicial Independence: Reflections at the Century Mark*, 96 JUDICATURE 257 (2013).

57. *See* ROSS, *supra* note 55, at 290–302; GEYH, *supra* note 50, at 79–80; 87–90.

58. *See* GEYH, *supra* note 50, at 109–10.

59. Charles Gardner Geyh, *The Choreography of Courts-Congress Conflicts*, in THE POLITICS OF JUDICIAL INDEPENDENCE: COURTS, POLITICS AND THE PUBLIC 19, 21 (2011).

60. *Id.* at 20–21.

61. *Id.*

62. US Population by Year, http://www.multpl.com/united-states-population/table (last visited Jan. 10, 2015).

63. Nat'l Ctr. for State Courts, State Court Caseload Statistics: Annual Report, 1977, at 35, *available at* https://www.ncjrs.gov/pdffiles1/Digitization/86854NCJRS.pdf, at 34–36 (last visited Jan. 10, 2015).

64. Court Statistics Project, http://www.courtstatistics.org/other-pages/~/media/microsites/files/csp/data%20pdf/csp_dec.ashx (last visited Jan. 10, 2015).

65. United States Courts, http://www.uscourts.gov/news/newsview/11–03-15/Filings_in_the_Federal_Judiciary_Continued_to_Grow_in_Fiscal_Year_2010.aspx (last visited Jan. 10, 2015).

66. *Id.*

67. Pound, *supra* note 47.

68. David Carlson, *Adapting Integer Programming Techniques to Circuit Restructuring*, 96 CORNELL L. REV. 583, 586–87 (2011) (discussing thirteen studies).

69. Court Statistics Project, http://www.courtstatistics.org/Other-Pages/~/media/Microsites/Files/CSP/DATA%20PDF/CSP_DEC.ashx, at 6 (last visited Jan. 10, 2015).

70. *Id.*

71. Judith Resnik, *The Mythic Meaning of Article III Courts*, 56 COLO. L. REV 581 (1985).

72. FED. R. CIV. P. 16 (amended 1983, 1987, 1993, 2006, 2007, and 2015).

73. FED. R. CIV. P. 16 (and accompanying Committee Notes).

74. Carl Tobias, *The Expiration of the Civil Justice Reform Act of 1990*, 59 WASH. & LEE. L. REV. 541 (2002).

75. FED. R. CIV. P. 26(b)(1) (eliminating broader discovery "relevant to the subject matter" of the action—in favor of discovery "relevant to any party's claim or defense"); FED. R. CIV. P. 30(a)(2) (requiring stipulation or leave of court to take more than ten depositions or retake a deposition); FED. R. CIV. P. 33(a)(1) (requiring stipulation or leave of court to submit more than twenty-five interrogatories); FED. R. CIV. P. 26(a) (specifying unsolicited disclosure obligations); FED. R. CIV. P. 26(b)(2)(B) (articulating court's authority to manage electronic discovery).

76. Lisa Bernstein, *Understanding the Limits of Court-Connected ADR: A Critique of Federal Court-Annexed Arbitration Programs*, 141 U. PA. L. REV. 2169, 2172 (1993); *see also* Kim Dayton, *The Myth of Alternative Dispute Resolution in the Federal Courts*, 76 IOWA L. REV. 889 (1991).

77. *Id.*

78. 28 U.S.C. §§651–58 Thomas J. Stipanowich, *ADR and the "Vanishing Trial": The Growth and Impact of "Alternative Dispute Resolution*," 1 J. EMPIR. LEGAL STUD. 843, 849 (2004).

79. Thomas J. Stipanowich & J. Ryan Lamare, *Living with ADR: Evolving Perceptions and Use of Mediation, Arbitration and Conflict Management in Fortune 1,000 Corporations*, PEPPERDINE UNIV. SCHOOL OF LAW LEGAL STUDIES RESEARCH PAPER SERIES 2013/16, at 3 (Mar. 2013).

80. Ashcroft v. Iqbal, 129 S. Ct. 1937, 1950 (2009); Bell Atlantic Corp. v. Twombly, 550 U.S. 544 (2007) (noting that "the problem of discovery abuse cannot be solved by

'careful scrutiny of evidence at the summary judgment stage,'" because "the threat of discovery expense will push cost-conscious defendants to settle even anemic cases before reaching those proceedings").

81. Fed. R. Civ. P. 11(b)(1).
82. Charles Alan Wright, Arthur Miller, & Mary Kay Kane, Federal Practice and Procedure §1753.
83. 28 U.S.C. §1407 (1976).
84. Judith Resnik, *Aggregation, Settlement, and Dismay*, 80 Cornell L. Rev. 918 (1995).
85. 28 U.S.C. 1369 (2002) (The Multiparty, Multiforum Trial Jurisdiction Act).
86. Fed R. Civ. P. 23(e).
87. 28 U.S.C. §1332(d) (2011).
88. Linda Mullenix, *Aggregate Litigation and the Death of Democratic Dispute Resolution*, 107 Nw U. L. Rev. 511, 537–41 (2013).
89. Charles Silver, *"We're Scared to Death": Class Certification and Blackmail*, 78 N.Y.U. L. Rev. 1357 (2003).
90. Richard Nagareda, *Class Certifications in the Age of Aggregated Proof*, 84 N.Y.U. L. Rev. 97, 171 2009) ("[C]ivil procedure is not about the preparation of cases for trial ... [T]rial is exceedingly rare, not only in class actions but in civil litigation generally. What the 1938 reformers cast as the Federal Rules of Civil Procedure effectively operate now, in the age of 'the vanishing trial,' as rules of civil settlement procedure").
91. Stephen C. Yeazell, *The Misunderstood Consequences of Modern Civil Process*, 1994 Wis. L. Rev. 631, 633 n. 3.
92. Marc Galanter, *The Vanishing Trial: An Examination of Trials and Related Matters in Federal and State Courts*, 1 J. Empirical Legal Stud. 459, 462–63 tbl. 1 (2004).
93. Brian J. Ostrom, Shauna M. Strickland & Paula L. Hannaford-Agor, *Examining Trial Trends in State Courts: 1976–2002*, 1 J. Empirical Legal Stud. 755, 768 (2004).
94. Judith Resnik, *Managerial Judges*, 96 Harv. L. Rev. 374 (1982).
95. Greg Berman, John Feinblatt, & Sarah Glazer, Good Courts: The Case for Problem-Solving Justice (2005).
96. Sarah Staszak , No Day in Court: Access to Justice and the Politics of Judicial Retrenchment (2015); Judith Resnik, *Diffusing Disputes: The Public in the Private of Arbitration, the Private in Courts, and the Erasure of Rights*, 124 Yale L. J. 2804 (2015).
97. Judith Resnik, *Judicial Independence and Article III: Too Little and Too Much*, 72 S. Cal. L. Rev. 657, 670 (1999).
98. Quoted in Lawrence Baum, *Law and Policy: More and Less than a Dichotomy, in* What's Law Got to Do With It?: What Judges Do, Why They Do It, and What's at Stake (Charles Gardner Geyh ed., 2011).
99. The Judiciary Act of 1891 (26 Stat. 826).
100. The Supreme Court Case Selections Act of 1988 (Pub. L. No. 100–352, 102 Stat. 662).
101. 13 Cong. Rec. 3464 (1872) (statement of Senator David Davis).
102. Court Statistics Project,http://www.uscourts.gov/uscourts/Statistics/JudicialBusiness/2011/appendices/A01Sep11.pdf (last visited Jan. 12, 2015).
103. Paul Carrington, Daniel Meador, & Maurice Rosenberg, Justice on Appeal 149 (1976).
104. *Id.* at 150.
105. Margaret Meriwether Cordray & Richard Cordray, *The Supreme Court's Plenary Docket*, 58 Wash. & Lee L. Rev. 737, 751 (2001); G. Alan Tarr, *State Judicial Selection and Judicial Independence*, App. D at 6–7, *in* Justice in Jeopardy, *supra* note 46.
106. John Jeffries & James Ryan, *A Political History of the Establishment Clause*, 100 Mich. L. Rev. 279, 341 (2001).

107. Stephen Gottlieb, *The Constitutionality of "Bending" History in Public Secondary Schools*, 62 N.Y.U. L. Rev. 497, 509 n. 52 (1987).

108. Geyh, *supra* note 50, at 198–200, 202.

109. *Id.* at 203–06.

110. Kermit Hall, The Politics of Justice: Lower Federal Court Judicial Selection and the Second Party System 1829–61 171–72 (1979).

111. Sheldon Goldman, Picking Federal Judges: Lower Court Selection from Roosevelt through Reagan 288–89 (1997); Sheldon Goldman, *Unpicking Pickering in 2002: Some Thoughts on Lower Court Selection and Confirmation*, 36 U.C. Davis L. Rev. 695, 698 (2003) (vetting prospective nominees).

112. Geyh, *supra* note 50, at 212–22.

113. William J. Brennan Jr., *State Constitutions and the Protection of Individual Rights*, 90 Harv. L. Rev. 489 (1977).

114. G. Alan Tarr, *State Judicial Selection and Judicial Independence*, App. D at 6–7, *in* Justice in Jeopardy, *supra* note 46.

115. *Id.* at 5–6.

116. James Sample, *Retention Elections 2.010*, 46 U.S.F. L. Rev. 383, 402–05 (2011).

117. Traciel V. Reid, *The Politicalization of Retention Elections: Lessons from the Defeat of Justices Lanphier and White*, 83 Judicature 68, 70–74 (1999); Amanda Frost & Stefanie Lindquist, *Countering the Majoritarian Difficulty*, 96 Va. L. Rev. 719, 749 (2010) ("An incumbent judge's decisions in criminal cases are easy targets for his opponents in the next election cycle, who can use almost any decision favorable to a criminal defendant, no matter how legally defensible, as grounds for portraying the incumbent as 'soft on crime'").

118. *See* Charles Gardner Geyh, *Why Judicial Elections Stink*, 64 Oh. St. L. J. 43, 49–50 (2003).

119. Michael L. Rustad & Thomas H. Koenig, *Taming the Tort Monster: The American Civil Justice System as a Battleground for Social Theory*, 68 Brooklyn L. Rev. 1 (2002).

120. Emily Heller & Mark Ballard, *Hard-Fought, Big Money Judicial Races: U.S. Chamber of Commerce Enters Fray with Ad Money*, National Journal at 42 (2000).

121. *Id.*

122. This is the title of a periodically updated publication of the Justice at Stake Campaign. *See* The New Politics of Judicial Elections Online, http://newpoliticsreport.org/ (last visited Jan. 13, 2015).

123. Quality Judges Initiative, iaals.du.edu/initiatives/quality-judges-initiative/(last visited Jan. 9, 2015).

124. Paul Carrington, *Politics and Civil Procedure Rulemaking: Reflections on Experience*, 60 Duke L. J. 597 (2010).

125. Adam N. Steinman, *The Irrepressible Myth of Celotex: Reconsidering Summary Judgment Burdens Twenty Years after the Trilogy*, 63 Wash. & Lee L. Rev. 81, 86 (2006).

126. Class Action Fairness Act of 2005, PL 109–2, 119 Stat. 4 (2005).

127. Ashcroft v. Iqbal, 129 S. Ct. 1937, 1950 (2009); Bell Atlantic Corp. v. Twombly, 550 U.S. 544 (2007). *See* Arthur Miller, *From Conley, to Twombly to Iqbal: A Double Play on the Federal Rules of Civil Procedure*, 60 DUKE L. J. 1, 18 (2010).

128. *Id.*

129. Stephen Yeazell, *Unspoken Truths and Misaligned Interests: Political Parties and the Two Cultures of Civil Litigation*, 60 U.C.L.A. L. Rev.1752 (2013); Elizabeth G. Thornburg, *Giving the "Haves" a Little More: Considering the 1998 Discovery Proposals*, 52 SMU L. Rev. 229, 254 (1999) ("Business groups seek to limit discovery precisely because those limits will make it more difficult for plaintiffs to prevail in products liability suits. Having failed to pass substantive tort reform legislation, these groups seek procedural

advantage"). Danya Shocair Reda, *The Cost and Delay Narrative in Civil-Justice Reform: Its Fallacies and Functions,* 90 ORE. L. REV. 1085 (2012).

130. DANIEL BOORSTIN, THE IMAGE: A GUIDE TO PSEUDO-EVENTS IN AMERICA (1961).

131. Neil Hicky, *Money Lust: How Pressure for Profit is Perverting Journalism, in* THE POWER OF THE PRESS 36 (Beth Levy & Denise Bonilla eds., 1999).

132. Gerry Yandel, *TV Watch,* THE ATLANTA JOURNAL AND CONSTITUTION, June 23, 1992; CMPA Election Watch, Oct. 30, 2000, http://cmpa.com/election2004/JournalistsMonopolize.htm.

133. *Partisanship and Cable News Audiences,* PewResearch.org, http://www.pewresearch.org/2009/10/30/partisanship-and-cable-news-audiences/ (last visited Jan. 9, 2015).

134. For example, for several years the progressive Brennan Center for Justice issued "Court Pester" Awards on its website, in response to the conservative Family Research Council's "Court Jester" Awards. http://www.brennancenter.org /press-release/brennan-center-hands-out-court-pester-awards, (last visited Jan. 9, 2015).

135. ABA Ctr. for Prof. Resp., MODEL CODE OF JUDICIAL CONDUCT 2.10(A) (ABA 2007).

136. Michael Salamone, *News Media Portrayal of Ideology and Division among Supreme Court Justices* (Oct. 15, 2013), *available at* http://www.academia.edu/5058189/News_Media_Portrayal_of_Ideology_and_Division_among_Supreme_Court_Justices (last visited July 20, 2015).

137. Cass Sunstein, *Unanimity and Disagreement on the Supreme Court,* 100 CORNELL L. REV. 769 (2015).

138. GEYH, *supra* note 50, at 277.

139. 135 S. Ct. 2071 (2015).

140. Bruce Weber, *The Deciders: Umpires v. Judges,* THE N.Y. TIMES, July 11, 2009.

141. 135 S. Ct. 2071 (2015) (Roberts, C.J., dissenting).

142. THE FEDERALIST NO. 81 (Alexander Hamilton), *supra* note 8 (arguing that the threat of impeachment would deter judges from "deliberate usurpations on the authority of the legislature").

143. For a discussion of the Canons of Judicial Ethics and their impact, *see* Charles Gardner Geyh, *Preserving Public Confidence in the Courts in an Age of Individual Rights and Public Skepticism, in* BENCH-PRESS: THE COLLISION OF THE COURTS, POLITICS AND THE MEDIA (Keith Bybee ed., 2007).

144. Whitney North Seymour, *The Code of Judicial Conduct from the Point of View of a Member of the Bar,* 1972 UTAH L. REV. 352, 352.

145. *Id.*

146. CHARLES GARDNER GEYH, JAMES ALFINI, JEFFREY SHAMAN, & STEVEN LUBET, JUDICIAL CONDUCT AND ETHICS 1–6-1–7 (5th ed. 2013).

147. CHARLES GARDNER GEYH, JAMES ALFINI, & DANA REMUS, JUDICIAL CONDUCT AND ETHICS § 1.06 (2015 supplement).

148. Judicial Transparency and Ethics Enhancement Act of 2006, H.R. 5219, 109th Cong., sec. 2(a), § 1021 (2006) (proposing the creation of an inspector general for the judiciary to investigate judicial misconduct).

149. 2011 Year-End Report on the Federal Judiciary, http://www.supremecourt.gov/publicinfo/year-end/2011year-endreport.pdf (last visited Jan. 13, 2015).

150. 541 U.S. 913 (2004).

151. Caperton v. A.T. Massey Coal Company, 556 U.S. 868 (2009).

152. Lisa Leff, *U.S. Court Rules Recusal of Gay Judge Not Necessary: Legal Battle on California's Prop 8 Continues,* HOUS. CHRON., June 15, 2011, at A5; Perry v. Schwarzenegger, 630 F. 3d 909 (2011).

153. Robert Barnes, *As Health Case Looms, Two Justices Targeted: Conservatives Attack Kagan While Liberals Slash at Thomas*, THE HOUSTON CHRONICLE, Dec. 4, 2011, at A23.
154. 2011 Year-End Report on the Federal Judiciary, *supra* note 149.
155. JACK BASS, UNLIKELY HEROES (1990).
156. MODEL CODE OF JUDICIAL CONDUCT, Canon 3B(5) and commentary (1990).
157. JUSTICE IN JEOPARDY, *supra* note 46, at 60–65.
158. Brad Heath, *Racial Gap in U.S. Arrest Rates: "Staggering Disparity,"* U.S.A. TODAY, Nov. 19, 2014.
159. Becky Pettit & Bruce Western, *Mass Imprisonment and the Life Course: Race and Class Inequality in U.S. Incarceration*, 69 AM. SOC. REV. 151 (2004).
160. *Id.*
161. DAVID B. ROTTMAN, RANDALL HANSEN, NICOLE MOTT, & LYNN GRIMES, PERCEPTIONS OF THE COURTS IN YOUR COMMUNITY: THE INFLUENCE OF EXPERIENCE, RACE AND ETHNICITY, FINAL REPORT 10 (2003), available at http://www.ncjrs.gov/pdffiles1/nij/grants/201302.pdf.
162. Jennifer Mann, *Missouri Supreme Court Takes Over Cases in Ferguson; Judge Resigns*, ST. LOUIS POST DISPATCH, Mar. 9, 2015.
163. Charlie Savage, *A Judge's View of Judging is on the Record*, N.Y. TIMES, May 14, 2009.
164. Howard B. Glaser, *Wachtler v. Cuomo: The Limits of Inherent Powers*, 78 JUDICATURE 12, 12 (1994).
165. James W. Douglas & Roger E. Hartley, *The Politics of Court Budgeting in the States: Is Judicial Independence Threatened by the Budgetary Process?* 63 PUBLIC ADMINISTRATION REVIEW 441, 446, 449–50 (2003).
166. ROBERT BORK, COERCING VIRTUE: THE WORLDWIDE RULE OF JUDGES 9 (2003).
167. Quoted in Ruth Marcus, *There's New Ferocity in Talk of Firing Activist Judges*, WASHINGTON POST, Apr. 11, 2005, at A19.
168. Center for a Just Society, *Activist Judges Undermine Government by the People*, May 22, 2008, http://www.centerforajustsociety.org/press/article.asp?pr=3445.
169. Marcus, *supra* note 167.
170. Tom Feeney, *Rep. Feeney Defends Measure to Thwart Sentencing by Whim*, PALM BEACH DAILY BUSINESS REVIEW, Apr. 28, 2003, at A7.
171. *Id.* at 4.
172. Michael Dayton, *Chief Justice Lake Defends Latest Changes in Judicial Code in N.C.*, N. CAR. LAWYERS WEEKLY, Oct. 20, 2003.
173. Haynes, *Sales Tax Case: Reform the System*, MILWAUKEE JOURNAL SENTINEL, July 17, 2008, Section A.
174. Barbara Hoberock, *Report Cites Need for Reform in Sentencing*, TULSA WORLD, Nov. 1, 2008, at A13.
175. American Bar Association, Report 118, adopted Aug. 11–12, 2008.
176. *Gov. Paterson Commends Former Mayor Rudy Giuliani for Ideas on State Constitutional Convention*, U.S. FEDERAL NEWS, June 26, 2009.
177. U.S. District Judge Paul Friedman, quoted in Michael Traynor, *Judicial Independence: A Cornerstone of Liberty*, 37 GOLDEN GATE U. L. REV. 487, 497 (2007).
178. STEVEN TELES, THE RISE OF THE CONSERVATIVE LEGAL MOVEMENT (2008); Staszak, *supra* note 96.
179. Bill Schneider, *Cynicism Didn't Begin with Watergate*, ALLPOLITICS, June 17, 1997 (discussing survey data showing deterioration of public confidence in government beginning with the Vietnam War and escalating after Watergate).
180. TELES, *supra* note 178.

CHAPTER 3

1. Morton J. Horwitz, *The Rise of Legal Formalism*, 19 AM. J. LEGAL HIST. 251, 251 (1975).
2. William W. Fisher III, Morton J. Horwitz, & Thomas Reed, *Introduction*, AMERICAN LEGAL REALISM, at xi, xii (William W. Fisher III et al. eds., 1993).
3. Horwitz, *supra* note 1, at 251.
4. *Id.* at 252.
5. LAWRENCE M. FRIEDMAN, A HISTORY OF AMERICAN LAW 383–84 (2d ed. 1985).
6. JOHN HENRY SCHLEGEL, AMERICAN LEGAL REALISM AND EMPIRICAL SOCIAL SCIENCE 25–26 (1995).
7. *Id.* at 27 (quoting Ames that law professors should create "a high order of treatises on all branches of law, exhibiting the historical development of the subject and containing sound conclusions based on scientific analysis"); *see also* Fisher et al., *supra* note 2, at xii (stating that "[p]roperly organized, law was like geometry" to classical educators) *and* Thomas Grey, *Langdell's Orthodoxy*, 45 U. PITT. L. REV. 1, 5 (1983) ("Langdell believed that through scientific methods lawyers could derive correct legal judgments from a few fundamental principles and concepts").
8. Oliver Wendell Holmes, *The Path of the Law*, 10 HARV. L. REV. 457 (1897).
9. Roscoe Pound, *Liberty of Contract*, 18 YALE L.J. 454, at 462 (1909).
10. *See generally* SCHLEGEL, *supra* note 6, at 16–18.
11. JEROME FRANK, LAW AND THE MODERN MIND 244 (1930).
12. *See* Benjamin Cardozo, *The Nature of the Judicial Process (1921), in* AMERICAN LEGAL REALISM, *supra* note 2, at 176–77; Felix Cohen, *Transcendental Nonsense and the Functional Approach*, 35 COLUM. L. REV. 809, 842 (1935).
13. SCHLEGEL, *supra* note 6, at 255.
14. BRIAN Z. TAMANAHA, BEYOND THE FORMALIST-REALIST DIVIDE: THE ROLE OF POLITICS IN JUDGING (2009).
15. *Id.* at 4.
16. *Id.* at 94.
17. *Id.*
18. *Id.* at 6–7.
19. Charles K. Rowley, *An Intellectual History of Law and Economics: 1739-2003, in* THE ORIGINS OF LAW AND ECONOMICS: ESSAYS BY THE FOUNDING FATHERS 3, 11–12 (Francesco Parisi & Charles K. Rowley eds., 2005) ("The path towards law and economics undoubtedly was smoothed by the legal realist challenge to formalism that opened up American legal education to the study of the social sciences"); *see also* Edmund W. Kitch, *The Intellectual Foundations of "Law and Economics,"* 33 J. LEGAL EDUC. 184, 184 (1983); Owen M. Fiss, *The Death of the Law*, 72 CORNELL L. REV. 1, 2 (1986). This is not to suggest, however, that law and economic scholars share intellectual roots with legal realism in the same way that political scientists and psychologists do. *See, e.g.*, RICHARD A. POSNER, OVERCOMING LAW 3 (1995).
20. *See generally* SAUL M. KASSIN & LAWRENCE S. WRIGHTSMAN, THE AMERICAN JURY ON TRIAL: PSYCHOLOGICAL PERSPECTIVES (1988).
21. LAWRENCE M. FRIEDMAN & STEWART MACAULAY, LAW AND THE BEHAVIORAL SCIENCES 1–8 (2d ed. 1977); Schlegel, *supra* note 6, at 248–50.
22. SCHLEGEL, *supra* note 6, at 254 (discussing "the second class citizenship that was implied by 'law and'"). Law and economics has fared somewhat better, in part because its approach is more compatible with a rules-based analysis. Rowley, *supra* note 19, at 12 ("[T]he relationship [between legal realism and law and economics] should not be exaggerated," in part because law and economics "turned out to be a movement that

incorporated some of the formalism of the Langdellian era, albeit a formalism which was based on the notion that laws should be economically efficient, rather than that they should rest on *stare decisis* and precedent").

23. FRIEDMAN & MACAULAY, *supra* note 21, at 7 ("[I]t is fair to note that a social science interest in law is outside the mainstream of scholarship in law, and in all social sciences, except perhaps political science").

24. Cornell W. Clayton, *The Supreme Court and Political Jurisprudence: New and Old Institutionalisms, in* SUPREME COURT DECISION-MAKING: NEW INSTITUTIONAL APPROACHES 15, 20 (Cornell W. Clayton & Howard Gillman eds., 1999).

25. *Id.*

26. Lee Epstein, Jack Knight, & Andrew D. Martin, *The Political (Science) Context of Judging,* 47 ST. LOUIS U. L.J. 783, 786 (2003) (discussing Pritchett); Pauline T. Kim, *Lower Court Discretion,* 82 N.Y.U. L. REV. 383, 384 (2007) (discussing linkage to social psychology).

27. C. HERMAN PRITCHETT, THE ROOSEVELT COURT: A STUDY IN JUDICIAL POLITICS AND VALUES, 1937–1947, at xii–xiii (1948).

28. *Id.* at 240.

29. Cass Sunstein, *Unanimity and Disagreement on the Supreme Court,* 100 CORNELL L. REV. 769 (2015).

30. Eileen Braman & J. Mitchell Pickerill, *Path Dependence in Studies of Judicial Decision-Making, in* WHAT'S LAW GOT TO DO WITH IT? WHAT JUDGES DO, WHY THEY DO IT, AND WHAT'S AT STAKE 114 (Charles Gardner Geyh ed., 2011).

31. *See* Barry Friedman, *Taking Law Seriously,* 4 PERSP. ON POL. 261, 263 (2006).

32. GLENDON SCHUBERT, THE JUDICIAL MIND: THE ATTITUDES AND IDEOLOGIES OF SUPREME COURT JUSTICES, 1946–1963 (1965).

33. JEFFREY A. SEGAL & HAROLD J. SPAETH, THE SUPREME COURT AND THE ATTITUDI-NAL MODEL 17, 62 (1993).

34. John M. Scheb II & William Lyons, *The Myth of Legality and Public Evaluation of the Supreme Court,* 81 SOC. SCI. Q. 928, 936 (2000).

35. Howard Gillman & Cornell W. Clayton, *Beyond Judicial Attitudes: Institutional Approaches to Supreme Court Decision-Making, in* SUPREME COURT DECISION-MAKING: NEW INSTITUTIONAL APPROACHES 1 (Cornell W. Clayton & Howard Gillman eds., 1999).

36. SUPREME COURT DECISION-MAKING: NEW INSTITUTIONAL APPROACHES, *supra* note 35; THE SUPREME COURT IN AMERICAN POLITICS: NEW INSTITUTIONALIST INTER-PRETATIONS (Howard Gillman & Cornell Clayton eds., 1999).

37. LEE EPSTEIN & JACK KNIGHT, THE CHOICES JUDGES MAKE xiii (1998).

38. Rogers Smith, *If Politics Matters: Implications for a "New Institutionalism,"* 6 STUD. IN AM. POL. DEV. 1 (1992).

39. Friedman, *supra* note 31, at 263 (2006) ("Today, attitudinalists devote too much time to . . . fending off claims that something other than attitudes matter").

40. *See generally Critical Legal Studies Symposium,* 36 STAN. L. REV. 1 (1984).

41. Frank Cross, *Political Science and the New Legal Realism: A Case of Unfortunate Interdisci-plinary Ignorance,* 92 NW. U. L. REV. 251, 257–58 (1997).

42. *Id.*

43. *Id.* at 252–53.

44. Michael Gerhardt, *Attitudes about Attitudes,* 101 MICH. L. REV. 1733, 1733 (2003) (reviewing JEFFREY A. SEGAL & HAROLD J. SPAETH, THE SUPREME COURT AND THE ATTITUDINAL MODEL REVISITED (2003)).

45. Patricia Wald, *A Response to Tiller and Cross,* 99 COLUM. L. REV. 235, 236 (1999).

46. *Id.*

47. Friedman, *supra* note 31, at 262 ("[L]egal scholars are now pursuing the same sort of empirical inquiries as positive scholars, creating exciting opportunities for true interdisciplinary collaboration"); Epstein, Knight, & Martin, *supra* note 26, at 783 ("It has been in only the last few years that law professors have shown much interest in political science approaches to judging").
48. Friedman, *supra* note 31; *see also* Harry T. Edwards, *Collegiality and Decision Making on the D.C. Circuit*, 84 Va. L. Rev. 1335, 1335 (1998)(denouncing two studies as "the heedless observations of academic scholars who misconstrue and misunderstand the work of the judges").
49. Cross, *supra* note 41, at 264; Stephen B. Burbank & Barry Friedman, *Reconsidering Judicial Independence*, *in* Judicial Independence at the Crossroads 9, 25 (Stephen B. Burbank & Barry Friedman eds., 2002) (discussing the problems attitudinal studies have had operationalizing law).
50. Lee Epstein & Gary King, *The Rules of Inference*, 69 U. Chi. L. Rev. 1 (2002); *see also* Gregory C. Sisk & Michael Heise, *Judges and Ideology: Public and Academic Debates about Statistical Measures*, 99 Nw. U. L. Rev. 743, 779–83 (2005) (discussing "the great empirical method debate of 2002," provoked by the Epstein and King article).
51. Gregory C. Sisk, *The Quantitative Moment and the Qualitative Opportunity: Legal Studies of Judicial Decision Making*, 93 Cornell L. Rev. 873, 876 (2008) (reviewing Frank B. Cross, Decision Making in the U.S. Courts of Appeals (2007)).
52. Segal & Spaeth, *supra* note 33, at 229.
53. Jeffrey A. Segal & Albert D. Cover, *Ideological Values and the Votes of U.S. Supreme Court Justices*, 83 Am. Pol. Sci. Rev. 557 (1989).
54. Theodore W. Ruger, Pauline T. Kim, Andrew D. Martin, & Kevin M. Quinn, *The Supreme Court Forecasting Project: Legal and Political Science Approaches to Predicting Supreme Court Decisionmaking*, 104 Colum. L. Rev. 1150 (2004); *see John Henry: The Steel Driving Man*, A Folk Version of the Ballad, Ibiblio.org, http://www.ibiblio.org/john_henry/folk.html (last visited Jan. 6, 2014).
55. Ruger et al., *supra* note 54.
56. *Id.* at 1164.
57. *Id.* at 1163. The six factors that the study employed, were: the circuit of origin for the case; the issue area of the case; the type of petitioner; the type of respondent, the ideological direction of the lower court ruling; and whether the petitioner argued that a law or practice was unconstitutional.
58. *Id.* at 1184.
59. *Id.* at 1184–85.
60. *Id.* at 1191.
61. Kim, *supra* note 26, at 404–05; Alexander Volokh, *Choosing Interpretive Methods: A Positive Theory of Judges and Everyone Else*, 83 N.Y.U. L. Rev. 769 (2008).
62. Volokh, *supra* note 61.
63. Professor Volokh, in contrast, speculates that the opposite may also be true—that justices will change their legal preferences to achieve preferred policy outcomes. *Id.*
64. Harold J. Spaeth & Jeffrey A. Segal, Majority Rule or Minority Will: Adherence to Precedent on the U.S. Supreme Court (1999).
65. Thomas G. Hansford & James F. Spriggs II, The Politics of Precedent on the U.S. Supreme Court (2006); Michael J. Gerhardt, The Power of Precedent (2008).
66. Lee Epstein, Andrew D. Martin, Kevin M. Quinn, & Jeffrey A. Segal, *Ideological Drift among Supreme Court Justices: Who, When, and How Important?* 101 Nw. U. L. Rev. 1483, 1504 (2007) (finding drift among twenty-two of twenty-six justices, with twelve becoming more liberal, seven more conservative, and three drifting "in more exotic

ways"); Andrew D. Martin & Kevin M. Quinn, *Assessing Preference Change on the U.S. Supreme Court*, 23 J.L. Econ. & Org. 365, 365 (2007) (finding drift among fourteen of sixteen justices who served on the Court for more than ten years).

67. Nancy Staudt, Barry Friedman, & Lee Epstein, *On the Role of Ideological Homogeneity in Generating Consequential Constitutional Decisions*, 10 U. Pa. J. Const. L. 361 (2008).

68. Cooper v. Aaron, 358 U.S. 1 (1958).

69. Donald R. Songer, Jeffrey A. Segal, & Charles M. Cameron, *The Hierarchy of Justice, Testing a Principal-Agent Model of Supreme Court-Circuit Court Interactions*, 38 Am. J. Pol. Sci. 673, 675 (1994).

70. McNollgast, *Politics and the Courts: A Positive Theory of Judicial Doctrine and the Rule of Law*, 68 S. Cal. L. Rev.1631 (1995).

71. Frank B. Cross, Decision-making in the U.S. Court of Appeals 51, 228 (2007) (finding results "generally consistent with what the legal model would dictate" and concluding that "just one legal standard, affirmance deference to the lower court decision, is consistently significant statistically and by far the most important single variable substantively in explaining circuit court outcomes").

72. *Id.* at 228–29 ("[T]he interposition of a legal threshold requirement obviously had a significant effect on judicial decisions").

73. *Id.* at 122 (arguing that the extent of circuit court compliance with Supreme Court precedent "might be considered evidence of remarkable power for the legal model").

74. *Id.* at 177.

75. *Id.* at 28.

76. Lee Epstein, William M. Landes, & Richard A. Posner, The Behavior of Federal Judges: A Theoretical and Empirical Study of Rational Choice (2013).

77. *See, e.g.,* Nancy C. Staudt, *Modeling Standing*, 79 N.Y.U. L. Rev. 612, 683 (2004) (finding that lower court standing decisions are "above politics" when "lower federal courts are subject to clear and unambiguous standing rules and when effective judicial monitoring exists"); Gregory C. Sisk & Michael Heise, *Judges and Ideology: Public and Academic Debates about Statistical Measures*, 99 Nw. U. L. Rev. 743, 746 (2005) ("[T]o suggest that partisan or ideological preferences are prevalent influences in deciding most cases or are invariably powerful variables in deciding even the most controversial and open-ended of legal issues is a dubious extrapolation from the empirical evidence").

78. Stefanie A. Lindquist, *Stare Decisis as Reciprocity Norm, in* What's Law Got to Do With It?: What Judges Do, Why They Do It, and What's at Stake 173 (Charles Gardner Geyh ed., 2011).

79. Daniel R. Pinello, *Linking Party to Judicial Ideology in American Courts: A Meta-Analysis*, 20 Just. Sys. J. 219 (1999).

80. Gregory A. Huber & Sanford C. Gordon, *Accountability and Coercion: Is Justice Blind when It Runs for Office?*,48 Am. J. Poli. Sci. 247 (2004); Carlos Berdejó & Noam Yuchtman, *Crime, Punishment, and Politics: An Analysis of Political Cycles in Criminal Sentencing*, 95 Rev. of Econ. & Stat. 741 (2013).

81. Lindquist, *supra* note 78.

82. Gregory C. Sisk, Michael Heise, & Andrew P. Morriss, *Charting the Influences on the Judicial Mind: An Empirical Study of Judicial Reasoning*, 73 N.Y.U. L. Rev. 1377, 1498 (1998).

83. Cass R. Sunstein et al., Are Judges Political?: An Empirical Analysis of the Federal Judiciary (2006).

84. Michael A. Bailey & Forrest Maltzman, The Constrained Court: Law, Politics, and the Decisions Justices Make (2011).

85. Stephen B. Burbank, *On the Study of Judicial Behaviors: Of Law, Politics, Science, and Humility, in* What's Law Got to Do With It?: What Judges Do, Why They Do

It, and What's at Stake, *supra* note 78, at 41, 51; Lawrence Baum, *Law and Policy: More and Less than a Dichotomy, in* What's Law Got to Do With It?: What Judges Do, Why They Do It, and What's at Stake, *supra* note 78, at 71; Frank Cross, *Law is Politics, in* What's Law Got to Do With It?: What Judges Do, Why They Do It, and What's at Stake, *supra* note 78, at 92.

86. Richard A. Posner, *What Do Judges and Justices Maximize? (The Same Thing Everybody Else Does)*, 3 Sup. Ct. Econ. Rev. 1, 2 (1993).

87. *Id.* at 13–23 (reviewing the factors and arguing that voting as a source of judicial utility is the most important); *see also* Frederick Schauer, *Incentives, Reputation, and the Inglorious Determinants of Judicial Behavior*, 68 U. Cin. L. Rev. 615 (2000).

88. *See* Huber & Gordon, *supra* note 80.

89. Andrew P. Morriss, Michael R. Heise, & Gregory C. Sisk, *Signaling and Precedent in Federal District Court Opinions*, 13 Sup. Ct. Econ. Rev. 63 (2005); *see also* Mark A. Cohen, *The Motives of Judges: Empirical Evidence from Antitrust Sentencing*, 12 Int'l Rev. L. & Econ. 13 (1992).

90. C.K. Rowland & Robert A. Carp, Politics & Judgment in the Federal District Courts 142–45 (1996).

91. Model Code of Judicial Conduct R. 2.2 (2007).

92. *Id.* R. 2.4(A).

93. *Id.* R. 2.4(B).

94. Rowland & Carp, *supra* note 90, at 158.

95. Evan R. Seamone, *Judicial Mindfulness*, 70 U. Cin. L. Rev. 1023, 1030 (2002).

96. Lawrence S. Wrightsman, Judicial Decision Making: Is Psychology Relevant? 55 (1999).

97. Lawrence Baum, *Motivation and Judicial Behavior: Expanding the Scope of Inquiry* (Mar. 2007), http://faculty.virginia.edu/judging/Documents/motivation.lb.pdf.

98. *Id.*

99. Eileen Braman, Law, Politics, and Perception: How Policy Preferences Shape Legal Reasoning 13–41 (2009).

100. Dan Simon, *A Psychological Model of Judicial Decision-Making*, 30 Rutgers L.J. 1, 20 (1998).

101. *Id.*

102. Eric Berger, *The Rhetoric of Constitutional Absolutism*, 56 Wm. & Mary L. Rev. 667 (2015).

103. Rowland & Carp, *supra* note 90, at 158.

104. Emily Pronin et al., *The Bias Blind Spot: Perceptions of Bias in Self Versus Others*, 28 Personality and Soc. Psychol. Bull. 369, 374 (2002).

105. Anthony G. Greenwald et al., *Measuring Individual Differences in Implicit Cognition: The Implicit Association Test*, 74 J. Personality & Soc. Psychol. 1464, 1465 (1998).

106. *See generally* Jerry Kang & Kristin Lane, *Seeing through Colorblindness: Implicit Bias and the Law*, 58 UCLA L. Rev. 465, 472 (2010).

107. Justin D. Levinson et al., *Guilty by Implicit Racial Bias: The Guilty/Not Guilty Implicit Association Test*, 8 Ohio St. J. Crim. L. 187, 207 (2010).

108. Jeffrey J. Rachlinski et al., *Does Unconscious Racial Bias Affect Trial Judges?* 84 Notre Dame L. Rev. 1195, 1210 (2009).

109. Victor D. Quintanilla, *Beyond Common Sense: A Social Psychological Study of Iqbal's Effect on Claims of Race Discrimination*, 17 Mich. J. Race & L. 1 (2011).

110. Victor D. Quintanilla, *Critical Race Empiricism: A New Means to Measure Civil Procedure*, 3 UC Irvine L. Rev. 187, 210–12 (2013).

111. Lawrence Baum, Judges and Their Audiences: A Perspective on Judicial Behavior (2006).

112. *See* Lindquist, *supra* note 78, at 184 fig.7.2.

113. David Klein & Darby Morrisroe, *The Prestige and Influence of Individual Judges on the U.S. Court of Appeals*, 28 J. LEGAL STUD. 371 (1999).

114. Frank B. Cross & Emerson H. Tiller, *Judicial Partisanship and Obedience to Legal Doctrine: Whistleblowing on the Federal Courts of Appeals*, 107 YALE L.J. 2155 (1998).

115. Harry T. Edwards, *The Effects of Collegiality on Judicial Decision Making*, 151 U. Pa. L. Rev.1639 (2003).

116. Alex Kozinski, *What I Ate for Breakfast, and Other Mysteries of Judicial Decision Making*, in JUDGES ON JUDGING: VIEWS FROM THE BENCH 71 (David M. O'Brien ed., 1997).

117. *See* Susan A. Bandes & Jeremy A. Blumenthal, *Emotion and the Law*, 8 ANN. REV. OF L. & SOC. SCI. 161 (2012).

118. Ryan C. Black et al., *Emotions, Oral Arguments, and Supreme Court Decision Making*, 73 J. OF POL. 572 (2011).

119. *Id.* at 577.

120. Chris Guthrie, Jeffrey J. Rachlinski, & Andrew J. Wistrich, *Blinking on the Bench: How Judges Decide Cases*, 93 CORNELL L. REV. 1 (2007); Chris Guthrie, Jeffrey J. Rachlinski, & Andrew J. Wistrich, *Inside the Judicial Mind*, 86 CORNELL L. REV. 777 (2001) (discussing anchoring, framing, hindsight, representative heuristic, and egocentric biases); Jeffrey J. Rachlinski, *Heuristics and Biases in the Courts: Ignorance or Adaptation?* 79 OR. L. REV. 61 (2000); Jeffrey J. Rachlinski, *A Positive Psychological Theory of Judging in Hindsight*, 65 U. CHI. L. REV. 571 (1998); Andrew J. Wistrich, Chris Guthrie, & Jeffrey J. Rachlinski, *Can Judges Ignore Inadmissible Information? The Difficulty of Deliberately Disregarding*, 153 U. PA. L. REV. 1251 (2005).

CHAPTER 4

1. Barry Friedman & Andrew Martin, *Looking for Law in All the Wrong Places: Some Suggestions for Modeling Legal Decision-Making*, in WHAT'S LAW GOT TO DO WITH IT?: WHAT JUDGES DO, WHY THEY DO IT, AND WHAT'S AT STAKE (Charles Gardner Geyh ed., 2011).

2. KEITH J. BYBEE, ALL JUDGES ARE POLITICAL—EXCEPT WHEN THEY ARE NOT: ACCEPTABLE HYPOCRISIES AND THE RULE OF LAW (2010).

3. *Id.* at 101–03.

4. BRIAN TAMANAHA, BEYOND THE FORMALIST-REALIST DIVIDE: THE ROLE OF POLITICS IN JUDGING (2010).

5. Shudraka, *The Little Clay Cart*, in 9 HARVARD ORIENTAL SERIES 134 (Arthur William Ryder trans., 1905) (2007), *available at* http://www.sacred-texts.com/hin/lcc.

6. KATHLEEN E. KENNEDY, MAINTENANCE, MEED, AND MARRIAGE IN MEDIEVAL ENGLISH LITERATURE 92, 96 (2009) (recounting the views of Nassington and Gower).

7. Theo Meder, *Tales of Tricks and Greed and Big Surprises: Laymen's Views of the Law in Dutch Oral Narrative*, 21 HUMOR 435, 438–40 (2008).

8. Wilfrid Prest, *Judicial Corruption in the Early Modern Period*, 133 PAST & PRESENT 67, 69 (1991) (quoting poem).

9. CELEBRATED CASES OF JUDGE DEE 5–6 (Robert Van Gulik trans., 1976).

10. WILLIAM SHAKESPEARE, MEASURE FOR MEASURE act 2, sc. 4.

11. GEOFFREY CHAUCER, THE CANTERBURY TALES 283–90 (J. U. Nicholson trans., Garden City Pub'g Co. ed. 1934).

12. FRANKLIN PIERCE ADAMS, FPA BOOK OF QUOTATIONS 466 (1952).

13. Shudraka, *supra* note 5.

14. HONORÉ DE BALZAC, *A Commission in Lunacy*, in 7 LA COMÉDIE HUMAINE OF HONORÉ DE BALZAC 171 (Katharine Prescott Wormeley trans., Hardy, Pratt & Co. 1904) (1836), *available at* https://archive.org/stream/lunac10/lunac10.txt.

15. HENRY FIELDING, AMELIA 16 (David Blewett ed., Penguin Books 1987) (1751).
16. *Id.*
17. 1 *Kings* 3:16–28.
18. Meder, *supra* note 7, at 445.
19. ADAMS, *supra* note 12, at 466.
20. BALZAC, *supra* note 14, at 171 (praising Judge Popinot's "heavenly temper").
21. Shudraka, *supra* note 5, at 134.
22. KENNEDY, *supra* note 6, at 96.
23. *Id.* at 111.
24. 2 MARK TWAIN, PERSONAL RECOLLECTIONS OF JOAN OF ARC 116 (1896).
25. LEWIS CARROLL, ALICE'S ADVENTURES IN WONDERLAND AND THROUGH THE LOOKING GLASS AND WHAT ALICE FOUND THERE (Barnes & Noble Books 2003) (1865).
26. *Id.* at 127.
27. *Id.* at 138, 140.
28. MARIE DE FRANCE, LANVAL, http://publishing.cdlib.org/ucpressebooks/ view?docId=ft4580069z&chunk.id=ch5&toc.id=ch5&brand=ucpress
29. Meder, *supra* note 7, at 438.
30. Prest, *supra* note 8, at 71.
31. *Quoted in* 2 LORD CAMPBELL, THE LIVES OF THE CHIEF JUSTICES OF ENGLAND 208 (1881).
32. FIELDING, *supra* note 15, at 17–19.
33. *Id.* at 19.
34. WILLIAM GODWIN, THINGS AS THEY ARE; OR, THE ADVENTURES OF CALEB WILLIAMS (Oxford Univ. Press 1982) (1794).
35. *Id.* at 276.
36. FIELDING, *supra* note 15, at 17.
37. Emile Zola, *J'Accuse!*, L'AURORE (Paris), Jan. 13, 1898, *available at* http://www. oxygenee.com/Zola-and-Dreyfus.pdf.
38. Shawn Tuma, *Law in Texas Literature: Texas Justice—Roy Bean Style*, 21 REV. LITIG. 551, 561 (2002).
39. MARY WOLLSTONECRAFT, THE WRONGS OF WOMAN 170–74 (Oxford Univ. Press 2007) (1798).
40. ROBERT LOUIS STEVENSON, THE WEIR OF HERMISTON 25 (Catherine Kerrigan ed., Edinburgh Univ. Press 1995) (1896).
41. RICHARD ERDOES, SALOONS OF THE OLD WEST 138 (1979).
42. CELEBRATED CASES OF JUDGE DEE, *supra* note 9, at 6.
43. *John* 19:12.
44. LEO TOLSTOY, RESURRECTION 97 (Penguin Books 2009) (1899).
45. ERDOES, *supra* note 41, at 138.
46. 2 CHARLES DICKENS, A CHILD'S HISTORY OF ENGLAND 124 (1852).
47. *Id.*
48. MARIE DE FRANCE, *supra* note 28.
49. Prest, *supra* note 8, at 82.
50. Shudraka, *supra* note 5, at 134.
51. FIELDING, *supra* note 15, at 16–18.
52. MARIE DE FRANCE, *supra* note 28.
53. ANTON CHEKHOV, *A Malefactor, in* 6 THE TALES OF CHEKHOV: THE WITCH & OTHER SHORT STORIES 269, 274 (Constance Garnett trans., Ecco Press 1985) (1885).
54. TWAIN, *supra* note 24, at 118.
55. CARROLL, *supra* note 25, at 140.

56. Sophocles, Antigone lines 453–55 (David Mulroy trans., Univ. of Wisconsin Press 2013) (441 B.C.E.).

57. Edgar Lee Masters, *The Circuit Judge, in* Spoon River Anthology 73 (1916), *available at* http://www.bartleby.com/84/73.html.

58. Charles Dickens, Bleak House 50 (Norman Page ed., Penguin Books 1971) (1853).

59. William Shakespeare, The Merchant of Venice act 4, sc. 1.

60. Celebrated Cases of Judge Dee, *supra* note 9, at 6.

61. Dickens, *supra* note 58, at 400.

62. Adams, *supra* note 12, at 466.

63. Balzac, *supra* note 14, at 157, 171.

64. Fielding, *supra* note 15, at 16.

65. Godwin, *supra* note 34, at 277.

66. Madison McGraw, Justify the Means 128 (2003), *available at* http://www.scholarisland.org/justice.htm.

67. Edgar Lee Masters, *Judge Selah Lively, in* Spoon River Anthology 94 (1916), *available at* http://www.bartleby.com/84/94.html.

68. Robert G. Ingersoll, Address on the Civil Rights Act in Washington, D.C. (Oct. 22, 1883), *transcript available at* http://www.gutenberg.org/files/38811/38811.txt.

69. David Dudley Field, *Judicial Integrity, in* 1 Speeches, Arguments, and Miscellaneous Papers of David Dudley Field 536 (New York, D. Appleton 1884).

CHAPTER 5

1. Am. Bar Assn, Justice in Jeopardy: Report of the Comm'n on the 21st Century Judiciary 17 (2003).

2. *Id.*

3. *Id.*

4. Campbell Pub. Affairs Inst., Maxwell Sch. of Syracuse Univ., Law and Courts Questions from 2005 Poll (2005).

5. *Id.*

6. The Annenberg Pub. Policy Ctr., Univ. of Pa, Fair and Independent Courts: A Conference on the State of the Judiciary: Summary of Survey Results/The Public and the Courts 3 (2006).

7. Keith J. Bybee, All Judges Are Political—Except When They Are Not: Acceptable Hypocrisies and the Rule of Law 8, 14 (2010).

8. Patricia Ewick & Susan S. Silbey, The Common Place of Law: Stories From Everyday Life 28 (1998).

9. Annenberg Public Policy Ctr., *supra* note 6.

10. Beldon, Russonello, & Stewart, *Access to Justice and Constitutional Rights versus Political Pressure: Defining the Battle for the Courts, in* Justice at Stake Campaign, Speak to American Values: A Handbook for Winning the Debate for Fair and Impartial Courts 13, 17 (2006).

11. Campbell Pub. Affairs Inst., *supra* note 4.

12. Beldon, Russonello, & Stewart, *supra* note 10.

13. Kathleen Hall Jamieson & Michael Hennessy, *Public Understanding of and Support for the Courts: Survey Results*, 95 Geo. L. J. 899, 900 (2007).

14. *See* Polling Report Inc., http://www.pollingreport.com/court.htm (listing poll data from various organizations).

15. Keith Bybee, *The Rule of Law is Dead! Long Live the Rule of Law!, in* What's Law Got to Do With It?: What Judges Do, Why They Do It, and What's at Stake (Charles Gardner Geyh ed., 2011).

16. David D. Kirkpatrick, *Senate Democrats Increase Resistance to Roberts*, N.Y. TIMES, Aug. 17, 2005, at A16.
17. Larry Margasak, *Obama Pick for Bench Blocked by GOP for First Time*, THE ASSOCIATED PRESS, May 19, 2011. ("The politics were reversed in 1987, when Democrats defeated Republican Supreme Court nominee Robert Bork by citing his conservative writings. Liberals said Bork was a conservative extremist . . . Bork's nomination was defeated in an up-or-down vote 58–42"); *see* Don Irwin, *Reagan Asks Public to Back Bork Nomination: Says Opponents are "Liberal Special-Interest Groups" that Seek to Politicize Court System*, L.A. TIMES, Oct. 4, 1987.
18. Linda Greenhouse, *Bork Sets Forth Spirited Defense of His Integrity*, N.Y. TIMES, Sept. 19, 1987, at A1.
19. David Lauter, *Senate Rejects Bork for Supreme Court, 58–42*, L.A. TIMES, Oct. 24, 1987, at 1.
20. Sheryl G. Stolberg & Adam Liptak, *Roberts Fields Questions on Privacy and Precedents*, N.Y. TIMES, Sept. 14, 2005, at A1.
21. Quoted in David G. Savage, *Roberts sees Role as Judicial "Umpire,"* L.A. TIMES, Sept. 13, 2005 at A1.
22. Sheryl G. Stolberg, *Senate Approval Likely as Roberts Clears Panel, 13–5*, N.Y. TIMES, Sept. 23, 2005, at A1. For other explanations for the outcomes, see Steven Lubet, *The Alito Confirmation: How Democrats Lost the Political Battle, San Diego Union-Tribune*, Feb. 1, 2006.
23. Quoted in *Obama's Remarks on the Resignation of Justice Souter*, N.Y. TIMES, May 1, 2009.
24. Charlie Savage, *Scouring Obama's Past for Clues on Judiciary*, N.Y. TIMES, May 9, 2009, at A17.
25. Lynn Sweet, *A "Real-Life" Story*, CHICAGO SUN-TIMES, May 27, 2009, at 13.
26. Amy Goldstein & Paul Kane, *Democrats Seek Political Gain from Sotomayor Vote*, WASH. POST, Aug. 5, 2009.
27. The Model Code of Judicial Conduct directs judges to "avoid . . . the appearance of impropriety," with the accompanying comment explaining that "public confidence in the judiciary is eroded by improper conduct and conduct that creates the appearance of impropriety." MODEL CODE OF JUDICIAL CONDUCT R. 1.2 (2007). Rule 2.2, in turn, states that judges "shall uphold and apply the law"; insofar as failing to uphold and apply the law is thus improper, creating the perception that judges do not uphold and apply the law (by openly acknowledging that judges base their decisions on extralegal factors instead) gives rise to an appearance of impropriety.
28. *Three Views from the Bench, in* WHAT'S LAW GOT TO DO WITH IT?: WHAT JUDGES DO, WHY THEY DO IT, AND WHAT'S AT STAKE 328, 328 (Charles Gardner Geyh ed., 2011) (Statement of Indiana Justice Frank Sullivan).
29. *Id.* at 328, 334 (Statement of Indiana Court of Appeals Judge Nancy Vaidik).
30. Gerald E. Rosen, *Remarks of Judge Gerald E. Rosen, Thomas M. Cooley Law School Distinguished Brief Award Banquet, July 19, 1997*, 14 T.M. COOLEY L. REV. 685 (1997) ("So, as judges, we must realize that we hold in our own hands the keys to the door of our continued independence from the political process. To the extent that the people and policy makers perceive that we are stepping beyond our proper role without substantial justification, and willy-nilly thwarting the will of the majority, the door of judicial independence will be slammed shut"); Diarmuid F. O'Scannlain, *The Rule of Law and the Judicial Function in the World Today*, 89 NOTRE DAME L. REV. 1383 (2014) ("There is always the risk that, in our efforts to police the boundaries that the Constitution . . . ha[s] erected, we will become overzealous, inventing constitutional 'rights' or enforcing restrictions existing only in our imaginations. This tendency, I submit, poses . . . threats to the Rule of Law").
31. Margaret H. Marshall, *The Promise of Neutrality: Reflections on Judicial Independence*, 36 HUM. RTS. 3, 4 (2009). ("Fair and neutral judges, knowing that each written opinion

may be scrutinized as a statement of political partisanship by interest groups, may feel tremendous pressure to look over their shoulders, to abandon the principles of judicial neutrality, when deciding cases"); *Law Day Speech by N.C. Superior Court Judge Thomas W. Ross*, N.C. LAW. WKLY., May 16, 2005 ("the constant, degrading and sometimes personal attacks on judges and the judiciary by political and other leaders are slowly eroding the credibility of the judiciary and will ultimately, I fear, undermine the rule of law.")

32. BYBEE, *supra* note 7.
33. *Confidence in Institutions*, GALLUP (June 5–8, 2014), http://www.gallup.com/poll/1597/confidence-institutions.aspx.
34. *See* Polling Report, Inc., *supra* note 14.
35. Joseph William Singer, *Legal Realism Now*, 76 CAL. L. REV. 465, 467 (1988).
36. Austen Sarat, *Book Review: Redirecting Legal Scholarship in Law Schools, Paul Kahn, The Cultural Study of Law: Reconstructing Legal Scholarship. Chicago: University of Chicago Press, 1999*, 12 YALE J. L. & HUMAN. 129, 144 (2000) ("Law's relation to culture is as complex, varied, and disputed as the concept itself"); CULTURAL STUDIES, CULTURAL ANALYSIS, AND THE LAW: MOVING BEYOND LEGAL REALISM (Austen Sarat & Jonathan Simon eds., 2003); PAUL W. KAHN, THE CULTURAL STUDY OF LAW: RECONSTRUCTING LEGAL SCHOLARSHIP (1999).
37. Sarat, *supra* note 36, at 144.
38. Naomi Mezey, *Law as Culture*, in CULTURAL STUDIES, CULTURAL ANALYSIS, AND THE LAW: MOVING BEYOND LEGAL REALISM 37, 42 (Austen Sarat & Jonathan Simon eds., 2003).
39. Judith Welch, *Legal Education's Wicked Problems*, 61 RUTGERS L. REV. 867 (2009).
40. W. SULLIVAN ET AL., EDUCATING LAWYERS: PREPARATION FOR THE PROFESSION OF LAW (2007).
41. Susan Sturm & Lani Guinier, *The Law School Matrix: Reforming Legal Education in a Culture of Competition and Conformity*, 60 VAND. L. REV. 515, 521 (2007).
42. Welch, *supra* note 39, at 909–10.
43. Sturm & Guinier, *supra* note 41, at 521–22.
44. *Id.*
45. TRACEY GEORGE & SUZANNA SHERRY, WHAT EVERY LAW STUDENT REALLY NEEDS TO KNOW (2009); Welch, *supra* note 39, at 908.
46. Welch, *supra* note 39, at 897–98.
47. Kurt Saunders & Linda Levine, *Learning to Think Like a Lawyer*, 29 U. SAN. FRAN. L. REV. 121, 129–30; Welch, *supra* note 39, at 895–900; Anne-Marie Slaughter, *On Thinking Like a Lawyer*, HARV. L. TODAY, May 2002.
48. Welch, *supra* note 39, at 919–24.
49. *Id.* at 597, 916–18; Slaughter, *supra* note 47.
50. Welch, *supra* note 39, at 913–16.
51. *Id.* at 916–18.
52. Saunders & Levine, *supra* note 47, at 130; Paul Wangerin, *Skills Training in Legal Analysis: A Systematic Approach*, 40 U. MIAMI L. REV. 409, 412–15 (1986).
53. MODEL RULES OF PROF'L CONDUCT R. 3.6 (2013); Margaret Tarkington, *A First Amendment Theory for Protecting Attorney Speech*, 45 U.C. DAVIS L. REV. 27 (2011).
54. MODEL RULES OF PROF'L CONDUCT R. 3.1, 3.3, 3.4, 3.5(a), 3.6(a), 3.8(a) (2013).
55. *See* Charles Gardner Geyh, *Why Judicial Elections Stink*, 64 OH. ST. L.J. 43, n. 71 (2003) (listing state laws); AMERICAN BAR ASSOCIATION, STANDING COMMITTEE ON THE FEDERAL JUDICIARY: WHAT IT IS AND HOW IT WORKS, Appendix II (2009) (evaluative questionnaire requiring judicial candidates to supply information in categories captioned: education (including "law school"); bar associations; bar and court admissions;

legal career; litigation; and legal activities), *available at* http://www.americanbar.org/content/dam/aba/migrated/scfedjud/federal_judiciary09.authcheckdam.pdf (last visited Jan. 25, 2015).

56. *See, e.g.,* AMERICAN BAR ASSOCIATION, MODEL CODE OF JUDICIAL CONDUCT R. 2.2, Comment 2 (2007) ("Although each judge comes to the bench with a unique background and personal philosophy, a judge must interpret and apply the law without regard to whether the judge approves or disapproves of the law in question").

57. Frank Cross & Emerson Tiller, *Judicial Partisanship and Obedience to Legal Doctrine: Whistleblowing on the Federal Courts of Appeals,* 107 YALE L.J. 2155 (1998).

58. Chris Guthrie, Jeffrey J. Rachlinski, & Andrew J. Wistrich, *Inside the Judicial Mind,* 86 CORNELL L. REV. 777, 811–16 (2001) (finding that judges participating in a study exhibited an egocentric bias by exaggerating their affirmance rates).

59. *See, e.g.,* Patrick Marley, *State Supreme Court Could Decide Whether John Doe Probe Proceeds,* MILWAUKEE JOURNAL-SENTINEL, Sept. 25, 2014 (discussing investigation into various groups for spending heavily in Wisconsin Supreme Court races).

60. Patrick Marley, *Supreme Court Tensions Boil Over,* MILWAUKEE JOURNAL-SENTINEL, Mar. 19, 2011; *In re* Disciplinary Proceedings Against Ziegler, 750 N.W.2d 710, 713 (Wis. 2008).

61. Patrick Marley, *Issue of Gableman Recusal Divides State Supreme Court,* MILWAUKEE JOURNAL-SENTINEL, Oct. 16, 2009.

62. *See* Patrick Marley, *Ethics Violations Filed against Prosser,* MILWAUKEE JOURNAL-SENTINEL, Mar. 16, 2012.

63. *See* Patrick Marley, *John Doe Probe Raises Issue of Potential Conflicts with Justices,* MILWAUKEE JOURNAL-SENTINEL, Apr. 28, 2014.

64. *See* Patrick Marley, *Gableman Decides to Stay on Criminal Case,* MILWAUKEE JOURNAL-SENTINEL, Sept. 25, 2009 (Gableman was accused of expressing anti-criminal defendant sentiments after airing a commercial in which he attacked his opponent for defending a child molester when the opponent was a public defender).

65. *See* Bill Lueders, *Recusal Disputes Drive Tension Among Supreme Court Justices,* WISCONSINWATCH.ORG, Mar. 10, 2012.

66. *See* Marley, *supra* note 60.

67. *See* Patrick Marley, *Bradley Reads Dissent before Recusal Rule is Set,* MILWAUKEE JOURNAL-SENTINEL, Dec. 7, 2009.

68. *See* Patrick Marley, *Justice Bradley Got More Security before Prosser Incident; Safety Concerns Remain,* MILWAUKEE JOURNAL-SENTINEL, Feb. 13, 2013.

69. *See id.*

70. *See* Patrick Marley, *Court Adopts New Campaign Donation Rules,* MILWAUKEE JOURNAL-SENTINEL, Jan. 21, 2010 (4-3 majority voted to approve the new campaign donation recusal rules).

71. *See* Patrick Marley, *Former Prosser Aide Made Recommendations for Judicial Panel,* MILWAUKEE JOURNAL-SENTINEL, Dec. 19, 2011 (the court split 3-3 on whether Gableman violated ethics rules with his campaign ad).

72. *See* Patrick Marley, *Ethics Violations Filed against Prosser,* MILWAUKEE JOURNAL-SENTINEL, Mar. 16, 2012. ("Prosser and some of his fellow conservatives who saw the incident said Bradley had her fists raised; she said she did not. Prosser said he put his hands up in a defensive gesture and they briefly went onto her neck.")

73. *See* Marley, *supra* note 68 ("Bradley also called for reforming the way justices are disciplined and wrote that the court should reconsider its decision not to hire a counselor to help justices work out their differences. The court rejected that idea 4-3 in September 2011.")

74. Sturm & Guinier, *supra* note 41, at 521; Mark Richards & Herbert Kritzer, *Jurispruden-tial Regimes in Supreme Court Decision-Making*, 96 AM. POL. SCI. REV. 305, 305 (2002); Joel Grossman et al., *Dimensions of Institutional Participation: Who Uses the Courts and How*, 44 J. OF POLITICS 86 (1982).

75. Rogers Smith, *If Politics Matters: Implications for a "New Institutionalism,"* 6 STUD. IN AM. POLIT. DEVELOPMENT 1 (1992).

76. LIEF H. CARTER & THOMAS F. BURKE, REASON IN LAW 8 (6th ed. 2002).

77. Susan Daicoff, *Lawyer, Know Thyself: A Review of Empirical Research on Attorney Attri-butes Bearing on Professionalism*, 46 AM. U. L. REV. 1337, 1408 (1997).

78. James Ogloff et al., *More than "Learning to Think Like a Lawyer": The Empirical Research on Legal Education* 34 CREIGHTON L. REV. 73, 111 (2000).

79. EILEEN BRAMAN, LAW, POLITICS AND PERCEPTION: HOW POLICY PREFERENCES IN-FLUENCE LEGAL REASONING 164 (2009).

80. *Id.*

81. MARK A. GRABER, A NEW INTRODUCTION TO AMERICAN CONSTITUTIONALISM 93 (2013).

82. *Id.*

83. *Id.* at 92.

84. Eileen Braman's study of how people with and without legal training analyze legal prob-lems differently is corroborative. See BRAMAN, *supra* note 79.

85. Bryan Lammon, *What We Talk about When We Talk about Ideology: Judicial Politics Scholarship and Naïve Legal Realism*, 83 ST. JOHN'S L. REV. 231, 271 (2009).

86. David Dunning et al., *Flawed Self-Assessment: Implications for Health, Education, and the Workplace*, 5 PSYCHOL. SCI. IN THE PUB. INT. 69, 71–73 (2004).

87. David Dunning et al., *Why People Fail to Recognize Their Own Incompetence*, 12 CUR-RENT DIRECTIONS IN PSYCHOL. SCI. 83, 86 (2003).

88. Emily Pronin et al., *The Bias Blind Spot: Perceptions of Bias in Self Versus Others*, 28 PER-SONALITY AND SOC. PSYCHOL. BULL.369, 374 (2002).

89. Emily Pronin, *Perception and Misperception of Bias in Human Judgment*, 11 TRENDS IN COGNITIVE SCI. 37, 38 (2006).

90. RICHARD POSNER, HOW JUDGES THINK 46 (2008); *see also* Harry T. Edwards, *Pitfalls of Empirical Studies That Attempt to Understand the Factors Affecting Appellate Decision-making*, 58 DUKE L.J. 1895, 1897 (2009) ("When the relevant legal materials are un-complicated, the issues are uncontroversial, and precedent is clear, judges' deliberations are straightforward and judgments are easily reached").

91. Jeffrey Segal, *What's Law Got to Do With It: Thoughts from "the Realm of Political Science,"* *in* WHAT'S LAW GOT TO DO WITH IT?: WHAT JUDGES DO, WHY THEY DO IT, AND WHAT'S AT STAKE 19 (Charles Gardner Geyh ed., 2011) (referencing, and rejecting, this conception).

92. Stephen B. Burbank, *On the Study of Judicial Behaviors: Of Law, Politics, Science and Humility, in* WHAT'S LAW GOT TO DO WITH IT? WHAT JUDGES DO, WHY THEY DO IT, AND WHAT'S AT STAKE (Charles Gardner Geyh ed., 2011).

93. Edward L. Rubin, *Independence as a Governance Mechanism, in* JUDICIAL INDEPEND-ENCE AT THE CROSSROADS 56, 70–71 (Stephen B. Burbank & Barry Friedman eds., 2002); Martin H. Redish, *Federal Judicial Independence: Constitutional and Political Perspectives*, 46 MERCER L. REV. 697, 708 (1995); Tom R. Tyler, *The Role of Perceived Injustice in Defendant's Evaluation of Their Courtroom Experience*, 18 LAW & SOC'Y REV. 51, 70 (1984).

94. U.S. CONST. amend. V, VI, XIV § 1; FED. R. EVID. 601–15; CHARLES GARDNER GEYH, JAMES J. ALFINI, STEVEN LUBET, & JEFFREY M. SHAMAN, JUDICIAL CONDUCT AND

ETHICS 2–26 (5th ed. 2013) ("Litigants have a right to expect . . . that their case will be heard in a public forum before an impartial judge or jury with representatives of both sides present"); *In re* Stuhl, 292 N.C. 379, 389, 233 S.E. 2d 562, 568 (1977) ("A judge should accord to every person who is legally interested in a proceeding, or his lawyer, full right to be heard according to law, and, except as authorized by law, neither initiate nor consider ex parte or other communications concerning a pending or impending proceeding"); MODEL CODE OF JUDICIAL CONDUCT R. 2.9, 2.11(A)(1) (2007).

95. Martin H. Redish & Lawrence C. Marshall, *Adjudicatory Independence and the Values of Procedural Due Process*, 95 YALE L.J. 455, 476 (1986).

96. Edward Rubin, *Independence as a Governing Mechanism*, in JUDICIAL INDEPENDENCE AT THE CROSSROADS: AN INTERDISCIPLINARY APPROACH 56, 70 (Stephen B. Burbank & Barry Friedman eds., 2002).

97. Tom R. Tyler, *The Role of Perceived Injustice in Defendants' Evaluation of Their Courtroom Experience*, 18 L & SOC. REV. 51, 69–70 (1984); TOM TYLER, ROBERT BOECKMANN, HEATHER SMITH, & YUEN HUO, SOCIAL JUSTICE IN A DIVERSE SOCIETY 82–83 (1997).

98. DAVID B. ROTTMAN, RANDALL HANSEN, NICOLE MOTT, & LYNN GRIMES, PERCEPTIONS OF THE COURTS IN YOUR COMMUNITY: THE INFLUENCE OF EXPERIENCE, RACE AND ETHNICITY, FINAL REPORT 60 (2003).

99. Tyler does not identify judicial independence per se as a factor contributing to public confidence in court procedure, but it is implicit in several of the factors he does identify, including the judge's efforts to be fair; the judge's honesty; the ethics of the judge's conduct; and the judge's bias. Tom Tyler, *What is Procedural Justice?: Criteria Used by Citizens to Assess the Fairness of Legal Procedures*, 22 L. & SOC. REV. 103, 121 (1988). If, for example, if a judge presents himself as neutral and fair, but is thought to be under the thumb of an energized legislature or interest group, the adverse impact on the judge's perceived fairness, honesty, ethics, and bias seems plain.

100. MODEL CODE OF JUDICIAL CONDUCT R. 2.2 (2007); *see, e.g.*, Reiser v. Residential Funding Corp., 380 F.3d 1027, 1029 (7th Cir. 2004) ("Just as the court of appeals must follow decisions of the Supreme Court whether or not we agree with them . . . so district judges must follow the decision of this court whether or not they agree"); *In re* Feinberg, 833 N.E.2d 1204, 1209 (N.Y. 2005) ("Petitioner's consistent disregard for fundamental statutory requirements of office demonstrates an unacceptable incompetence in the law").

101. Steven D. Smith, *The Pursuit if Pragmatism*, 100 YALE L.J. 409 (1990) (explaining that the pragmatist will choose between outcomes by deciding which is likely to produce the "best" consequences).

102. Thomas C. Grey, *Holmes and Legal Pragmatism*, 41 STAN. L. REV. 787, 791 (1989) ("In social theory generally, and legal theory more particularly, the pragmatist tendency is to promote trade rather than warfare between normative and descriptive theorists, storytellers and model-builders, interpreters and causal explainers").

103. Richard Rorty, *The Banality of Pragmatism and the Poetry of Justice*, in PRAGMATISM IN LAW AND SOCIETY 89, 90 (Michael Brint & William Weaver eds., 1991).

104. POSNER, *supra* note 90, at 230, and sources cited at n. 2.

105. *Id.* at 18–46 (2008).

106. Smith, *supra* note 101, at 423–24.

107. Tom R. Tyler, *The Role of Perceived Injustice in Defendants' Evaluation of Their Courtroom Experience*, 18 L & SOC. REV. 51, 69–70 (1984); TOM TYLER, ROBERT BOECKMANN, HEATHER SMITH, & YUEN HUO, SOCIAL JUSTICE IN A DIVERSE SOCIETY 82–83 (1997).

108. Franklin Pierce Adams, FPA Book of Quotations 466 (1952).
109. Model Code of Judicial Conduct R. 2.10 (2007).
110. Judith Kaye, *Safeguarding a Crown Jewel: Judicial Independence and Lawyer Criticism of Courts*, 25 Hofstra L. Rev. 703, 712 (1997).
111. Daniel M. Schaffzin, *Memorandum on Ethical Constraints Limiting a Judge's First Amendment Freedom of Speech*, in Uncertain Justice: Politics and America's Courts 173, 176–83 (2000).

CHAPTER 6

1. Stephen B. Burbank, *On the Study of Judicial Behaviors: Of Law, Politics, Science and Humility, in* What's Law Got to Do With It?: What Judges Do, Why They Do It, and What's at Stake 41, 53 (Charles Gardner Geyh ed., 2011) (expressing a preference for "the messiness of lived experience to the tidiness of unduly parsimonious models"). While Burbank was writing about quantitative models, his point applies equally to theory: there is a line between simplification and over-simplification that scholars should not cross.
2. *Compare* 28 U.S.C. § 455, *with* Code of Conduct for United States Judges, Canon 3 C.
3. Model Code of Judicial Conduct R. 2.2, Comment 1 (judges must "perform all duties of judicial office . . . impartially" to "ensure impartiality and fairness to all parties"); R. 2.6, Comment 1 (judges must guarantee parties "the right to be heard according to law" which is "an essential component of an impartial system of justice").
4. *See, e.g.,* Model Code of Judicial Conduct R. 1.2 (2007) ("A judge shall act at all times in a manner that promotes public confidence in the . . . impartiality of the judiciary, and shall avoid impropriety and the appearance of impropriety").
5. *See* discussion at *infra*, notes 87–92, and accompanying text (discussing impeachment as a remedy for less than "good" behavior).
6. Anthony B. Sanders, *The New "Judicial Federalism" before Its Time: A Comprehensive Review of Economic Substantive Due Process under State Constitutional Law since 1940 and the Reasons for Its Recent Decline*, 55 Am. U. L. Rev. 457, 469 (2005).
7. *In re* Murchison, 349 U.S. 133, 136 (1955).
8. Tumey v. Ohio, 273 U.S. 510, 535 (1927).
9. Martin H. Redish & Lawrence C. Marshall, *Adjudicatory Independence and the Values of Procedural Due Process*, 95 Yale L.J. 455, 476 (1986); *see also* Paul R. Verkuil, *Separation of Powers, Due Process, and the Idea of Judicial Independence*, 30 Wm. & Mary L. Rev. 301, 315 (1989).
10. Tumey, 273 U.S. 510, 523 (1927).
11. Stephan O. Kline, *Judicial Independence: Rebuffing Congressional Attacks on the Third Branch*, 87 Ky. L.J. 679, 747 (1999) ("Due process guarantees an impartial and competent judge"); Martin H. Redish, *Same-Sex Marriage, The Constitution, and Congressional Power to Control Federal Jurisdiction: Be Careful What You Wish For*, 9 Lewis & Clark L. Rev. 363, 368 (2005) ("The Due Process Clause . . . requires that a neutral, independent, and competent judicial forum remain available in cases in which the liberty or property interests of an individual or entity are at stake").
12. Charles Gardner Geyh, *Why Judicial Disqualification Matters. Again*, 30 Rev. Litig. 671, 677–78 (2011).
13. John P. Frank, *Disqualification of Judges*, 56 Yale L.J. 605, 611–12 (1947).
14. Caperton v. A.T. Massey Coal Co., 129 S. Ct. 2252, 2267 (2009) (Roberts, C.J., dissenting) ("There is a 'presumption of honesty and integrity in those serving as adjudicators.'

(citation omitted) All judges take an oath to uphold the Constitution and apply the law impartially, and we trust that they will live up to this promise").

15. Caperton, 129 S. Ct. 2252.

16. Inhabitants of Northampton v. Smith, 52 Mass. 390 (1846) ("[A]n interest in a question or subject matter, arising from feeling and sympathy, may be more efficacious in influencing the judgment, than even a pecuniary interest; but an interest of such a character would be too vague . . . a test"); *see also* Frank, *supra* note 13, at 611–12 ("English common law practice at the time of the establishment of the American court system was simple in the extreme. Judges disqualified for financial interest. No other disqualifications were permitted, and bias . . . was rejected entirely").

17. 129 S. Ct. 2252.

18. 129 S. Ct. at 2267 (Roberts, C.J., dissenting).

19. 129 S. Ct. at 2265–66.

20. Aetna Life Ins. Co. v. Lavoie, 475 U.S. 813, 828 (1986).

21. Ashwander v. Tennessee Valley Auth., 297 U.S. 288, 346–49 (1936) (Brandeis, J., concurring) ("The Court will not pass upon a constitutional question although properly presented by the record, if there is also present some other ground upon which the case may be disposed of").

22. 28 U.S.C. § 455.

23. State courts, like their Federal counterparts, adhere to *Ashwander* avoidance principles. *See, e.g.,* Jack Tuholske, *Going with the Flow: The Montana Court's Conservative Approach to Constitutional Interpretation,* 72 MONT. L. REV. 237, 242–43 (2011) (noting that the state supreme court implemented *Ashwander* principles).

24. In Tumey v. Ohio, for example, the Court opined that "[a]ll questions of judicial qualification may not involve constitutional validity. Thus matters of kinship, personal bias, state policy, remoteness of interest, would seem generally to be matters merely of legislative discretion." 273 U.S. 510, 523 (1927). Given the stories recounted in chapter 4, which showed a centuries-old antipathy toward judges who presided in the teeth of relational conflicts and personal biases, the suggestion that kinship and bias did not implicate core due process concerns can only be explained in terms of historical, pragmatic, and prudential constraints.

25. Around twenty, mostly western, states have preemptory disqualification (or substitution) of judges procedures that permit a party to request the removal of an assigned judge without the showing required by disqualification rules. Judicial Disqualification Project, *Taking Disqualification Seriously,* 92 JUDICATURE 9 (2008).

26. *In re* Kadur (N.Y. Comm'n, May 28, 2003) (judge removed from office for knowingly presiding over cases involving seven relatives whom she accorded lenient treatment); *In re* Deyo, Unreported Determination (N.Y. Comm'n, Dec. 18, 1980) (judge removed for failing to recuse himself from a case he decided in favor of his brother).

27. *In re* Anderson, 252 N.W.2d 592 (Minn. 1977) (judge disciplined for presiding over case in which he owed money to attorney); *In re* Yandell, 772 P.2d 807 (Kan. 1989) (judge disciplined for presiding over a case in which he was in default on a loan from one of the parties).

28. WILLIAM BLACKSTONE, III COMMENTARIES ON THE LAWS OF ENGLAND *361 (1768) (stating that "judges or justices cannot be challenged" because "the law will not suppose a possibility of bias or favour in a judge, who is already sworn to administer impartial justice, and whose authority greatly depends upon that presumption and idea").

29. RICHARD E. FLAMM, JUDICIAL DISQUALIFICATION: RECUSAL AND DISQUALIFICATION OF JUDGES 54–59 (2d ed. 2007) (discussing proof problems limiting disqualification for actual bias).

30. Geyh, *supra* note 12, at 678–79 (discussing the presumption of impartiality and the tension it creates with disqualification rules).

31. *Id.* at 690–92.

32. *Id.* at 703–04 (discussing tension between the appearance of partiality in disqualification proceedings, and the ethical directive to avoid the appearance of impropriety); MODEL CODE OF JUDICIAL CONDUCT R. 1.2, Comment 5 (directing judges to avoid the appearance of impropriety and explaining that "the test" for an appearance of impropriety is, *inter alia*, whether the judge's conduct would "create in reasonable minds a perception" that "reflects adversely on the judge's . . . impartiality").

33. JEFFREY M. SHAMAN, JONA GOLDSCHMIDT, JUDICIAL DISQUALIFICATION: AN EMPIRICAL STUDY OF JUDICIAL PRACTICES AND ATTITUDES 69 (1995) ("[T]he survey showed a sensitivity to conflicts of interest and a concern for judicial impartiality").

34. *Id.* at 1.

35. *See* Cassandra Burke Robertson, *The Right to Appeal*, 91. N.C. L. REV. 1219, 1222 (2013).

36. GENE R. SHREVE & PETER RAVEN-HANSEN, UNDERSTANDING CIVIL PROCEDURE 479 (4th ed. 2009)("One purpose of appeal is to *ensure the correctness* of lower court dispositions").

37. For example, at common law, where disqualification for bias was not permitted, appeal was recognized as the primary remedy for parties victimized by judicial partiality. McCauley v. Weller, 12 Cal. 500, 523–24 (1859) (explaining that jurors are disqualified more readily than judges and that the premature "expression of an unqualified opinion on the merits" will disqualify a juror but not a judge because a judges decisions are subject to appeal).

38. Charles Gardner Geyh, *Informal Methods of Judicial Discipline*, 142 U. PA. L. REV. 243, 297–302.

39. *See* Toby J. Heytens, *Reassignment*, 66 STAN. L. REV. 1 (2014); 28 U.S.C. § 2106; CHARLES GARDNER GEYH, JUDICIAL DISQUALIFICATION: AN ANALYSIS OF FEDERAL LAW 109–13 (2d ed. 2010) (discussing the circumstances in which circuit courts have reassigned cases to a different judge under § 2106).

40. Fed. R. Civ. P. 2.

41. *Id.* Rule 8(a).

42. Moore's Federal Practice, § 12.34[1][b] (2011).

43. Fed. R. Civ. P. 56(a).

44. Judith Resnik, *On the Bias: Feminist Reconsiderations of the Aspirations for Our Judges*, 61 S. CAL. L. REV. 1877 (1988).

45. Lon L. Fuller, *The Forms and Limits of Adjudication*, 92 HARV. L. REV. 353, 383 (1978).

46. Fed. R. Civ. P. 1.

47. U.S. CONST. art. 6, § 3.

48. 28 U.S.C. § 453.

49. *See, e.g.,* N.Y. CONST. art. XIII, § 1; CAL. CONST. art. XX, § 3; PA. CONST. art. VI, § 3; WYO. CONST. art. VI, § 20; OR. CONST. art. VII, § 7; TEX. CONST. art. XVI, § 1; IND. CONST. art. XV, § 4.

50. WILLIAM BLACKSTONE, I COMMENTARIES ON THE LAWS OF ENGLAND, *368(1768); *see also* JOSEPH STORY, III COMMENTARIES ON THE CONSTITUTION § 1838 (1833) ("Oaths have a solemn obligation upon the minds of all reflecting men, and especially upon those, who feel a deep sense of accountability to a Supreme being").

51. Michael A. Wolff, *Chief Justice Michael A Wolff: 2006 State of the Judiciary Address*, 62 J. MO. B. 56, 57 (2006).

52. William H. Pryor Jr., *Judicial Independence and the Lesson of History*, 68 ALA. LAW. 389, 390 (2007).

53. Gerald E. Rosen, *Judicial Independence in an Age of Political and Media Scrutiny*, 14 T.M. COOLEY L. REV. 685, 689 (1997).

54. Judith Ann Lanzinger, *What Have You Done for Me Lately? Lessons Learned from Judicial Campaigns*, 38 U. BALT. L. REV. 11, 26 (2008).

55. Leslie W. Abramson, *Appearance of Impropriety: Deciding When a Judge's Impartiality "Might Reasonably Be Questioned,"* 14 GEO. J. LEGAL ETHICS 55, 55 (2000).

56. MODEL CODE OF JUDICIAL CONDUCT, pmbl.

57. CANONS OF JUDICIAL ETHICS, pmbl. (1924).

58. MODEL CODE OF JUDICIAL CONDUCT, pmbl. ("The United States legal system is based upon the principle that an independent, impartial, and competent judiciary, composed of men and women of integrity, will interpret and apply the law that governs our society").

59. CHARLES E. GEYH [*SIC*] & W. WILLIAM HODES, REPORTERS' NOTES TO THE MODEL CODE OF JUDICIAL CONDUCT 19 (2009).

60. MODEL CODE OF JUDICIAL CONDUCT, pmbl.

61. *Id.*

62. *Id.* at R. 2.2 ("A judge shall uphold and apply the law"); *id.* at R. 2.4, Comment 1 ("An independent judiciary requires that judges decide cases according to the law and facts, without regard to whether particular laws or litigants are popular").

63. *Id.* at R. 2.6 ("A judge shall accord to every person . . . the right to be heard according to law"); *id.* at Comment 1 ("The right to be heard is an essential component of a fair and impartial system of justice"); *id.* at R. 2.12, Comment 2 ("Public confidence in the judicial system depends upon timely justice").

64. *Id.* at R. 1.2, Comment 4 ("A judge should participate in activities that promote . . . access to justice for all").

65. *Id.* at pmbl.

66. 28 U.S.C. § 351.

67. JUDICIAL CONFERENCE COMMITTEE ON JUDICIAL CONDUCT AND DISABILITY, RULES FOR JUDICIAL-CONDUCT AND JUDICIAL-DISABILITY PROCEEDINGS 5 (2008).

68. *Id.* at R. 2.9.

69. CHARLES GARDNER GEYH, JAMES J. ALFINI, STEVEN LUBET, & JEFFREY M. SHAMAN, JUDICIAL CONDUCT AND ETHICS §5.02 (5th ed. 2013).

70. MODEL CODE OF JUDICIAL CONDUCT R. 2.10; *id.* at Comment 1.

71. *See, e.g.,* United States v. Microsoft Corp., 253 F.3d 34 (D.C. Cir. 2001) (requiring disqualification for statements to reporters); FLAMM, *supra* note 29 at 374–75 ("[W]here the judge violates this rule [against ex parte communications], he is ordinarily obliged to recuse himself from presiding over that proceeding. . . .").

72. GEYH ET AL, *supra* note 69, at 4–21; *see also* FLAMM, *supra* note 29, at 406, n. 2 ("[T]he fact that a judge has engaged in ex parte communications, standing alone, is not necessarily sufficient to warrant disqualification"); LESLIE W. ABRAMSON, JUDICIAL DISQUALIFICATION UNDER CANON 3 OF THE CODE OF JUDICIAL CONDUCT (STUDIES OF THE JUSTICE SYSTEM) 27–30 (American Judicature Society, 2d ed. 1992).

73. United States v. Barry, 961 F.2d 260, 263–65 (D.C. Cir. 1992); GEYH ET AL., *supra* note 69, at 4–24 ("Even strong statements made out-of-court about a pending case are not disqualifying if they do not stem from an extrajudicial source and so long as they do not go so far as to show that the judge's mind is closed").

74. *Compare* 28 U.S.C. § 455, *with* CODE OF CONDUCT FOR UNITED STATES JUDGES, Canon 3 C.

75. GEYH ET AL., *supra* note 69, at 4–3("[A] judge will be subject to discipline (as distinct from reversal on appeal) for incorrectly failing to disqualify himself only where the failure was willful").
76. MODEL CODE OF JUDICIAL CONDUCT R. 2.7, Comment 1 (judges must "decide . . . matters assigned to the judge, except when disqualification is required," because of "the burdens that may be imposed on a judge's colleagues" by "unwarranted disqualification").
77. GEYH ET AL, *supra* note 69, at 1–11.
78. *Id.* at 2–4.
79. MODEL CODE OF JUDICIAL CONDUCT R. 2.2.
80. GEYH ET AL., *supra* note 69, at 2–4 to 2–15. In the federal system, the issue is resolved by the disciplinary statute itself, which directs chief judges to dismiss judicial conduct complaints that are "directly related to the merits of a decision or procedural ruling"; 28 U.S.C. § 352(b)(1)(A)(ii).
81. *See, e.g.,* Republican Party of Minnesota v. White, 536 U.S. 765 (2002).
82. *Id.*
83. 135 S. Ct. 1656 (2015).
84. Charles Gardner Geyh, *The Criticism and Speech of Judges in the United States*, in JUDICIARIES IN COMPARATIVE PERSPECTIVE 257, 271 (H.P. Lee ed., 2011) (citing and discussing cases).
85. MODEL CODE OF JUDICIAL CONDUCT R. 2.2, Comment 2.
86. FLAMM, *supra* note 29, at 274.
87. Peter M. Shane, *Who May Discipline or Remove Federal Judges? A Constitutional Analysis*, 142 U. PA. L. REV. 209, 213–22 (1993).
88. U.S. CONST. art. II, § 4.
89. THE FEDERALIST NO. 65 (Alexander Hamilton) (Clinton Rossiter ed. 1961).
90. 28 U.S.C. § 351–64.
91. CHARLES GARDNER GEYH, WHEN COURTS & CONGRESS COLLIDE: THE STRUGGLE FOR CONTROL OF AMERICA'S JUDICIAL SYSTEM 125–31 (2006).
92. *See, e.g.,* the impeachment and removal of judges Archbald, Ritter, Nixon, and Hastings as discussed in EMILY FIELD VAN TASSEL & PAUL FINKELMAN, IMPEACHABLE OFFENSES: A DOCUMENTARY HISTORY FROM 1787 TO THE PRESENT (1999).
93. GEYH ET AL., *supra* note 69, at 15–11.
94. *Id.* at 15–1 to 15–17.
95. *Id.* at 15–1 to 15–2.
96. Randy J. Holland & Cynthia Gray, *Judicial Discipline: Independence with Accountability*, 5 WIDENER L. SYMP. J. 117, 121 (2000).
97. Charles Geyh, *The Choreography of Courts-Congress Conflicts*, in THE POLITICS OF JUDICIAL INDEPENDENCE: COURTS, POLITICS, AND THE PUBLIC 19, 32–33 (Bruce Peabody ed., 2011).
98. Don Van Natta., *A Publicized Drug Courier Pleads Guilty to 3 Felonies*, N.Y. TIMES, June 22, 1996.
99. GEYH ET AL., *supra* note 69, at 15–10.
100. *Id.* at 15–14.
101. VAN TASSEL & FINKELMAN, *supra* note 92, at 91 (discussing Jeffersonian Republicans campaign to remove "all of [the judges]. . . indiscriminately").
102. GEYH, *supra* note 91, at 3.
103. The five systems include: gubernatorial appointment; gubernatorial appointment from a candidate pool selected by a judicial nominating commission ("merit selection"), typically followed by periodic retention elections; partisan election; non-partisan

election; and legislative appointment. Charles Gardner Geyh, *The Endless Judicial Selec-tion Debate and Why It Matters for Judicial Independence*, 21 GEO. J. LEGAL ETHICS 1259, 1263 (2008). For a summary of which states use what selection methods, see: http://www.judicialselection.us/.

104. AMERICAN BAR ASSOCIATION STANDING COMMITTEE ON JUDICIAL INDEPENDENCE, REPORT OF THE COMMISSION ON PUBLIC FINANCING OF JUDICIAL CAMPAIGNS ix (2002).

105. In 2005, Harriet Miers withdrew her nomination for the Supreme Court because of the public's negative reaction to it, which was due in part to the belief that Miers was unqualified for the position, implicating competency concerns. David Stout & Timothy Williams, *Miers Ends Supreme Court Bid after Failing to Earn Support*, N.Y. TIMES, Oct. 27, 2005.

106. Former Illinois Supreme Court Justice James Heiple declined to run for another term in 2000, which the press and public attributed to an issue of integrity arising out of allegations that he abused the prestige of his office by attempting to avoid traffic tickets. *See* Christi Parsons, *Heiple Won't Run for Court Again: Controversial Jurist Calls It Quits*, CHI. TRIB., May 6, 2000.

107. In a 2007 Wisconsin Supreme Court race, candidate Annette Ziegler was accused (as a court of appeals judge) of, and later reprimanded, for presiding over cases in which her husband was affiliated with a corporate party. *In re* Disciplinary Proceedings Against Ziegler, 750 N.W.2d 710, 716–17 (Wis. 2008).

108. A candidate's dependence on his campaign supporters is typically couched in terms of impartiality concerns, but clearly implicates independence issues. *See, e.g.,* Toby Coleman, *Massey CEO Gives $1.7 Million to Anti-Warren McGraw Group*, WEST VIR-GINIA CITIZEN ACTION GROUP (Oct. 15, 2004), http://www.wvcag.org/news/fair_use/2004/10_15a.htm; *see also* Adam Liptak & Janet Roberts, *Campaign Cash Mirrors a High Court's Rulings*, N.Y. TIMES, Oct. 1, 2006 (all justices in the Ohio Supreme Court 4-3 majority had taken money from the defendant companies' affiliates, while justices in the minority had received contributions from the plaintiffs' lawyers. Retired chief justice of the West Virginia Supreme Court of Appeals Richard Neely explains the influ-ence of campaign contributions: "It's pretty hard in big-money races not to take care of your friends. It's very hard not to dance with the one who brung you").

109. Geyh, *supra* note 84, at 265–66.

110. Geyh, *supra* note 103, at 1262 (noting that "the merit selection movement has stalled").

111. Campaigns have been launched in several states to replace merit selection systems with contested elections. *Id.* To date, however, those efforts have failed. http://www.judicialselection.us/judicial_selection/reform_efforts/failed_reform_efforts.cfm?state=; *see also* Charles Gardner Geyh, *Judicial Independence: Judicial Selection Reconsidered: A Plea for Radical Moderation*, 35 HARV. J.L. & PUB. POL'Y 623 (2012) (arguing for in-cremental reform of judicial selection, "[w]hen, as now, the latest movement has run its course and the political will for fundamental change is absent").

112. *See, e.g.,* Charles Gardner Geyh, *Why Judicial Elections Stink*, 64 OHIO ST. L.J. 43, 53–54 (2003); Rebecca White Berch & Erin Norris Bass, *Judicial Performance Review in Ari-zona: A Critical Assessment*, 56 ARIZ. L. REV. 353 (2014).

113. Survey research suggests that contested elections foster general public support for the courts. JAMES L. GIBSON, ELECTING JUDGES: THE SURPRISING EFFECTS OF CAM-PAIGNING ON JUDICIAL LEGITIMACY (2012).

114. Note, *Disqualification of Judges and Justices in the Federal Courts*, 86 HARV. L. REV. 736, 736 n. 1 (1973); GEYH, *supra* note 91, at 202.

115. Note, *supra* note 114 at 736 n. 2.

116. GEYH, *supra* note 91, at 203.

117. *Id.* at 204.
118. *Id.* at 206.
119. *See* chapter 3.
120. Christopher E. Smith & Scott P. Johnson, *Newcomer on the High Court: Justice David Souter and the Supreme Court's 1990 Term*, 37 S.D. L. Rev. 21, 24 (1992) (Souter "successfully avoided providing concrete answers to senators' specific inquiries about controversial issues facing the contemporary Supreme Court"); Maureen Dowd, *Doing the Alito Shuffle*, N.Y. Times, Jan. 11, 2006 (discussing Alito's strategic answers to inquiries into ideological issues).
121. Michael J. Gerhardt, *Toward a Comprehensive Understanding of the Federal Appointments Process*, 21 Harv. J.L. & Pub. Pol'y 467, 479 (1998).
122. Evan Harris, *First President in US History to Have Voted to Filibuster a Supreme Court Nominee Now Hopes for Clean Process*, ABCNews, May 30, 2009.
123. Charles Gardner Geyh, *The Elastic Nature of Judicial Independence, in* The Improvement of the Administration of Justice 167, 168–70 (ABA Press, 7th. 2002).
124. 28 U.S.C. §§ 455, 2071–77.
125. 28 U.S.C. § 351.
126. Geyh, *supra* note 123, at 167, 168.
127. 28 U.S.C. § 1332(a).
128. 28 U.S.C. § 1332(d).
129. Jurisdiction of the Courts of the United States, H.R. Rep. No. 50–942, at 3–4 (1888); Act of Mar. 3, 1891, ch. 517 26 Stat. 826.
130. Geyh, *supra* note 91, at 268–69.
131. *Id.* at 3–4.
132. Emily Field Van Tassel, *Challenges to Constitutional Decisions of State Courts and Institutional Pressures on State Judiciaries, in* American Bar Association, Justice in Jeopardy app. E (2003).
133. Kline v. Burke Constr. Co., 260 U.S. 226 (1922).
134. U.S. Const. art. I, § 8, cl. 18; *id.* at art. III, § 2.
135. Geyh, *supra* note 123, at 170.
136. Geyh, *supra* note 91, at 10–14.
137. *Id.* at 254–55.
138. Stephen B. Burbank & Barry Friedman, *Reconsidering Judicial Independence, in* Judicial Independence at the Crossroads: An Interdisciplinary Approach 9, 16–22 (Stephen B. Burbank & Barry Friedman eds., 2002).
139. Geyh, *supra* note 112, at 49–50.
140. Geyh, *supra* note 91, at 212–22.
141. 28 U.S.C. §§ 2071–77. Procedural rule reform thus straddles dimensions: Congressional rule amendments represent a political dimension foray into the adjudicative dimension, while judicial rule promulgation is an adjudicative dimension undertaking with political dimension implications.
142. Bell Atl. Corp. v. Twombly, 550 U.S. 544, 555–56 (2007); Ashcroft v. Iqbal, 556 U.S. 662, 678–79 (2009).
143. Videofile: *Has the Supreme Court Limited Americans' Access to Courts?: Hearing before the S. Comm. on the Judiciary* (Dec. 2, 2009), http://judiciary.senate.gov/hearings/hearing.cfm?id=4189.
144. Geyh, *supra* note 91, at 215.
145. Caperton v. A.T. Massey Coal Co., 129 S. Ct. 2252 (2009).
146. *See* notes 14–19, *supra*, and accompanying text.
147. Caperton v. A.T. Massey Coal Co., 129 S. Ct. 2252, 2263 (2009).
148. Judicial Disqualification Project, note 25 at 12, 16.

149. *Id.*
150. *See, e.g.,* 541 U.S. 913 (2004) (Justice Scalia explained his disinclination to err on the side of disqualification, given the risk of a 4–4 tie on the Court).
151. Geyh, *supra* note 12, at 700.
152. The Judicial Disqualification Project, *supra* note 25. I served as Director of and consultant to the ABA Disqualification Project from 2007 to 2009. The views I express here are not necessarily those of the ABA Disqualification Project, the ABA Standing Committee on Judicial Independence to which I reported, or the American Bar Association itself.
153. Draft Report of the Judicial Disqualification Project 58 (2008).
154. *Id.* Discussion Drafts (on file with the author).
155. Geyh, *supra* note 12, at 727–28.
156. Discussion Draft dated July 16, 2010 (on file with the author).
157. Geyh, *supra* note 12, at 727–28.
158. Resolution, American Bar Association, Adopted by the House of Delegates (August 8–9, 2011), http://www.americanbar.org/content/dam/aba/administrative/judicial_ independence/report107_judicial_disqualification.authcheckdam.pdf.
159. *Examining the State of Judicial Recusals after* Caperton v. A.T. Massey *before the Subcomm. on Courts and Competition Policy of the H. Comm. on the Judiciary,* 111ᵗʰ Cong. (2009).
160. *Poll: Huge Majority Wants Firewall between Judges, Election Backers,* JUSTICE AT STAKE (Feb. 22, 2009), http://justiceatstake.org/node/125 (81% thought that a different judge should decide disqualification motions).
161. *See, e.g.,* Lise Olsen, *Secrecy of Chief Federal Judges Questioned: Judging the Judges: Veil of Secrecy Stirring Calls for Change,* HOUS. CHRON., Dec. 31, 2009, at A1.
162. *Operations of Federal Judicial Misconduct Statutes: Hearing before the Subcomm. on Courts, the Internet, and Intellectual Property of the H. Comm. on the Judiciary,* 107th Cong. (2001).
163. *Impeaching Manuel L. Real, a Judge of the United States Dist. Court for the Cent. Dist. of Cal., for High Crimes and Misdemeanors: Hearing before the Subcomm. on the Courts, the Internet and Intellectual Property of the H. Comm. on the Judiciary,* 109th Cong. (2006).
164. H.R. 5219, 109th Cong. (2006); Bruce Moyer, *Proposals Resurface to Create a Judicial Branch Watchdog,* FEDERAL BAR ASSOCIATION (Mar./Apr. 2011), http://fedbar.org/ Advocacy/Washington-Watch/WW-Archives/2011/MarchApril-2011.aspx.
165. Fair and Independent Federal Judiciary Act of 2003, S. 787, 108th Cong., 1st Sess. (2003).
166. *See* Caprice L. Roberts, *The Fox Guarding the Henhouse?: Recusal and the Procedural Void in the Court of Last Resort,* 57 RUTGERS L. REV. 107, 111 (2004).
167. 2011 Year-End Report on the Federal Judiciary, http://www.supremecourt.gov/ publicinfo/year-end/2011year-endreport.pdf.
168. Judicial Code of Conduct Committee, Advisory Opinion 46 ("The Commentary to Canon 4 C states that '[a] judge may attend fund-raising activities of law-related and other organizations although the judge may not be a speaker, a guest of honor, or featured on the program of such an event.' When a judge is chosen to receive an award, it would appear likely that the judge would be either a 'guest of honor' or a 'speaker' at such an event. Additionally, the judge should consider whether the judge's presence is being employed as a device to promote publicity and the sale of tickets"). The annual dinner would seem to be a "fundraising activity" in the obvious sense that the Federalist Society wants revenues from ticket sales to exceed costs, and so will sell as many tickets as possible by promoting the justices as featured speakers. There are good reasons to relax this restriction (the Model Code has, in Rule 3.7(A)(4)), particularly for justices on the Supreme Court whose appearance as featured speakers at such events can enrich public understanding of the Court and its justices. The point, for purposes here,

however, is that Justices Thomas and Scalia felt unencumbered by the Code of Conduct for United States judges, which retains the restriction.

169. *See* Bruce Moyer, *Four Supremely Provocative Proposals*, FEDERAL BAR ASSOCI-ATION (May 2009), http://www.fedbar.org/Advocacy/Washington-Watch/WW-Archives/2009/May-2009.aspx.
170. Williams-Yulee v. The Florida Bar, 135 S. Ct. 1656 (2015).
171. About half the states have adopted a rule in the ABA Model Code that calls for the disqualification of a judge whose public statements "appear to commit" the judge to reaching a particular result in a future case, but that rule does not address the ethical propriety of making such statements in the first place.
172. Terry Carter, *The Big Bopper: This Terre Haute Lawyer is Exploding the Canons of Judicial Campaign Ethics*, 92 A.B.A. J. 31, 32–33 (Nov. 2006). (Characterizing the message sent by questionnaires as: "judge, you can no longer hide behind the code of judicial conduct, in light of the U.S. Supreme Court's decision in Republican Party of Minnesota v. White, and if you decline to answer what my client constituency wants to know, it'll most likely cost you their votes").

CHAPTER 7

1. Lillian Hellman, *Love Letters, Some Not So Loving*, N.Y. TIMES, Oct. 13, 1974.
2. Lisa Leff, *U.S. Court Rules Recusal of Gay Judge not Necessary: Legal Battle on California's Prop 8 Continues*, HOUSTON CHRONICLE, June 15, 2011.
3. *Id.*
4. 28 U.S.C. §455(b)(4) and (d)(4) (requiring disqualification when a judge "has a financial interest in . . . a party to the proceeding," with "financial interest" defined as "ownership of a legal or equitable interest, however small").
5. Darryl Fears, *Nominee's Past Opens Old Wounds; Appeals Court Pick Raises Tempers, Divides Blacks*, WASHINGTON POST, Mar. 3, 2002 (discussing opposition to Pickering in terms of his ideology compromising his impartiality); Charles Hurt, *Senators Send a Signal, Reject Judicial Pick*, THE PHILADELPHIA INQUIRER, Mar. 15, 2002 (reporting on Senate Judiciary Committee rejection of Pickering).
6. RICHARD FLAMM, JUDICIAL DISQUALIFICATION: RECUSAL AND DISQUALIFICATION OF JUDGES §10.7 (2d ed. 2007) (there is a "strong presumption against disqualifying a judge" solely on the basis of the judge's judicial philosophy or views on matters of public policy).
7. Republican Party of Minnesota v. White, 536 U.S. 765 (2002).
8. *Id.* at 777-78.
9. *Hearing on the Nomination of Judge Antonin Scalia to be Assoc. Justice of the Supreme Court of the United States before the S. Comm. on the Judiciary*, 99th Cong., 2d Sess. 58 (1986).
10. *Id.* at 37.
11. Quoted in J. CAMPBELL, LIVES OF THE CHIEF JUSTICES OF ENGLAND 208 (1873).
12. Ashcroft v. Iqbal, 129 S. Ct. 1937, 1950 (2009); Bell Atlantic Corp. v. Twombly, 550 U.S. 544 (2007).
13. C.K. ROWLAND & ROBERT A. CARP, POLITICS AND JUDGMENT IN FEDERAL DISTRICT COURTS 147 (1996).
14. This theory posits that a decision-maker's ideological and other motivations affect her reasoning process in ways that persuade her to favor legal arguments for preferred outcomes. EILEEN BRAMAN, LAW, POLITICS & PERCEPTION: HOW POLICY PREFERENCES INFLUENCE LEGAL REASONING 13–40 (2009) (outlining a theory of motivated reasoning and exploring potential weaknesses); Lawrence Baum, *Motivation and Judicial Behavior: Expanding the Scope of Inquiry, in* THE PSYCHOLOGY OF JUDICIAL DECISION

MAKING 3, 5 (David Klein & Gregory Mitchell eds., 2010); Dan Simon, *A Third View of the Black Box: Cognitive Coherence in Legal Decision Making,* 71 U. CHI. L. REV. 511, 541–42 (2004) (exploring motivated reasoning in several contexts where facts were distorted to ensure a desired outcome).

15. Hellman, *supra* note 1.

16. *Id.*

17. FLAMM, *supra* note 6, at §10.7.

18. Julie Hirschfeld Davis, *Sotomayor is Confirmed in Historic Vote,* CHARLESTON GAZETTE, Aug. 7, 2009, at A4; FLAMM, *supra* note 6, at §10.3.

19. Davis, *supra* note 18.

20. CHRIS W. BONNEAU & MELINDA GANN HALL, IN DEFENSE OF JUDICIAL ELECTIONS 41 (2009) (finding no statistically significant post-*White* impact on contestation rates in judicial elections).

21. Ashcroft v. Iqbal, 129 S. Ct. 1937, 1950 (2009).

22. Arthur Miller, *From Conley, to Twombly to Iqbal: A Double Play on the Federal Rules of Civil Procedure,* 60 DUKE L.J. 1, 18 (2010).

23. Victor D. Quintanilla, *Beyond Common Sense: A Social Psychological Study of Iqbal's Effects on Claims of Race Discrimination,* 17 MICH. J. OF RACE & L. 1 (2011).

24. John Locke, Concerning Civil Government, Second essay ¶119 (1690).

25. *Id.* at ¶221.

26. *Id.* at ¶222.

27. 2 THE COMPLETE WRITINGS OF THOMAS PAINE 273 (P.S. Foner 1945).

28. 1 THE COMPLETE WRITINGS OF THOMAS PAINE 250 (P.S. Foner 1945).

29. Letter from James Madison to Daniel Webster, Mar. 15, 1833, in 1 *The Founders' Constitution,* 94 (Philip Kurland & Ralph Lerner eds., 1987).

30. *Id.*

31. James Gibson, Gregory Caldeira, & Lester Kenyatta Spence, *Why Do People Accept Public Policies They Oppose? Testing Legitimacy Theory with a Survey-Based Experiment,* 58 POLITICAL RES. Q. 187 (2005).

32. For Solum, the "thin" virtues include (1) incorruptibility and judicial sobriety, which correspond to the instrumental value of integrity or honesty; (2) civic courage, which corresponds loosely to the instrumental value of independence (although independence is a somewhat broader concept that includes but is not limited to factors relating to the judge's character); (3) judicial temperament and impartiality, which I likewise grouped together in chapter 4, as the instrumental value of impartiality; (4)-(6) diligence, carefulness, intelligence, learnedness, craft, and skill, which I cluster as subsets of the instrumental value of "capability." Lawrence Solum, *A Tournament of* Virtue, *available at* http://papers.ssrn.com/sol3/papers.cfm?abstract_id=588322 (last visited Feb. 2, 2015). *See also* Lawrence B. Solum, *Virtue Jurisprudence: A Virtue-Centered Theory of Judging,* 34 METAPHILOSOPHY 178 (2003).

33. Solum bundles lawfulness and wisdom as subsets of justice that together comprise what he characterizes as "thick" virtues. Solum, *Tournament of Virtue, supra* note 32, which correlate to my law, process, and justice objectives of good judging, particularly if process is conceptualized, as the procedural side of law.

34. JOEL M. GORA, DUE PROCESS OF LAW 1-3 (1977); JOHN V. ORTH, DUE PROCESS OF LAW: A BRIEF HISTORY 7-8 (2003).

35. *See* WILLIAM M. SULLIVAN, ANNE COLBY, JUDITH WELCH WEGNER, LLOYD BOND, & LEE S. SHULMAN, EDUCATING LAWYERS: PREPARATION FOR THE PROFESSION OF LAW 74 (2007) (illustrating the use of policy analysis in the law school setting).

36. Judith Welch Wegner, *A Legal Education Prospectus: Reframing Legal Education's "Wicked Problems,"* 61 RUTGERS L. REV. 867, 918 (2009).

37. *Id.* at 917.
38. *Id.* at 918.
39. *Id.* at 918.
40. *Id.* at 916.
41. Theodore W. Ruger, Pauline T. Kim, Andrew D. Martin, & Kevin M. Quinn, *The Supreme Court Forecasting Project: Legal and Political Science Approaches to Predicting Supreme Court Decisionmaking,* 104 Colum. L. Rev. 1150 (2004).
42. *Id.* at 1178 (detailing that the sample size consisted of only twelve attorneys from a pool of eighty-three experts).
43. Pamela Casey, Roger Warren, Fred Cheesman II, & Jennifer Elek, Helping Courts Address Implicit Bias 22 (2012), *available at* http://www.ncsc.org/~/media/Files/PDF/Topics/Gender%20and%20Racial%20Fairness/IB_report_033012.ashx (last visited June 14, 2015).
44. Mark Hansen, *Flunking Civics: Why America's Kids Know So Little,* A.B.A. J., May 1, 2011.
45. James Gibson & Gregory Caldeira, *Knowing the Supreme Court? A Reconsideration of Public Interest on the High Court,* 71 J. Pol. 429 (2009).
46. Model Code of Judicial Conduct R. 1.2, Comment 6 (2008).
47. Eric Berger, *The Rhetoric of Constitutional Absolutism,* 56 Wm. & Mary L. Rev. 667 (2015).
48. Marjorie Cohn & David Dow, Cameras in the Courtroom: Television and the Pursuit of Justice 113 (2002).
49. Press Release, Admin. Office of the U.S. Courts, Judicial Conference Opposes Sweeping Restrictions on Educational Programs (Sept. 19, 2000), http://www.uscourts.gov/News/NewsView/00–09-19/Judicial_Conference_Opposes_Sweeping_Restrictions_on_Educational_Programs.aspx (last visited Feb. 2, 2015).
50. *Id. Compare* U.S. Judicial Conference Comm. on Codes of Conduct, Advisory Opinion No. 67: Attendance at Independent Educational Seminars (revised June 2009), *available at* http://www.uscourts.gov/uscourts/RulesAndPolicies/conduct/Vol02B-Ch02.pdf (setting forth the factors a judge must consider when deciding whether to attend an expenses-paid seminar), *with* Bruce A. Green, *May Judges Attend Privately Funded Educational Programs? Should Judicial Education Be Privatized?: Questions of Judicial Ethics and Policy,* 29 Fordham Urb. L.J. 941, 954–60 (2002) (quoting extensively from the 1998 version of Advisory Opinion No. 67).
51. Judicial Transparency and Ethics Enhancement Act of 2006, H.R. 5219, 109th Cong., § 2(a), (2006) (proposing the creation of an inspector general for the judiciary to investigate judicial misconduct); *Impeaching Manuel L. Real, a Judge of the United States District Court for the Central District of California, for High Crimes and Misdemeanors: Hearing on H.R. Res. 916 before the Subcomm. on Courts, the Internet, and Intellectual Prop. of the H. Comm. on the Judiciary,* 109th Cong. 2–4 (2006); *Judicial Transparency and Ethics Enhancement Act of 2006: Hearing on H.R. 5219 before the Subcomm. on Crime, Terrorism, and Homeland Sec. of the H. Comm. on the Judiciary,* 109th Cong. 1–4 (2006).
52. *See Hearing on H.R. 5219, supra* note 50, at 61.
53. *See* Tony Mauro, *Binding National Rules Adopted for Handling Judicial Misconduct Complaints,* Law.com (Mar. 12, 2008), http://www.law.com/jsp/article.jsp?id=1205232267963&slreturn=1&hbx;see *also* Rules for Judicial-Conduct and Judicial-Disability Proceedings (2008), *available at* http://www.uscourts.gov/uscourts/RulesAndPolicies/Misconduct/jud_conduct_and_disability_308_app_B_rev.pdf (last visited Feb. 2, 2015).
54. *Bill Summary & Status 109th Congress (2005-2006) H.R. 5219,* THOMAS, http://hdl.loc.gov/loc.uscongress/legislation.109hr5219 (last visited Sept. 6, 2011).

55. S. Rep. 101–416, S. Rep. No. 416, 101st Cong., 2d Sess. (1990), at 6834.
56. *Id.* at 6807.
57. 28 U.S.C. § 2071–77.
58. Ashcroft v. Iqbal, 556 U.S. 662 (2009); Bell Atlantic Corp. v. Twombly, 550 U.S. 544 (2007).
59. *See, e.g.,* Notice Pleading Restoration Act of 2009, S.1504 (111th Cong.); Open Access to Courts Act of 2009, H.R. 4115 (111th Cong.).
60. Letter to Congressmen Henry Johnson and Howard Coble, from the National Association of Manufacturers, December 15, 2009, *available at* http://www.nam.org/Issues/Legal-Policy-and-Product-Safety/Legal-Policy/Coalition-Letter-Opposing-H_R_-4115-That-Would-Overturn-Ashcroft-v_-Iqbal/ (last visited Feb. 2, 2015).
61. Swierkiewicz v. Sorema, 534 U.S. 506 (2002).
62. 28 U.S.C. § 2072(a).
63. Fabio Arcila Jr., *Discoverymania: Plausibility Pleading as Misprescription,* 80 Brook. L. Rev. 1487 (2015).
64. Fed. R. Civ. P. 26 (2006 Advisory Committee Note).
65. 2011 Year-End Report on the Federal Judiciary 3-5 (Dec. 31, 2011), http://www.supremecourt.gov/publicinfo/year-end/2011year-endreport.pdf (last visited Feb. 2, 2015).
66. *Id.* at 4.
67. *Id.* at 3, 4-5.
68. *Id.* at 6, 7.
69. The federal statute establishing a disciplinary process for the federal courts defines a "judge" subject to its provisions as a "circuit judge, district judge, bankruptcy judge, or magistrate judge." 28 U.S.C. § 351.
70. Nick Wing, *Supreme Court Ethics Act Proposed in Response to Controversial Behavior By Justices Scalia, Thomas,* Huffington Post, Aug. 1, 2013.
71. Press release, Alliance for Justice, Justices Scalia and Thomas to Attend Federalist Society Fundraising Dinner, Demonstrating Ongoing Lack of Respect for Judicial Ethics (Nov. 9, 2011), http://www.afj.org/press-room/press-releases/justices-scalia-and-thomas-to-attend-federalist-society-fundraising-dinner-demonstrating-ongoing-lack-of-respect-for-judicial-ethics (last visited Feb. 3, 2015).
72. Model Code of Judicial Conduct R. 3.7(a)(4).
73. Charles Gardner Geyh, *Why Judicial Disqualification Matters. Again* 30 Rev. of Litig. 671, 672 (2011).
74. Dr. Bonham's Case, 77 Eng. Rep. 646, 652 (1609); Tumey v. Oho 273 U.S. 510 (1927).
75. Goldwater's 1964 Acceptance Speech, *available at* http://www.washingtonpost.com/wp-srv/politics/daily/may98/goldwaterspeech.htm (last visited Feb. 3, 2015).
76. *See, e.g.,* Chris W. Bonneau & Melinda Gann Hall, In Defense of Judicial Elections 2 (2009); Julius Uehlein & David H. Wilderman, *Opinion: Why Merit Selection Is Inconsistent with Democracy,* 106 Dick. L. Rev. 769, 769, 772 (2002); Dennis B. Wilson, *Electing Federal Judges and Justices: Should the Supra-Legislators Be Accountable to the Voters?* 39 Creighton L. Rev. 695, 732 (2006).
77. *See, e.g.,* American Bar Association, Justice in Jeopardy: Report of the Commission on the 21st Century Judiciary 70–71 (2003); Charles Gardner Geyh, *Why Judicial Elections Stink,* 64 Ohio St. L.J. 43, 49 (2003).
78. For an elaboration on the incremental reforms summarized here, *see* Charles Gardner Geyh, *Judicial Selection Reconsidered: A Plea for Radical Moderation,* 35 Harv. J. of L. & Pub. Pol. 623 (2012).
79. These proposals are fraught with constitutional questions concerning the First Amendment limits on the "speech" of campaign contributors, that I have elided to avoid

getting bogged down. *See* James Sample, *Democracy at the Corner of First and Fourteenth: Judicial Campaign Spending and Equality*, 66 N.Y.U. ANN. SURVEY OF AM. L. 727 (2010). I have excluded the option of publicly financing judicial campaigns because eliminating direct contributions to candidates leaves standing the elephant in the campaign finance parlor: massive, independently organized, privately funded, campaigns in support of judicial candidates.

80. Seth S. Andersen, *Judicial Retention Evaluation Programs*, 34 LOY. L. REV. 1375 (2001).
81. For example, federal district court docket delays declined after the Civil Justice Reform Act was enacted in 1990, which directed federal district judges to report data on such delays. Charles Gardner Geyh, *Adverse Publicity as a Means of Reducing Judicial Decision-Making Delay: Periodic Disclosure of Pending Motions, Bench Trials and Cases under the Civil Justice Reform* Act, 41 CLEV. ST. L. REV. 511 (1993).
82. For example, judges are subject to discipline for violating rules that require them to uphold the law, to be courteous and patient with litigants, lawyers, and witnesses, to afford parties their right to be heard, and to avoid abusing the prestige of judicial office to advance their own interests. MODEL CODE OF JUDICIAL CONDUCT R. 1.3, 2.2, 2.6, and 2.8.
83. James Gibson, *New-Style Judicial Campaigns and the Legitimacy of State High Courts*, 71 J. OF POLITICS 1285, 1294 (2009).
84. *Compare* Republican Party of Minnesota v. White, 536 U.S. 735 (2002) (invalidating rule prohibiting judicial candidates from announcing their views), and Williams-Yulee v. Florida State Bar, 135 S. Ct. 1656 (2015) (upholding rule barring judicial candidates from soliciting company contributions from supporters directly).
85. MODEL CODE OF JUDICIAL CONDUCT R. 2.10.
86. Judith Kaye, *Safeguarding a Crown Jewel: Judicial Independence and Lawyer Criticism of Courts*, 25 HOFSTRA L. REV. 703, 712 (1997).
87. Chris Bonneau, Melinda Gann Hall, & Matthew Streb, *White Noise: The Unrealized Effects of Republican Party of Minnesota v. White on Judicial Elections,* 32 JUST. SYS. J. 247 (2011).
88. For example, the Model Code Rule 2.10 bar on judges making public statements on pending and impending cases as it pertains to cases in other jurisdictions could be relaxed; and commentary illustrating the kinds of public statements that will not impair the fairness of a pending or impending proceeding might be added.
89. The Court could, for example, subject restrictions on such speech to intermediate scrutiny analogous to that which the Supreme Court has applied to restrictions on the speech of government employees (which all judges are) or licensed lawyers (which effectively all judicial candidates must be). *See* Charles Gardner Geyh, *The Jekyll and Hyde of First Amendment Limits on the Regulation of Judicial Campaign Speech*, 68 VAND. L. REV. EN BANC 83 (2015). The Court rejected this approach in Williams-Yulee v. Florida State Bar, 135 US. Ct. 1656 (2015), but it effectively applied a softer form of strict scrutiny to the end of upholding a state-imposed content based restriction on speech that rarely passes constitutional muster.

INDEX